ALTERED EVIDENCE

ALTERED EVIDENCE

Flight 800: How and Why the
Justice Department
Framed a Journalist and His Wife

By

JAMES D. SANDERS

WWW.ALTERED-EVIDENCE.COM

Library of Congress Cataloging-in-Publication Data
(to come)

ISBN: 0-9676658-0-9

First Printing: November, 1999
10 9 8 7 6 5 4 3 2 1

Printed in the United States of America
Offset Paperback Mfrs., Inc.
Dallas, Pa 18612

This book is dedicated to my wife.
She became a hostage of the federal government
April 19, 1997.

Liberty cannot be preserved without a general knowledge among the people, who have a right ... and a desire to know; but besides this, they have a right, an indisputable, unalienable, indefeasible, divine right to that most dreaded and envied kind of knowledge, I mean of the characters and conduct of their rulers.

John Adams, 1765

ACKNOWLEDGMENTS

The last time I wrote an acknowledgment to thank those who touched my life in some meaningful way during the investigation of government wrongdoing was March 1977 as *The Downing of TWA Flight 800* went to press.

Virtually everyone thanked in that acknowledgment, from publisher to agent to friends, soon became victims of federal harassment and intimidation. The Justice Department used the book's acknowledgment section as a virtual roadmap to neutralize that which placed them at risk.

It has been a long journey from March 1977 to November 1999. My wife Liz and I have survived.

Because of the efforts of many people I have been able to use the ordeal of indictment to accumulate additional, compelling evidence of federal lawlessness and corruption.

Those who helped me know who you are.

Thanks.

TABLE OF CONTENTS

	Introduction	1
1	Willful Blindness	6
2	The Paranoid Herd	10
3	Eyewitnesses	16
4	What the Radar Really Observed	36
5	The White House	42
6	Altering the Debris Field	47
7	Justice at the Scene of the Crime	55
8	Hangar Man	57
9	Power Struggle	59
10	St. Louis Canine Scheme	72
11	The Sanders' Gang Emerges	81
12	The Chairman's Report	88
13	Red Residue	98
14	Prelude to War	106
15	The *Press-Enterprise* Article	116
16	Glue Repels Missiles	123
17	Dyslexic Fog	129
18	CIA Disinformation	138
19	The Third Piece of Residue	148
20	Expert Opinion?	150
21	Face to Face With the "Justice" Department	154
22	Scrupulous Detail?	158
23	Guess Who's Coming to Dinner	160
24	The House Aviation Subcommittee	169
25	Congressman Trafficant	177

26	Final Response	180
27	Kallstrom's Last Press Conference	183
28	The Arrest Warrants	185
29	Arrest Warrants as Propaganda	190
30	The Government Leans on TWA	197
31	Pre-Trial Discovery	201
32	The Infidel Responds	218
33	Clinton Administration "Police-State Tactics"	236
34	Defense, Final Discovery	238
35	The Judge's Opinion	250
36	Pre-Trial Maneuvering	266
37	The Trial Begins	271
38	Day Two	278
39	Day Three	286
40	Closing Arguments	297
41	Sentencing	306
42	Propaganda or Journalism?	312
43	Prior Restraint	335
44	Neutralize the Message, Destroy the Messenger	340
45	Conclusion	351
	Exhibit A[1]	352
	Notes	364

INTRODUCTION

I'm a retired police officer and investigative journalist. For almost 15 years I have used the skills learned on the job in Southern California law enforcement to investigate wrongdoing within the federal government. This is my fourth book related to that subject.[1]

On July 17, 1996, TWA Flight 800, a Boeing 747 with 230 passengers and crew, crashed less than 10 miles south of Long Island. All 230 onboard died.

During the first hours after the crash, the airwaves were filled with eyewitness accounts of a missile streaking up into the air and a plane falling from the sky.

Within two months *The New York Times* was carrying Flight 800 stories that sounded more like FBI propaganda than journalism. And NBC Evening News became the preferred method by which the NTSB began to spin a story around a mysterious mechanical event that may have been the cause of it all.

Reporters began to tell me stories that questioned the official government line, intimating that it had been spiked. Stories about Navy divers removing highly sensitive debris from the ocean floor within 48 hours after the crash; about military officers admitting off the record that a major "screw-up" had caused the crash; that Navy sources were talking of a large concentration of Navy ships south of Long Island, the launch of a drone, and "friendly fire."

I eventually developed sources within the government and the Flight 800 investigation. A stream of documents—and forensic evidence—became available establishing beyond a reasonable doubt that obstruction of justice was ongoing at the senior-most levels of those government agencies that controlled the investigation.

I wrote a book entitled *The Downing of TWA Flight 800.* Released in April 1997, it provided the American public with a view of the TWA Flight 800 investigation never before revealed.

Government documents used to write the book told of a much different initiating event than the government's version. These documents reported that FAA radar technicians saw a missile on their scopes and immediately notified the White House. The documents also revealed there was damage to the recovered debris consistent with a missile warhead explosion in the center wing tank (CWT).[2]

The documents said there was an initial, narrow area of damage that crossed the 747 in the area immediately in front of the CWT, generally in a right-to-left direction. My best source inside the investigation said there was a reddish-orange residue trail in this exact area. Eventually, he obtained two small samples of the residue, which I had tested.[3] They were consistent with the residue from a solid-fuel missile. Further investigation, coming after the publication of *The Downing of TWA Flight 800*, established that more than 98% of the residue's volume was consistent with an explosive event.

The government counterattacked, arguing that the residue was glue. After months of ducking and dodging, the NTSB finally announced that the residue was 3M 1357 HP Adhesive. They pointed to NASA Chemist Charles Bassett as the scientist who confirmed this fact.

I obtained a notarized affidavit from Charles Bassett. His written statement debunks the government's glue allegation. I sent a sample of 3M 1357 HP Adhesive to Florida State University (FSU) to be tested and compared to my residue sample's elemental analysis. FSU confirmed beyond any doubt that the government lied about my residue sample being 3M glue.

Then, Dr. Merritt Birky, the NTSB bureaucrat in charge of the Flight 800 Fire and Explosion team, admitted that the government had *never* tested my residue. Why? He indicated the government was afraid of the results.

By this time you can almost visualize Department of Justice agents swooping down and hauling away the responsible miscreants, parading the guilty through a frenzied throng of media. Unfortunately, the Department, including the FBI, was involved in this scheme to obstruct justice and rewrite the history of TWA Flight 800. They were not about to investigate and imprison themselves.

Three months after my book was published, the head of the National Transportation Safety Board, Jim Hall, under oath, before Congress, admitted that the NTSB had essentially removed a "mechanical" malfunction as possible cause of the downing of Flight 800:

Congressman Trafficant: I would just like the panelists to answer my questions yes or no. If you can't, just say you can't answer it. First question, Mr. Hall. Hypotheses and theories and opinion, not a fact, correct? Hypothesis is theory, correct?

NTSB Chairman Jim Hall: Yes.

Trafficant: To this point, has any physical evidence, conclusive forensic evidence, to prove it was a mechanical failure that caused the explosion of the center fuel tank? Yes or no.

Hall: We're looking at that.

Trafficant: I want a one [word] answer. I know it is tough at this point.

Hall: No.[4]

The NTSB has exhaustively searched for a politically-correct "mechanical" answer. Forty-million dollars later the answer is still "No."

The book you are about to read reveals what really happens in America when powerful interests are threatened by aggressive journalism—when the politically-correct answer is exposed as fraudulent.

The same bureaucrats within the FBI and Justice Department I was investigating used the awesome power with which they were entrusted to harass, intimidate and persecute. They were imperiled by the truth, and used their power in an attempt to neutralize my investigation.

The Justice Department turned my wife into a hostage to their demands on April 19, 1997. In a face-to-face confrontation with the FBI and Justice Department, they said they would "target" and indict my wife if she did not assist them in their investigation of me. She refused, and we were both indicted for conspiring with a source inside the TWA Flight 800 investigation to obtain additional evidence of their lawlessness.

We were arrested, bound, and dragged through throngs of reporters. My phone and financial records were seized in violation of Justice Department rules, regulations and case law. My computer was seized without a warrant.

And major media remained silent.

When the government demanded that the First Amendment be excised from the trial, major media did not speak out in protest. When the judge agreed, major media acquiesced. When the government's star witness failed to perform on the stand as the government said he would, *The New York Times* printed a story misrepresenting what was said under oath.

We were convicted of conspiring with a source to obtain additional evidence of government wrongdoing. The case is under appeal.

If we lose the appeal, federal case law will allow the wife

of any journalist to be made the target of a federal investigation, even in the absence of any evidence, real or imagined, upon which to justify the targeting. It will establish conspiracy as a legal tool to inhibit aggressive investigation of government lawlessness.

And major media still remains silent.

If you have seen or heard anything about this case in major media reports, it has been the government's version of the truth, devoid of balance. My side of the story has not been told—until now.

In spite of the best efforts of those placed at risk by my investigation, I have obtained compelling evidence of the government's motivation to illegally use its power to cover up and halt the dissemination of the truth.

The reason for the government's shrill, vindictive attack upon my wife and on me becomes apparent as you read the following chapters. Less apparent is the motivation for major media to cooperate with powerful interests rather than pursuing balanced journalism.

1

WILLFUL BLINDNESS

If a nation expects to be ignorant and free, in a state of civilization, it expects what never was and never will be.

Thomas Jefferson

The Freedom of the Press guarantee of the First Amendment has little meaning if the federal judiciary steps aside and allows the lawless within the federal government to use the court process for evil. But that is precisely what the federal justice system has descended to as we approach the millenium. A presumption of normalcy is the current theory under which the federal judicial system blissfully operates, demonstrating a classic willful blindness to lawlessness within the Justice Department.

Government officials are presumed to always operate in a lawful manner and their conduct, pre-trial, will not be questioned. These are angels with badges, guns, and the awesome power of the most powerful bureaucracy on the face of the earth, accountable to no one except themselves. Should the angelic behavior more closely resemble Lucifer than Gabriel, there is no interlocutory (pre-trial) appeal of their lawlessness.

The federal judiciary fails to comprehend the most basic, elementary fact of human nature: There are no angels within the federal bureaucracy, only corruptible humans—humans who are more frequently corruptible through arrogance combined with power than payoffs, and infinitely corruptible when not continually subjected to scrutiny by the judicial system.

Long ago the federal judiciary used to believe that "Decency, security and liberty alike demand that government officials shall be subjected to the same rules of conduct that are commands to the citizen. In a government of laws, existence of the government will be imperiled if it fails to observe the law scrupulously."[1] This concept is now under attack.

Fundamental to the institution of our democracy is the right of a journalist to investigate significant wrongdoing on the part of government officials without the requirement that he and his family survive injury, oppression, threats, intimidation, arrest and trial, all at the hands of those he is investigating. Only after successfully negotiating this multi-year "trial by ordeal"[2] can the journalist attempt to renew the pursuit of government wrongdoing; a trail that has grown cold through the passage of time. It should be a myth that such mental, physical, marital and financial strength must be a prerequisite to pursuing a fundamental First Amendment journalistic mandate to protect and defend the Constitution by uncovering wrongdoing within the top levels of the federal government.

It should be a myth—but isn't.

What should not be a myth, but is, is the standard used to judge the veracity of the federal government when it has been confronted with allegations of lawlessness within an investigation. Witness statements constitute compelling evidence in criminal trials, particularly when a significant number describe the same event. American citizens are frequently sentenced to death or lengthy prison terms based on one or two witnesses. But when hundreds of witnesses see a missile bring down a commercial jetliner, it is a mystifying event to major media rather than compelling evidence. The standard of evidence required to put an American citizen to death is considered by major media to be far too low a standard to use when investigating wrongdoing at the highest levels of the federal government.

An inference can be drawn from circumstantial evidence. If senior members of the National Transportation Safety Board (NTSB) leak false information to major media, an inference can be formed of a consciousness of guilt. But within major media, such acts are mystifying.

There is a major media presumption that leaks from high-level official sources constitute fact which can be regurgitated to the public without confirmation. We know this is so because the NTSB has not been able to produce one fact to back up its leaks. In 1996 and 1997, NBC news portrayed the NTSB as closing in on the mechanical reason for the demise of TWA Flight 800. Forty-million dollars later the NTSB cannot yet produce even one document to buttress any of its leaks to NBC.

If credible evidence is presented that the NTSB and FBI lied about residue found inside the airliner being 3M glue rather than from missile exhaust, an inference can be drawn of a consciousness of guilt. To major media, however, it is mystifying how such evidence could really exist. Such compelling evidence of a coordinated attempt within the federal government to lie to and manipulate major media constitutes *prima facie* evidence of a conspiracy. But conspiracies cannot happen inside the federal government because too many people would know about it and blow the whistle.

Whenever reasonable evidence is presented that the government broke the law, lied or suffered willful blindness, it represents compelling circumstantial evidence that government wrongdoing is responsible. Circumstantial evidence, like witness testimony and documents, all constitute evidence used to convict individual American citizens. But this level of proof is far too low for major media to use when journalistically judging the highest levels of the federal bureaucracy—at least when that bureaucracy is controlled by people of the same political persuasion as 92 percent of those in major media.

We need not use a higher standard to judge acts of federal officials. The rules by which We the People are judged is sufficient to judge the actions of those within the federal government suspected of engaging in lawlessness.

In the following pages, compelling evidence will be presented that: (1) The FBI and NTSB altered the radar data presented to the press in December 1997 in order to hide a major military presence in the immediate area of TWA Flight 800 when it was shot down; (2) The NTSB and FBI altered the Flight 800 reconstruction at the Calverton hangar to hide evidence of damage caused by a missile, and have blocked the publication of photos revealing the altered evidence; (3) The FBI and NTSB conspired to misrepresent the reddish-orange residue found on seats in rows 17, 18 and 19, claiming it was 3M 1357 HP Adhesive; (4) The FBI and NTSB altered the debris field to create a "mechanical" façade; (5) The Clinton administration, at the highest levels, including the Justice Department, controlled the cover-up; and (6) My wife and I were maliciously vilified, harassed, persecuted and framed by the *same* FBI and Department of Justice officials placed at risk by my investigation.

Above all else this is a story about institutional deviancy in America's federal bureaucracy and political structure. It is also the shameful story of major media's inability to pursue a story that might topple an administration with which they are politically enamored.

2

THE PARANOID HERD

"What about the books?" Breistroff [his son was aboard Flight 800] asked.
"Like The Downing of TWA Flight 800 ..."
"Some people are hyping the books," Kallstrom replied, "promoting conspiracies to make a quick buck off this tragedy, doing their demented PR stunts."

Statement attributed to FBI agent Jim Kallstrom
In the Blink of an Eye, Patricia Milton
(Random House, 1999), p. 331.

December 22, 1998. The paranoid herd of FBI and NTSB agents[1] stood just inside the Calverton hangar as their hated adversary entered, followed by two attorneys. It had been a year-long battle, but I was at long last inside Flight 800's resting place, the scene of the crime, certain there was additional evidence of government lawlessness waiting to be uncovered.

For the last year the Justice Department had blocked my entry to the hangar where the remnants of TWA Flight 800 were stored and where a huge portion of the 747 had been reconstructed from the debris pulled from the bottom of the Atlantic Ocean by Navy divers. The collective intelligence of these government agencies had overlooked the downside of indicting a journalist who was investigating their lawlessness. If my wife and I managed to survive the harassment, persecution, indictment, emotional and financial distress brought on by the herd, than I had earned the right to inspect and photograph the crime scene sometime prior to trial.

Now, I stood inside the door, 35mm camera and a brief-case full of film in-hand, two attorneys alongside for protection. The agencies' spokesman reiterated the rules: The photos were for my legal defense. They were not to be shared with other members of the media or with the public. J. Bruce Maffeo signed the agreement as my legal representative.

As far as I was concerned, the agreement had a limited shelf life. Rule 16, which mandated my right to inspect and photograph the crime scene, did not call for or recognize such an agreement. It was just another roadblock set up by the authorities controlling the investigation. A further abuse of power and the public trust, I thought, standing there, aware of the discomfort and hatred my presence created.

Unbeknownst to the agencies involved, I had gained access to a large number of NTSB photos taken inside the Calverton hangar in early 1997 and videotape from August 1996. Many hours had been consumed studying the photos, looking for the most promising areas to photograph once inside the hangar.

Finally, my "escorts" began to grudgingly move toward the long hall that would take us to the assembled wreckage. Within seconds of entering the hangar, I had to suppress a laugh. There in front of me was the disassembled left wing. Until recently, according to sources, it had been intact, waiting to have extremely important evidence photographed. Now it was gone—telling testimony to the consciousness of guilt by those within the herd, and those who controlled its actions.

Across the way was what remained of the right wing. The government had always been too paranoid of the right wing damage to contemplate a reconstruction. But my videotape included several minutes of right wing viewing. Interior-to-exterior damage of the number three fuel tank, closest to the fuselage, is apparent in the video, but could not be seen in the right wing debris that day. Major Fritz Meyer, a New York Air

National Guard pilot, had transported a large piece of the right wing leading edge to Washington, D.C., for FBI lab testing. It had tested positive for explosives and had several apparent high-velocity penetration holes. This piece was no longer in the hangar.

So I headed for the 60,000-pound mockup, electing to begin the three-hour photo shoot inside the passenger cabin. I wanted photographic evidence of the reddish-orange residue deposited by the exhaust of a missile and/or warhead explosion. Shortly after entering the mockup, it became apparent that the residue had been stripped from the seats. There was no reddish-orange path. Had my informant lied? Perhaps no such trail ever existed. That possibility was debunked when FBI Supervisory Senior Agent Kenneth J. Maxwell, the senior FBI agent at the Calverton hangar, admitted under oath at my trial that a residue path had been observed by other FBI agents, who then escorted him to the passenger cabin mockup to observe it.[2]

When it was revealed that I had tested a sample of the reddish-orange residue in a page-one story that broke across America the morning of March 10, 1997, the federal government had shrilly proclaimed the residue to be glue. But the government chemist who allegedly made this determination signed a notarized affidavit indicating the government was not telling the truth. And, the senior government scientist attached to the Flight 800 investigation had been caught on audiotape admitting the government had never tested the residue because they were afraid of the answer.

My next mental assignment was to photograph the back of row 19, seat 2. The FBI had removed a sample from the back of that seat and sent it to NASA for testing. I had been given a heads-up that someone had smeared a red dye on the sample. Sure enough, the information was correct. No red dye appeared on the area surrounding the area where the sample had been moved—a pathetic effort by someone in the government to alter evidence.

Next stop was the right side of the passenger cabin, row 23, and seats 8, 9 and 10. *The New York Times* had reported "fist-sized" holes in the backs of these seats. But these seats had been removed prior to my arrival. They were particularly important because of the location directly above a 3 x 4-foot hole in the right side of the center wing tank [CWT].

Directly up the aisle from row 23 were four seats I also wanted to photograph, rows 17 and 18, seats 8 and 10. But they had also been removed prior to my arrival. The rules mandated that I not communicate with any of the agents on hand. So I took Bruce Maffeo aside and pointed out the problem of the missing seats.

Maffeo then walked over to FBI agent Jim Kinsley. Kinsley is a large man, from whom no sign of a sense of humor or intellect could be detected. Maffeo, in simple words, pointed out the missing seats and asked where they were located. There was no response from Kinsley, just a vacant look. It was impossible to discern comprehension of what seemed like an easy question. So Maffeo repeated the question, louder, and received the same blank stare.

Maffeo is not a shy attorney. Nor does he suffer fools diplomatically. "Where are the fucking seats?" rushed from his lips.

Finally, comprehension could be discerned within Kinsley's eyes. "They're not here," was the response.

"No shit, Sherlock," Maffeo retorted. "Where *are* they?"

"In the evidence locker at Melville," Kinsley replied. Melville is the FBI's Long Island office.

Maffeo calmly pointed out that he had specifically told the Justice Department we wanted to photograph all seats in rows 17, 18 and 19. "Why weren't we told these seats were not available?" Maffeo questioned.

"You didn't ask," was Kinsley's reply.

I fully appreciated the arrogance that rolled from Kinsley's lips. As I had learned over a career investigating lawlessness within the federal government, the bureaucracy has a surplus of that commodity. Kinsley should be the federal government's poster boy, I thought, as the scene unfolded.

Next, I went over to the CWT, where many rolls of film were taken. The front spar had obviously been altered, as had a significant portion of span-wise beam number three. I also noticed that the NTSB's potable water bottle damage description was false. [Two, 1,000-pound, six-foot-tall water bottles were attached to the front of the CWT.] I took photos from each side and above, shooting down through the wire mesh in the passenger cabin area. By this time, I was far past identifying consciousness-of-guilt sins committed by the government and its agents. "Cover-up" flashed like a neon sign as the altered evidence was photographed.

It was also obvious that two major pieces of the center wing tank right-side (RSOB) reconstruction had been moved by fiat from the red to yellow zone. [The red zone is the area closest to JFK Airport where the first debris fell from the 747. The yellow and green zones follow.] They were among the earliest pieces blown from the plane, adjacent to a 3 x 4-foot hole in the RSOB—and the government had now moved them.

I had noticed that relatively few pieces of debris from the RSOB were entered in the NTSB computer printout obtained from my source, TWA Captain Terry Stacey, a prominent member of the investigating team—leading me to suspect some of the reconstruction pieces may have been pulled from the pre-red zone and/or early red zone. So the telephoto lens was used to get close-up shots of the RSOB tag numbers. Later, it would be determined that 13 pieces of the RSOB had not been entered into the NTSB computer, making the RSOB a high suspect area for missile penetration and altered evidence.

When I tried to photograph the landing gear, government agents protested and scrambled to block the shot. The same thing happened when I attempted to photograph the cockpit. Both times, Bruce Maffeo had to spend five minutes negotiating for a single photograph, when each needed an entire roll of film.

I turned toward two large debris-field maps fastened to the wall. When I began to photograph them, one of the agents moved quickly to where the NTSB investigative leader, Al Dickinson, was standing. A discussion ensued. Dickinson, in turn, hurried over to observe what I was photographing, then turned to a member of the assembled agents and announced, "It's okay. That's not the classified version."

When the three hours were up, my lawyers and I left with a briefcase full of film. As we headed for the front door, I heard an FBI agent say they wanted a duplicate set of all the photos.

They are still waiting.

The members of the herd were selected to be there for one very obvious reason, I believe. They knew what had been altered and were monitoring me to see if I photographed the altered evidence.

When I walked out of the hangar, the government knew it had a problem. Their response was to assign to the Department of Justice the task of legally blocking the publication of any photos I took that day. Simultaneously, Jim Kallstrom, who headed the FBI Flight 800 "investigation," publicly decried the fact that his critics "have seen none of the evidence."[3]

When the December 22, 1998, photos are compared to photographs taken at the hangar between late 1996 and mid-1997, they tell a story of altered evidence.

3

EYEWITNESSES

*CIA analysts have determined that the eyewitness sightings thought to be
that of a missile actually took place after the first of several explosions on
the aircraft. Our technical analysis concludes that what these eyewitnesses
saw was in fact the burning [Flight 800] 747 in various stages of crippled
flight, not a missile.*

Carolyn Osborn, CIA spokesperson
September 24, 1997

*At the time of the crash, and during the investigation, ABC News thor-
oughly considered the evidence available ... and considered a wide variety
of possible explanations. After a careful review, we concluded that there
was no credible evidence supporting the hypothesis of a missile being involved and that the eyewitness accounts were explained by the falling debris. ...*

David L. Westin, ABC News[1]

"I saw the missile. I was facing eastward, toward the
Hamptons, the ocean on my right, the deck of the house on
my left," Lisa Perry remembered as she talked to Jerry Cimisi,
a reporter with *Dan's Papers*, Long Island.[2] "The deck is about
22 feet above the beach. On a clear day, as you look straight
down the beach along the line of the shore, you can see the
parking lot at Smith Point Beach, 12 miles away. There was a
plane in the sky ... out on the left, from the north, something
was moving north to south over the dunes ... from the direction of the Great South Bay. The object came over the dunes of
Fire Island. It was shiny, like a new dime; it looked like a plane

without wings. It had no windows. ... It was as if there was a flame at the back of it, like a Bunsen burner. ... It was like a silver bullet. ... It was moving much faster than the plane. The silver object took a left turn, and went up to the plane. The plane stopped for an instant, as something would when it had suffered an impact, not just an explosion. Then it began to fracture—as if you had slammed a frozen candy bar down onto a table. You could see the spaces in between the parts of the plane. Then a moment later there was another explosion and the plane broke jaggedly in the sky. It was sideways to the way it had been ... there was smoke, fire ... the plane starts to fall apart in the sky ... the nose is continuing to go forward: the wing is gliding off in its own direction, drifting in an arc grace-fully down; the right wing and passenger windows are doing the same in their direction out to the right; and the tail with its fireball leaps up and then promptly into the water below. The sounds were a huge BOOM!—then another BOOM! There was a huge rumbling-rolling in the sky. ... I told the FBI the nose of the plane had come off, and I told them this before the Navy pulled it out of the water. [Mrs. Perry was interviewed by the FBI.] The two agents were very supportive; I was very com-fortable with them. ... I got the impression that they them-selves thought a missile had hit the plane. After the NTSB hear-ings I spoke with one of the agents, who told me the FBI had concluded I was too far away from the accident to see what I had seen. [Referencing the CIA Flight 800 video.] It wasn't like that at all. They [CIA and FBI] said most people turned to the sound and then saw something. I was already looking at the event, before any explosion."[3]

There were many compelling eyewitness accounts of the shootdown of TWA Flight 800. From various positions on the south shore of Long Island and in boats on the ocean, they saw the 747 destroyed by missile fire. The eyewitnesses include two Air Force National Guard pilots, engineers, and a missile expert:

Paul Angelides (July 12, 1998, public statement): "After work on July 17, 1996, I went to our ocean-front summer rental house to have dinner with my wife and one-year-old son. After dinner my wife was bathing our son before putting him to bed, so I decided to go to the ocean-side deck to enjoy the view. As I walked through the sliding doors to the deck, a red phosphorescent object in the sky caught my attention. The object was quite high in the sky (about 50 to 60 degrees) and slightly to the west and off-shore of my position. At first it appeared to be moving slowly, almost hanging and descending, and was leaving a white smoke trail. The smoke trail was short, and the top of the smoke trail had a clockwise, parabolic-shaped hook towards the shore. My first reaction was that I was looking at a marine distress flare that had been fired from a boat. I said to myself, someone must be in trouble.

"I quickly realized that the object was too large and then began moving too fast to be a distress flare. I followed the object as it moved out over the ocean in the direction of the horizon. I lost sight of the object, as it was about 10 degrees above the horizon. In the same area of the sky out over the ocean, I saw a series of flashes, one in the sky and another closer to the horizon. I remember straining to see what was happening as there seemed to be a lot of chaos out there. There was a dot on the horizon near the action, which I perceived to be a boat. The flashes were then followed by a huge fireball, which dropped very quickly into the sea. I yelled to my wife, 'come here, quickly, you've got to see this.'

"My first reaction was that I had seen a military exercise that went awry. Then the sounds started. There was a very loud and prolonged boom, which reminded me of thunder rolling above the house.[4] The noise continued and concluded with a series of two distinctly louder bursts and a final extremely loud burst. The sounds shook the house. My wife, who was on the bathroom floor drying our son from the bath, felt the floor shaking as she heard the noise, and I heard her cry out, 'What is going on?' After some silence there were two more extremely loud explosion-like bursts of sound that also shook the house. I thought to myself that I had witnessed some big weapons being used.

"I noticed several smoke patterns, which remained in the sky after the action took place. In the area where I lost sight of the object, there was a long, wide, white cigar-shaped cloud, which extended parallel to the horizon and eastward to the point where I had seen the huge fireball erupt. At the eastern end of the white cloud was a wide, black smoke trail, which followed the same path as the fireball, which had dropped to the horizon. The path of the black smoke left a trail that was slightly to the east of a vertical drop. There was also a thin, white parabolic contrail, which extended upward and westward from the cigar-shaped cloud.

"I called 911 and told the operator that I had just witnessed an explosion and crash, which had occurred offshore. … I then called the Moriches Coast Guard Station. I stated that I had seen the explosion offshore. I was told, 'Oh, that's the Air National Guard, they are firing flares tonight.' I told the Coast Guard operator that what I had seen was no flare and that I had witnessed a major explosion. I had then returned to the beach to see if anything else was going on.

"The dot on the horizon, which I thought was a ship, had disappeared. I could see flames beginning to appear above the horizon in the area where the fireball had dropped. I saw lights from aircraft and boats heading toward the scene. As I thought about what I had seen and what the Coast Guard had just told me, I felt I had witnessed an aircraft explode during a military exercise. …

"… I called the FBI hotline and a few days later was interviewed by three FBI representatives at my home in Laurel Hollow, New York, which is about 50 miles from Westhampton. I told the FBI my observations. I gave the FBI a sketch with a sequence of the events, which I had recalled at the time. I told the FBI that I had drawn no conclusions from my observations and that I was confident that the investigators would find the cause of the disaster. I was asked, 'What was your first impression?' and I replied, 'I thought it was a military exercise and someone shot themselves in the foot.' I was asked if I had ever seen a missile before and I replied, 'No.' I was asked if I was ever in the military and replied, 'No.' During the FBI interview, I noticed they had a questionnaire with an item that read, 'When did you first see the missile?' At the conclusion of the interview one of the FBI representatives told me not to talk to too many people about what I had seen since, 'Someone could say you said this and someone could say you said that.'

"I followed the news coverage of the event during the months that followed and I became increasingly concerned that the investigation was off the mark. In hindsight I realized that the delayed long rolling-thunder sound that I heard, probably corresponded to the object traversing the sky. The first two bursts corresponded to the two white flashes; the third loud burst corresponded with the fireball. After the silence, the last two sound bursts would likely correspond with the aircraft hitting the water. In early 1997, I called the FBI stating that I wanted to tell my observations again and that I felt what I had seen was very important to their investigation. I was disappointed by what seemed to be their lack of interest. My friends and family have told me that I should not be persistent with the FBI since they are afraid that the government would reprise against me.

"Months later I saw the CIA video reenactment on various TV newscasts. It does not correlate in any way with my observations, especially with regard to the descending fireball of the aircraft, which is shown in the video from the perspective of an observer onshore. Nor is there any explanation of the characteristic location and movement of 'the object' I saw traversing the sky. The FBI has explained eyewitness sighting of a 'flare' as the body of the aircraft as it ascended, (prior to exploding) after the nose section fell off. I strongly disagree. My observations tell me that the aircraft was not just flying along and then suddenly blew up as the center fuel tank exploded. The large fireball, which would have occurred from a fuel explosion in the sky, was a later event in the sequence of my observations. The red, phosphorescent object which first attracted my attention, traveled a great distance and at great speed to the area of Flight 800's demise. The object originated in a vastly different sector of the sky than the Flight 800 path. The object traveled in a generally north-south direction, whereas Flight 800 traveled west-east. The official explanations do not address the flashes of light I observed prior to the fireball and long, rolling sonic boom, which ended with two small bursts and one large burst, followed by silence and then two additional loud bursts. The [CIA] videotape does not explain the long, white, cigar-shaped cloud that was left in the sky.

"I have been disappointed with the results of the investigation so far. The official explanations of the disaster are vastly inconsistent with my observations. Considering the resources at the disposal of the investigators and the extent of the investigation, which has been performed over the past two years, I do not believe that the cause of the disaster remains unknown. At the time of the incident I was 48 years old. I received a B.S. degree in Mechanical Engineering in 1971 [and] received licensure as a Professional Engineer in 1997. I am self-employed full time as a consulting engineer and have been qualified as an expert witness before courts in Nassau, Suffolk, Queens and Bronx counties. … I watched the negative official and press reaction to the reports by Mr. Salinger, which more accurately describe my observations. I have reasoned that if Mr. Salinger, who is a former prestigious government official, could be treated so poorly, what is in store for me if I speak out? I am concerned for my security and fear government reprisal against me for what I have seen."

Richard Goss [located a short distance from Angelides when he made the following observation]: "That evening [July 17, 1996] I was just finishing up a sunfish race at West Hampton Yacht Club … it was a Wednesday night … and that particular night every week we have an informal sunfish race and then it's followed by a 'bring your own' barbecue dinner on the back porch of the yacht club. That porch faces south, and my position at the table I was sitting at, I was looking right out at Moriches Bay and, you know, just leaning back, resting, just enjoying the moment of that part of the evening. It was near dusk and it was then that I saw a flare-type object go up, and feeling that, oh, someone along Dune Road has fireworks, and other members of the club saw it also and said, 'Hey, look at the fireworks.' And everybody turned to look, and we all watched it climb, and I particularly watched it and it was bright, very bright … that almost bright pink … and orange glow around it, and it traveled up and it looked to go straight up from the area that I was observing it, and then it reached its peak and seemed to go away in the distance toward the south, and that's when I saw it veer left, which would bring it out east. It was a sharp left, and then it did not disappear. From my vantage point there was a direct explosion that followed, and then, after that, there was a second explosion that was off to the east a little farther, which was much larger … it was like something broke off of whatever that was, and caught on fire. … And then it took some time to come down … probably three or four seconds, and there was just a stream of black and white smoke, and then it hit the horizon over the barrier beach ... Dune Road ... and when it hit the horizon there was a bright flash."

Vincent Bilodeau and Joseph McBride [both observed the same object as the two previous eyewitnesses, but from a location further west]: "Bilodeau and McBride state that on 7-17-96 at 2045 they were at the Moriches Inlet, South Shore, facing south to southeast. Bilodeau and McBride observed a reddish glowing flare ascend skyward from due east, but they could not tell if from land or water. [The] flare was tight, corkscrew shapes, with even but fast speed. [They] did not see what [the] flare struck, but it exploded in air into a large orange fireball. Two large flaming chunks of debris fell from the fireball. Both recall hearing a deep, thunderous rumble during the explosion." [The FBI and CIA presume all sounds heard by eyewitnesses equate to an explosion. The missile these two saw was, by description, much larger than a shoulder-fired weapon. The launch and rocket motor exhaust noise creates a rumble. We can infer by the fact that the missile was initially half the distance to Flight 800, and that the 747 continued flying five to eight seconds before the first large explosion, that the sound of a missile launch and acceleration toward the target would reach them about the time they observed the explosion.] (Suffolk County, New York, Police report #96-435598.)

Anthony Curreri [His observations correlate to the above eyewitness accounts when plotted on a map] was sitting on the beach "at the Bellport Dock at the south end of Station Road. Facing southeast toward Smith Point Bridge he saw 'a red streak rise from the horizon.' Curreri said he thought 'it was from fireworks being fired from Smith Point Beach over the ocean.' He said the streak 'ascended at a slight angle to the right, very high, then curved downward slightly, leveled off and appeared to explode, resulting in two similar objects falling down.' He thought that it might be two aircraft colliding. He estimated that the event occurred three miles offshore."[5]

Tom Dougherty also saw the projectile veer left. "I was in Docker's restaurant in Quogue. ... I was leaving there and I was with two other people and we were headed ... south ... we were walking toward the water. I heard what I thought to be thunder ... very loud thunder up in the sky, and I looked up in the direction of where the thunder was coming from and I didn't see any clouds to indicate that there was any kind of thunderheads. So I said, 'You know, that's strange,' to the friend of mine. So we continued a few more paces and I guess ... I don't know how many seconds later there was another thundering noise that I heard, and I looked up again and said, 'that's very strange just to hear this when there was no thunder and no clouds of that type around. So I continued to look in that direction because of the noises I heard, and within a few more seconds I saw a red-orange flare go up that I thought was like a Guicci fireworks, and I watched it go up away from me in a south-westerly direction toward the West Hampton beach area and it ... what I was waiting for was the flare to reach its trajectory peak and to come down and explode like fireworks. And it didn't. What happened was it kept traveling south-west, growing ever smaller in the distance, then [it] seemed to veer toward the east more and then it disappeared in the clouds or the fog area ... the haze ... a second later ... I saw this 'glowing' in the sky and it looked like a UFO. ... I was kidding around with my friends and I turned and said, 'Look at the fireworks [that] turned into a UFO.' A few seconds later I saw something just ... flop out of the sky ... seconds later ... I heard another explosion and that's when I saw this big fire come out of the sky, and it looked like the sun coming down, actually."[6]

Donald Eick and his family were on a boat off the south
shore of Long Island when they saw "a reddish flare-like object
just off the water heading upward, zigzagging a little in an
unmistakable vertical climb, a fireball erupting at the end of
the ascent. The initial drama took no more than 12 to 15 seconds, Eick estimates. Then, the meteorologist, his wife and
12-year-old daughter, saw three sections of aircraft 'fluttering'
toward the Atlantic Ocean. ... Eick's description, previously
given only to FBI investigators, is different than the others because he says he and his family saw the plane separate: two
parts in flame and one part seeming to arch upward before
heading toward the Atlantic. All other published accounts, including reports from airline pilots in the air, tell only of seeing
lights, explosions or fireballs, but not the fuselage. The Islip,
New York, family was returning to Long Island's Great South
Bay after a day of boating and swimming when Eick's daughter
noticed the reddish light headed upward. Eick does his work
as a meteorologist for TWA. ... He also is a civilian pilot and
has participated in accident investigations. 'It was what we
would best describe as a boat flare, a reddish object going up,'
Eick said. 'It went up and a few seconds later we saw an explosion in the sky. I can't say if it came [from] offshore or onshore.
At first we thought it was a boat flare. It zigzagged a little. ...
Then, several seconds later, we saw an eruption of fire. We
never heard anything. We saw a fireball, and at that point we
identified what was an aircraft. We could see it fluttering down.
... When I was interviewed by the FBI the next day, they were
interested in the wreckage I saw go upward,' Eick said. 'I think
it was probably the nose.' Eick said it was 'completely errone-
ous' to believe that the red flare he and his family saw was fuel
or other descending plane debris. There 'was something going
up to it beforehand,' he said. 'Yes, I saw flaming debris go down.
Something attracted us to the area before it exploded. And even
my wife and my oldest daughter, we were witnesses to it. There

definitely was something there first before the aircraft went down.'"[7]

Ed Wagner was fishing in Moriches Inlet the evening of July 17, 1996. He first noticed a "white flare" shortly after it was launched off the ocean. It shot upwards then curved to the west, toward Flight 800, which was not visible 10 miles away.[8]

Wagner was asked, "if what he saw could have been the plane [or fuel] going down." Wagner "put his thumb up and said, 'This is up, right?'"[9]

Brandi Ellison and John Gang "were on a boat with five other persons, on the Peconk Bay" near the Harbor Cove Inn. They were facing west and saw a flare-like object shoot upwards, "from the water, ascend with a bright orange-red glow skyward and at its apex, burst into numerous red flames. [The] flare had a very large orange-red tail. Neither heard any noise."[10]

According to the Suffolk County [New York] police report: "Margaret Greig was sitting on the Smith Point Beach slightly to the west of the bath house, facing southeast when she saw a 'flare' shoot upwards from the ocean. The flare went 'upwards in a concave arc.' The flare 'had a pink flame at first which turned into an orange flame' about a quarter of the way up. A thin trail of black smoke followed behind [the] flare. The flare shot upward for about five seconds and then turned into a fireball of orange fire. The black-smoke trail lingered afterwards for about six minutes. She estimated that the flare was about one mile out to sea."

"Long Island's Channel 55 cameraman James Hughes, said during an interview that he and another camera crew from one of the networks were at the airport when the C-130 [New York Air National Guard] landed. The crew, he said, stated they saw a missile heading toward Flight 800 just before they witnessed the explosion. The C-130 crew members were pulled away from the camera crews by what Hughes said appeared to be their superiors and came back claiming they had seen nothing."[11]

All the witnesses saw the same event. A plot of their sighting of the missile places it at the same point on the map, about 10 miles north-northeast of Flight 800 about 20 seconds before the missile impact. Description of the exhaust, launch noise, rocket motor noise and terminal explosions are all consistent.

A surface ship can be tracked on the Islip radar in the same area where these witnesses heard and saw a missile launch. The Islip radar also has a primary hit consistent with a missile launch, in the same area as this surface ship, about 17 seconds before Flight 800's transponder is silenced by a missile strike.

This surface track was expunged from the radar images presented by the NTSB in its "factual report" 13A. The NTSB also expunged an entire "armada" from the radar images released to the press and public. More than one-dozen ships, all steaming in the same direction, about 20 miles from the Flight 800 crash site, inside military warning zone W-105, can be seen on the radar fleeing the scene of the crime.

The above witnesses represent only one cluster of eyewitness accounts of a missile launch. A second missile was also launched from a point almost due south of Flight 800. A second cluster of witnesses, in boats and planes off the south shore of Long Island, describe the missile that struck the right side of Flight 800:

Robert Casola was off the south shore of Long Island; about 12 miles from what would become Flight 800's graveyard, when "he noticed what he thought was a distress flare. He saw a smoke trail rising from the ocean"[12] in the projectile's wake. Where the projectile's climb into the evening sky terminated, he "saw a small explosion, then a much larger explosion. He heard nothing over the noise of his motor."[13]

Albert Gipe, a "self-employed consultant, engineer and ex-naval officer, was transiting 25 nautical miles offshore aboard a sailboat in passage to Block Island. He was standing in the boat ladder well, facing Long Island, attempting to place a cellphone call. Mr. Gipe saw a streak of light like a 'tracer bullet' rise from the surface, going from south to north [toward Long Island] on a 30- to 45-degree elevation, which terminated six seconds later in an explosion that was followed shortly thereafter by another explosion. Mr. Gipe immediately wrote down his position and what he observed. Mr. Gipe was 17 nautical miles, or 34,000 yards, from TWA Flight 800 when it exploded. ... Mr. Gipe's recorded observations fit precisely to a successful short-range surface-to-air engagement of TWA Flight 800 with a large anti-aircraft missile fired from the immediate vicinity of the 30-knot radar contact" [one of the few surface vessel contacts not expunged from the radar records released by the NTSB].[14]

"William Gallagher, a commercial fisherman, had just finished trolling for squid when he saw a reddish light in the sky. 'I thought it was fireworks. And then I didn't know what to think because from the white ball, I saw two wide orange bands of light fall down, obviously the fuel igniting.' It was TWA Flight 800. When he returned to port he called the FBI. 'I'll lay my ass on the table and tell the president or the FBI, and someone can hypnotize me: there was no way that red light was descending,' Gallagher said. 'It was ascending. It made contact with what turned out to be that airplane and made a white bright light and then split in two.' He thinks something is wrong with the investigation. 'If I were in a courtroom and the prosecutor says I've got an eyewitness, then I become a trump card,' he said. 'We're not just one witness but 135 or more strong.' Officials say more than 400 eyewitnesses were interviewed, many reporting a red flare-like or fireworks-like object ascending toward the plane. 'I saw something hit the right side of the plane,' said Gallagher. 'My opinion was it blew the wing off on impact. I assumed something went through the airplane, like behind first class and into the wing.' Gallagher, of New Jersey, has worked the ocean waters near the crash for more than 15 years. 'My honest opinion, my gut feeling, is that we have the most brilliant people in the world and the best technology,' Gallagher said. 'If they've been on-scene for a year and they've not come up with something, as a critical thinker I have to ask, could they be covering up something?'[15] Gallagher also said the missile altered course, turning upward just prior to impacting the 747."

Commander William Donaldson[16] tape-recorded an interview with Roland Penney: "The FBI said, 'Are you sure you didn't see something going down … and not going up?' I said, 'No … gosh sakes I ain't that stupid, I ought to be able to tell if something is going up in the air or going down in the air. … No, and I said I'm not changing my mind about it. … I'll stick to that until I die. I said I saw something going up, and I said there was no question in my mind. I said I'm telling you what I saw. I'm not telling you what I think I saw. I said I saw something and … that's the way I am stating it. I'm not trying to make up a story just to be on the news or whatever. … I said I have no desire to be on the news—I don't even want to get involved in this stuff anymore. But I said there was definitely something going up and then it went behind … I said I'm assuming it's a cloud and then we saw this white light.'"

Donaldson: "Okay [when the tape recorder was off], you mentioned that a neighbor … we won't mention the name …

but had a similar experience apparently with an FBI interview, that they were trying to get her to say that it was going the other way."

Penney: "That's right."

Donaldson: "And she talked to you on the phone and got a little bit ..."

Penney: "She was upset because she says, 'I'm a grown woman—I don't drink,' and she says 'it wasn't because I had alcohol in me.' She says, ' I saw something definitely going up, and there is no question in my mind about that,' and she says, 'I'm not going to change my mind, either.'"

Lou Desyron was interviewed by ABC World News, Sunday, July 21, 1996, four days after Flight 800 went down: "We saw what appeared to be a flare going straight up. As a matter of fact we thought it was from a boat. It was a bright reddish-orange color. Once it went into flames I knew that it wasn't a flare."

Art Bell, December 1, 1998, interviewed Bill Lisle during his radio show:

Bell: Bill, where are you located?

Lisle: I'm located in Lindenhurst, Long Island.

Bell: Lindenhurst, Long Island. All right. You apparently were a mate on a commercial fishing boat of some kind?

Lisle: Yes, I was first mate on a charter boat fishing for blue fish about six miles off the beach.

Bell: On that night?

Lisle: Right.

Bell: So you had the advantage of being offshore—let's see ... six miles more or less west of the missile launch point, and it says here you watched it go from the surface into the cloud and then observed two explosions. Is that correct?

Lisle: Well, everything is correct. What I saw was, after it got up into the cloud cover I saw a large flash up in the clouds and then after that, another large flash, and then ... I saw stuff coming down.

Bell: Right. Let's back up. What were you able to see at ground level ... from the ocean where you were?

Lisle: Well, we were heading west and I was standing on the stern of the boat because we were trolling what they call blue fish, and I was watching the two lines running out the back of the boat. And all of a sudden I saw this large orange and red thing just take off from the surface of the ocean southeast of me.

Bell: I know it's difficult to estimate distance, but how far would you say this launch was from your ... ?

Lisle: It had to be maybe six miles.

Bell: Six miles.

Lisle: Maybe a little further—it's kinda tough to estimate how far, but I'd say something in that area.

Bell: Was there any question in your mind what you saw?

Lisle: None, not at all. From day one ... nobody will ever convince me any different about what I saw.

Bell: So you saw a missile leave the sea and streak up into the clouds. You saw one explosion, then you saw a secondary explosion.

Lisle: Right, I saw ... an explosion up in the cloud cover. I saw a flash—looked like sometimes you see lighting up in the clouds, and then I saw another one, and that was it.

Bell: You heard Suzanne before you, and I'm going to have to ask you some of the same questions. Number one—did you talk to the FBI?

Lisle: Yes I did. The second day after the accident they came down to the dock and interviewed me down at the dock.

Bell: At the dock?

Lisle: Right. I was a mate on a charter boat ... and when

we were coming in from a trip they were on the dock and they wanted to talk to me then, after we got tied up.

Bell: So you told them roughly what you just told me.

Lisle: Yes.

Bell: And their reaction?

Lisle: Their reaction to me was, "You actually want us to believe that you saw a missile go up there and shoot that plane down?" And I said "Yes."

Bell: That was their reaction? My God! So it's as though they were incredulous ... "You want us to believe that?" That kind of reaction?

Lisle: That's the impression I got—yes.

Major Fritz Meyer[17] was perhaps the closest eyewitness to Flight 800. "Meyer's attention was first called to the area ... 'by a streak of light moving from my right (west) to my left (east),' the same direction as the TWA flight, he said. ... [Captain Chris] Baur, on the left side of the cockpit, saw a streak moving from the left to right toward the approaching TWA aircraft before the initial explosion. The streak of light Meyer saw ... was red-orange in color ... there was what Meyer describes as a hard, very sudden, yellowish-white explosion that looked identical to the detonation of an anti-aircraft shell. ... 'It left a cloud of smoke just like a flak explosion does,' Meyer said. 'One or two seconds later, there was a second, hard explosion, almost pure white in color ... almost immediately there was a third explosion and fireball.' ... Baur also saw three explosions ... he contends they started from left (east) and went to the right (west). ... According to the crew, Baur called over the intercom to his flight engineer, MSgt. Dennis Richardson, 'Hey, Denny, is that pyro?' Within seconds he saw a hard explosion. Richardson, shifting in his seat from behind Baur, did not see the streak but did see the explosions."[18]

Shortly after retiring from the New York Air National

Guard, one of Meyer's speeches was captured on tape:

"Now, I went out to give aid as I told you, and found no survivors, and went back to my unit and went home that night. The next day at 4:00 P.M. we gave a press conference, and some reporters came to base and we sat in an auditorium on the base, and I came down from my office to participate in this press conference in which the crew of the C-130 and the rest of my crew and two para-rescue men who had seen a light in the sky, were all called in to tell what we saw to the news media. When I went into that press conference the public affairs officer from my unit gave me three criteria—he said 'do not speculate, do not give your opinion,' and 'do not discuss the condition of the bodies.' So those were the conditions under which we held that press conference. I described my streak of light and everything to the people there. I walked out of that room about an hour and 15 minutes later, and a fellow was watching a television in a room across the hall from the briefing room and he said, 'Hey, I just saw you on television—Peter Jennings says you said it was a missile.'

"Well, all hell broke loose because I had apparently violated the parameters of the press conference. The AJ of the New York State Air Guard was on the phone with me and wanted to know why I did that. I told him, 'General, the entire press conference was videotaped—look at the videotape. I never said it was a missile.' Well, the media had picked it up as a missile and therefore I was given the task to go back to the media and tell them 'I didn't say it was a missile.' So I went back—at that time the next day—two days later—the Friday after the accident. I went back to the Coast Guard station at East Moriches where I gave in excess of 40 interviews to news media crews in which I told them I did not say it was a missile. They, of course, reported, 'Pilot on the scene says it was not a missile.' There came a period in here where we decided—and it was a mutual decision, it was not an order—that we were just going to stop talking to the media because no matter what we told them they screwed it up. We stopped talking to the media. We also decided we were witnesses to an accident—that there were pros in the NTSB who were going to come in and do a first-rate job. And we waited for a year for those pros to do a first-rate job and we don't believe they did. ..."

Dwight Brumley was a "U.S. Navy electronic-warfare technician" en route to Providence, Rhode Island, aboard USAir Flight 217. He was seated on the right side of the aircraft when he "saw a flare-like streak" pass USAir Flight 217 as it approached Long Island at 21,000 feet. Both the plane and projectile were headed in the same general direction—toward TWA Flight 800, a few miles ahead and to the east of USAir Flight 217. "Brumley saw a small explosion in the area where he had last seen" the projectile. Then he observed a much larger explosion, a few thousand feet below Flight 217, which was at 21,000 feet.[19]

James Nugent was also a passenger aboard Flight 217, seated on the right side of the plane immediately behind Brumley. "Nugent said he could see the cabin lights inside the plane a moment before it erupted into a fireball."[20]

This second clump of eyewitnesses had all seen a missile launched from a point south of TWA Flight 800's west-to-east flight path, south of Long Island and northwest of military warning zone W-105. Major Fritz Meyer, on duty with the New York Air National Guard and in the air a few miles from Flight 800, had seen the same streak a U.S. Navy officer, Dwight Brumley, had also seen from close range. Eyewitnesses on boats south of Long Island, one who immediately recorded his position and what he had seen, make it possible to plot a launch point and trajectory leading straight to Flight 800.

This launch site correlates closely to a large ship traveling in excess of 30 knots that was tracked by the FAA radar at Islip, New York. The ship continued at 30 knots after the missile launch, narrowly escaping the flaming debris from Flight 800. It escaped to the south, joining up with a flotilla of at least 30 large ships, all steaming in the same direction at the same speed: east, away from the shootdown of Flight 800. Some of the flotilla's ships were inside W-105, the military warning zone that had been reserved for military activity.[21] The rest were rapidly approaching the western W-105 boundary.

4

WHAT THE RADAR REALLY OBSERVED

"I won't go so far as to say it was terrorism, but there was sabotage here,"
[Senator] Hatch said. "We're looking at a criminal act. We're looking at
somebody who either put a bomb on it or shot a missile, a surface-to-air
missile." Hatch said, "the National Transportation Safety Board should
now turn the investigation over to the FBI because the crash was not re-
lated to an aviation problem. ... It's very—almost 100 percent unlikely
that this was a mechanical failure. ... It looks pretty darn conclusive that
it was an explosion caused either internally or externally by a criminal
act." Investigators told CNN that there is no indication that the Boeing 747
suffered a catastrophic mechanical failure.

CNN
July 19, 1996

FAA air traffic controllers saw a series of events unfold on
the radar screen. The controller responsible for monitoring TWA
Flight 800 watched what he believed was a high-speed object
on the radar screen intersect Flight 800's path. He then saw the
747's transponder go into "coast," and an ever-increasing number of hits tracked the debris as parts of the plane fell toward
the ocean.

But that was not all that was captured on the 11 radar
covering the area. More than 30 ships and aircraft without transponders were also tracked in the vicinity of Flight 800, one
within 2.9 miles of the airliner when it was hit. This 30-knot
target continued moving south at a high rate of speed until it
approached an armada of ships that could also be seen by the
FAA radar. The 30-knot track then disappeared from the radar

screen, suggesting that the ships even further from the Islip radar were larger.

Flight 800 exploded and was breaking up in a brilliant series of explosions and fireballs just 3.5 miles away from the 30-knot track speeding south, but it never slowed or turned to race to the scene and search for survivors.[1]

Also visible on the FAA radar were two ships close to shore, about 10 miles north-northeast of Flight 800 when the first missile struck. An FAA radar may have captured a possible "backstop" missile in its early stage of flight. A primary radar hit can be seen in the immediate area of one of these ships, at the precise time required to launch and impact Flight 800, 10 miles away—less than 20 seconds.

Early in the investigation, a retired senior intelligence officer told me that if the Navy was stupid enough to conduct a missile exercise south of Long Island, they would have a "backstop" anti-missile missile platform between the missile launch point and Long Island. A cluster of witnesses pinpoints an apparent backstop missile launch from a point due north of the missile shot further out in the Atlantic that was observed by a second cluster of witnesses. The FAA radar has a one-hit primary consistent with the launch of a backstop missile where the witness cluster reported seeing and hearing a missile launch.

FAA personnel were so certain that a missile brought the plane down, they notified the White House Situation Room[2], which immediately brought the entire United States government national security apparatus online.

Television screens across America were soon filled with eyewitness accounts of a missile streaking into the sky. At least one military aircrew was interviewed live, on Long Island television, telling the interviewer they had seen a missile take out an aircraft.

Eyewitnesses covering a 360-degree arch on the south side of Long Island—in boats, on the ground, and in the air—

observed a reddish-orange or white streak ascending into the sky. Some saw it strike a plane, a few said they actually saw the missile, not just the bright flame blowing out the tail of the rocket motor as it pushed the projectile along at speeds in excess of Mach 2. Many never heard any noise.

The FAA radar in the area of Flight 800 saw multiple 300-plus-knot blips, without transponders, before and after the 747 crashed. More than 30 ships, headed east in apparent formation with helicopters and planes flying overhead, were also seen on the radar.

Over the coming months and years the FBI and Navy would vehemently deny any Navy assets were in the area except for a P-3 antisubmarine plane about three miles south of Flight 800 when it blew-up. Those denials are factually false.

The Navy had "significant Naval units" in the area. When confronted with a journalist's Freedom of Information Act request to turn over the documents, the government elected to invoke national security [5 U.S.C., Section 552 (b)(1)].[3]

At issue was an August 5, 1996, message: "Subject/FBI Request for Information—TWA Flight 800." The Joint Chiefs of Staff had requested the data be accumulated. Three paragraphs were included in the message detailing Navy assets in the area of TWA Flight 800 when it went down. Paragraph two was withheld for national security reasons because it contained "information concerning the movement of significant Naval units" in the area of TWA Flight 800.

A Navy radar database, from the Navy radar at Riverhead, New York (RP-44), was released under the Freedom of Information Act (FOIA). It confirms the presence of an even larger number of ships being tracked south and southeast of Flight 800. Surface ships 195 miles away were tracked, meaning the Riverhead Navy radar was being fed multiple radar signals from an airborne platform.

Something far more significant was hidden within the

pages of radar data—a military asset with transponder code number 1275 was also in the vicinity of Flight 800, flying at 98,000 feet. A sensitive source closely connected to the military and projects within Lockheed's famous "Skunk Works," when shown this radar data, confirmed that only two military assets are capable of flying that high: the SR-71, and a highly classified craft from the Skunk Works that can fly or hover for extended periods of time at that altitude.

The SR-71 flies at about 2,000 miles per hour, while the Skunk Works craft can hover or fly at extremely slow speeds at 98,000 feet. The craft seen on the Navy radar was going about 20 knots, confirming that the vehicle attached to transponder code 1275 could only be the new Skunk Works craft.

It is a platform from which multiple 21st-century military operations can be performed. Two of these operations may relate to what happened the evening of July 17, 1996. It can provide a surveillance, tracking and information relay platform for Cooperative Engagement Capability (CEC) Army, Navy and Air Force units working in a littoral warfare environment.

It is also a platform from which missiles or other exotic weapons can be used to destroy a ballistic missile attack on military forces operating in a littoral warfare environment. This ability may violate current anti-ballistic missile (ABM) treaties with the Russians.

There is only one explanation for using a transponder in an environment 60,000 feet above any other air traffic: to allow it to be seen by those who were witnessing some type of military exercise.

Also "seen" by the Riverhead Navy radar, according to a source of New York Air National Guard pilot, Major Fritz Meyer, were "two targets approaching TWA Flight 800 before the impact—one a high-speed supersonic, and one subsonic." Four lines of the Riverhead radar database, 2.8 seconds prior to the event that initiated the Flight 800 crash, were partially expunged from the Riverhead radar database I obtained.

New York Air National Guard pilot Meyer was one of two pilots in the air the evening of July 17, 1996, when Flight 800 went down. Each saw a high-speed object approach Flight 800. Meyer saw the high-speed object travel from west to east. Captain Chris Bauer, also a New York Air National Guard pilot, saw a streak traveling from east to west.

Major Meyer gave the confidential-source information to Congressman Duncan, who heads the House Aviation subcommittee. Congressman Duncan, in turn, sent a letter to the FBI asking for the Riverhead radar tape.

Even though the FBI, up to that point, had not admitted they possessed the Riverhead tape, they told Congressman Duncan it was in their possession, but he could not see it. They assured the congressman that "it didn't show anything unusual."[4]

In addition to the 98,000-foot transponder, the Riverhead radar confirms the FBI and NTSB fabricated a story to discredit radar data leaked to the French magazine *Paris Match* in 1997.

Paris Match published a series of radar images in conjunction with former John F. Kennedy Press Secretary Pierre Salinger, publicly stating the images provided evidence that a missile was seen by the radar. The FBI and NTSB mounted a major media campaign to vilify and destroy Salinger. The government alleged the blips were anomalies because no other radar "saw" the blips.

That can now be definitely demonstrated to be false. The Navy Riverhead radar, as well as the FAA Islip [New York] and Boston radar, all confirm that the blips published by *Paris Match* were not anomalies—they were "seen" by three radar.

Because the FBI and NTSB so viciously attacked Salinger, while in possession of classified data proving beyond any doubt the blips recorded an event within a few miles of Flight 800 shortly before its demise, it is reasonable to infer the blips did record a missile in flight. There is no other rational explanation.

5

THE WHITE HOUSE

The FAA had alerted the national security apparatus. The White House Situation Room, where such events are closely monitored, began to perform its function. The President, head of the National Security Council, was inside the White House that night. He was the decision maker. Others could offer advice, but he made the final decision.

The president knew the FAA believed a missile had brought down Flight 800. He knew the United States had significant assets in the immediate area. He knew America's most closely guarded military asset was in the vicinity.

The radar did not show these assets change course to pursue a fleeing terrorist. The radar showed ships at high speed evacuating the area. So we know from radar data that no order was given to pursue fleeing terrorists.

I had a White House source[1] that described the White House Situation Room in the minutes prior to the loss of TWA Flight 800. There was a large gathering of senior military and civilian government personnel. It is not known if any senior members of Congress were also present.

This group was watching in real time, on a battlefield monitor, a Navy demonstration of a new, secret anti-aircraft missile developed for the Seawolf-class of attack submarines that would be used for self-defense when sailing ahead of the fleet without air cover, the source said. Because the submarine's new mission is closely aligned with the "littoral" warfare concept—shallow water—these multi-billion-dollar submarines

would need protection from enemy shore-based defenses—
both air and sea—and an underwater-launched anti-aircraft
missile would be a new, potent defensive shield when operating solo in dangerous waters.

It was a vertical launch system contained within the hull
of the Seawolf. [The source did not state that the Seawolf was
the boat involved.] The multi-tube launcher swivels to point
the missile in the desired direction before launch. Once out of
the tube, the missile is no longer under control of the submarine's weapons software. A second [Navy] source confirmed
that an underwater-launched missile was responsible for the
downing of TWA Flight 800. A third [Navy] source described
the missile and swivel-tube concept, taken from a British design and upgraded for use in Seawolf-class submarines.

It was like boys' night out, according to the White House
source. A fun evening watching America's tax dollars at work.
A military platform high in the sky was transferring radar data
to the White House Situation Room in real time, as events unfolded south of Long Island.

But something went wrong. Everyone watched the live
demonstration as the missile streaked into the sky in the wrong
direction and hit TWA Flight 800, the source said.

There was a long silence. Finally, someone said, "Oops."

That seemed to galvanize the senior people in the room
into action. This senior group huddled, and within a few minutes quietly announced that national security was being in-
voked.

This explains the seemingly irrational decision by President Clinton not to immediately activate all U.S. military assets capable of hunting down and destroying the "terrorists"
who made this attack on the sovereignty of the United States,
killing 230 citizens. The order was not given because the President knew who pulled the trigger.

At 0200 hours, July 18, 1996, about 5.5 hours after hundreds of eyewitnesses saw a missile rise into the evening sky, a video teleconference was held between the White House and other sites, with high-level government personnel participating, certainly including Attorney General Janet Reno, Jim Kallstrom and his senior FBI staff in New York, and FBI Director Louis Freeh in Washington, D.C. "Top intelligence and security officials were told in a video-teleconference from the White House Situation Room that radar tapes showed an object headed at the plane before it exploded."[2]

The Navy Riverhead, New York, radar is believed to have had a primary (non-transponder) missile radar hit 2.8 seconds prior to Flight 800's last transponder hit. This hit was explained as an "unknown msg" in the database printout, but someone forgot to also remove the time of the hit and the channel [A, B or C] that recorded the event.

A few hours after the White House Situation Room teleconference told high-level government officials there was hard evidence of a missile, "White House Press Secretary Mike McCurry said investigators were 'trying to clarify any abnormalities' that turned up on the radar screen."[3]

Only a president who needs time to formulate a scheme to deceive the American people would have his press secretary deliver such a message.

Asked about speculation on a missile, McCurry replied, "There's no American official with half a brain who ought to be speculating on anything of that nature. There's no concrete information that would lead any of us in the United States government to draw that kind of conclusion."[4]

As McCurry was speaking those words, a senior Fox News reporter who had been out all night running down eyewitnesses, was quietly taken aside by a military officer and, off the record, told that they had been ordered to "stand down" for 24 hours while the White House decided how to handle a "major screw-up."[5]

The next day, July 18, the NTSB formed a Witness Group to begin the process of interviewing the eyewitnesses to a missile as mandated by federal law, which makes the NTSB the "priority" investigator. Other federal agencies may also investigate, but none may interfere with the NTSB's priority mission. But the FBI immediately stepped in and demanded the NTSB Witness Group be disbanded. Only the FBI would conduct missile-witness interviews.

An FBI/Justice Department Flight 800 team was to be used as an integral part of a White House-controlled operation to alter the history of TWA Flight 800. Those in control could not know the precise end-game until they had: (1) launched a psychological operation to neutralize major media; (2) witnessed the degree to which major media could be controlled; (3) determined to what extent debris could be pre-screened and removed from the investigation and (4) to what degree significant debris that made it past the pre-screening process could be altered before a final plan of action could be determined.

The Commerce Department's National Oceanographic and Atmospheric Administration's (NOAA) ship Rude began surveying the ocean bottom south of Long Island on July 18. By the next day it had finished mapping the debris field, giving the NTSB and FBI a highly accurate roadmap from which to make diving decisions. An analysis of the NTSB and Supervisor of Salvage databases provides compelling evidence that this information was used during the month of July to recover sensitive debris so officials could begin to formulate a plan to alter the debris field.

A corrupt administration contaminated the bureaucratic decision-making structure. Sensitive military assets in the area made it impossible to lay all the facts before the American public. An admission that a missile[s] downed TWA Flight 800, regardless of who pulled the trigger, would have legitimized a politically-correct major media feeding frenzy.

Honesty is a slippery slope that a reasonably honest administration would have difficulty dealing with. A corrupt administration with a finely-honed team of experienced disinformation practitioners would not have a clue how to proceed in a reasonably honest manner that had a significant downside but no discernable benefit.

Government action in the immediate aftermath of the crash proves beyond a reasonable doubt that honesty was never a serious consideration.

6

ALTERING THE DEBRIS FIELD

Part of Navy Seal Team 6 was airlifted to the scene shortly after TWA Flight 800 crashed.[1] Recovery of key debris from the ocean floor began within 48 hours after the crash.

I confirmed the early removal of debris from the ocean floor when I inspected the Calverton hangar on December 22, 1998. The starboard potable water bottle carries the recovery date in two places: 7/19. [Photos taken December 22 showing this recovery date cannot be shown because they have been blocked from being published in this book by the Justice Department.] Had they been recovered floating in the Atlantic, the Supervisor of Salvage and NTSB databases would have logged "floating." [I obtained a copy of the "SUPSALV" database printout dated August 17, 1996, from a sensitive source. Floating debris was logged in under this heading.]

This did not happen. Instead, these critical pieces of the recovery operation were withheld from the NTSB database accessible to many Flight 800 investigators. And, they were also withheld from the more secure Supervisor of Salvage database.

The potable water bottles, attached at the factory to the forward side of the front spar, each weighed about 1,000 pounds.[2] Unlike the aluminum structure surrounding these extremely large and heavy cylinders—each almost six-feet tall and 2.5 feet in diameter—when propelled by an explosive blast, they will cause extensive damage wherever they strike.

Potable water bottle exit points are key analytical factors on which any non-politicized investigation would focus. If an explosion came from the cargo containers forward of the bottles, they would have caused enormous damage when propelled aft into the center wing tank (CWT). That did not occur. They would have caused an equal amount of damage if propelled forward by a blast from the center area of the CWT. That also did not happen.

The initiating event propelled the water bottles from right to left. At least one of the bottles smashed through the aluminum structure of the left side at the point where the left wing joins the fuselage. This damage is interior to exterior, creating a hole through which a water bottle could easily pass. Nothing else from the interior of the plane had the mass to leave such devastation at the exit point. Significant right-to-left damage was inflicted on the front spar, to which the bottles were attached. This damage can be seen in photos taken of the front spar in early 1997. The right-to-left force propelled the bottles to the left and upward. An easily discernable, massive path of destruction can be tracked. The probable path of the bottles can then be seen in the radar database recording the disintegration of Flight 800.

When I inspected and photographed the mockup on December 22, 1998, the front spar had undergone significant alteration to remove the right-to-left damage. Blast damage emanating from a hole in the right-side-of-body [RSOB], i.e., the right side of the CWT, leading to the right-to-left front spar damage, had also been removed. Debris piece CW-601, in a direct line between the RSOB and the right-to-left front spar damage, had undergone significant alteration sometime after April 1997.[3] I took extensive photographs of the altered version of CW-601. [The Justice Department has blocked publication of the photos in this book.]

Once the potable water bottle[s] exited through the left side of the 747, a path opened for CW-504 to fall away from the stricken plane with little damage. CW-504, a piece of aluminum about the size of a sheet of plywood, is the first significant debris the NTSB/FBI allowed to be entered into the non-classified NTSB debris-field database. NASA chemist Charles Bassett tested residue from CW-504 and found nitrate, a possible indicator of an explosive event. When he advised the NTSB of this discovery, he was ordered to cease further testing.

The starboard water bottle has three equidistant horizontal strike marks that appear to be a perfect match for the rectangular exit point in the port [left]-side roof of Flight 800, above rows 10 to 15. [The Justice Department has blocked publication of the photo in this book.]

The FAA radar at Islip, New York, tracked debris blasted out of Flight 800. Two objects from the 747, each with the mass to be propelled at an initial velocity in excess of 1,000 mph, can be seen. Less than four seconds after Flight 800's transponder quit, one of these two objects was 15,000 feet north-northeast of the 747, while the second object was 9,000 feet east. Each object had a second radar hit as it fell toward the ocean.

Neither of these objects was the fuselage of the plane, which continued to be tracked by Islip radar, with no loss of forward momentum—meaning it was not climbing.

In an unguarded moment of unbridled honesty, accurate latitude and longitude numbers identifying the true location on the ocean floor from which some of the debris was removed were inserted in the Supervisor of Salvage database during the early phase of the debris-recovery operation. Other debris had the latitude entered, but the longitude was left blank in order to move the debris further east if necessary.

Clearly no one anticipated the removal of the NTSB database and the Supervisor of Salvage database from the exclusive control of those bent on rearranging the debris field.

Cross-referencing the two databases provides a rare opportunity to see a cover-up in action. The following graph provides a small sample of the actual location of debris and victims. Some of the debris was moved thousands of feet to the east, while other critical evidence was never inserted in the NTSB November 13, 1996, database. [Go to www.altered-evidence.com to see graph.]

During the final days of the July diving operation, Navy divers recovered two seats from row 18, seats 8 and 10. Recovered on July 30, the NTSB alleged they were not recovered until August 4. They were recovered too far to the west, so a fictitious latitude/longitude was entered into the NTSB computer [page 8 of the 11-13-96 NTSB database printout obtained by me. Line 4 has longitude 72-38-54.89 and latitude 40-38-45.77]. The actual recovery date, July 30, and location, longitude 72-39-16.1 and latitude 40-38-44.9, were obtained by me using a telephoto lens to get at the red A-TAG containing this information. [Go to www.altered-evidence.com to see photo.]

This photo represents direct evidence that the NTSB inserted a false recovery location about 1,500 feet east of the actual location into its database.

The first 100 A-TAGS, affixed to the first 100 pieces of debris removed from the ocean floor between July 18 and August 2, 1996, provides an excellent example of the extent the debris field was tampered with. The first three A-TAGS were not entered into the Supervisor of Salvage database,[4] and only 47 of the next 97 A-TAGS were logged in.

Fifty-three A-TAGS, issued at the onset of debris recovery in the western-most red zone, were issued to debris too sensitive to place in databases accessed by most of the Flight 800 investigators. Two were issued to the potable water bottles. A few more were issued to pieces from the nose-wheel area[5].

The tags were issued to a diving team[s] that, by August 2, 1996, was operating in the western-most red zone, in an area about 2,000 feet north-south, and 1,500 feet east-west.

A-TAG 004 was issued to one of the four forward cargo containers, AKN7415, found within this area on August 2. In the NTSB database it was moved 3,000 feet east.

The DME, A-TAG 051, located in the electronics bay underneath the forward part of the 747, was also located in this diving area on August 2. It was moved almost 3,000 feet east. Row 11, seat 6, A-TAG 068, was recovered the same day, from the same area and moved about 3,000 feet to the east.

A-TAG 051 is particularly interesting. Recovered at latitude 40-39-03.8, debris target 2981.2S, the forward-right lower cargo door, just to the rear of the cockpit area, was blasted into two major pieces. Its true location on the ocean floor was so sensitive that the longitude, revealing how close to JFK airport it was found, was not listed on the Supervisor of Salvage database. The A-Tag was entered into the SUPSALV database but not the NTSB's.

(Preceeding photo shows the right side of the cockpit, including the Flight Engineer station.)

The reason is apparent. A tremendous force was required to rip the cargo door in half. The entire forward area of the 747 receiving the greatest external blast damage was eliminated from the Calverton mockup. The following two photos—(1) the lower area of the right side of the cockpit; and (2) the right front of the 747—both reveal tremendous blast damage, damage that could only come from an external source.

The right side of the TWA Flight 800 mockup, looking forward. The shredded lower right side of the cockpit is a few feet forward of the mockup's termination point.

The NTSB would concoct an explanation that this damage is consistent with water impact. But the right side of the 747 was not pushed inward by water impact. A force originating below and slightly to the starboard side of the cockpit obliterated the lower front and right side of the airplane.

The 747 was moving east-northeast [71 degrees] at six-feet per .01 second. The damage in this area of the airplane is consistent with Flight 800 flying through an external blast. The blast force entered the forward cargo bay area and blew out the right-forward side of the aircraft. In .06 seconds the 747 traveled 42 feet, the distance down the right side of the airplane with the most extensive damage. The two starboard [right] cargo containers in this area of the 747 received significantly more damage than the port-side containers. One of the containers, AKN7415, left Flight 800 so early it was moved 3,000 feet east in the NTSB database.

The following radar graph shows debris being blasted from Flight 800 in a west-southwest direction, consistent with the external explosion described above. [Go to www.altered-evidence.com to see graph.]

Remembering Pan Am Flight 103 that was downed by an on-board bomb, probably the most famous of all the photos from this crash is the one with the cockpit laying intact on the ground after free-falling from about 30,000 feet. Yet, the damage it suffered when impacting hard Scottish dirt was insignificant when compared to the lower right side of Flight 800's cockpit that separated from the fuselage at about 13,000 feet.

The forward-right, lower cargo bay door is within a few feet of the lower-right cockpit. It too suffered exterior-to-interior blast damage so severe that it tore the cargo door into two pieces. The cargo door was entered in the SUPSALV database, but not the NTSB's, nor included in the mockup.

Much more was required, however, to alter this portion of Flight 800's demise. The nose gear, B-TAG 001, and nose wheel, B-TAG 002, were not entered into the NTSB database. Three of the four nose-gear doors, located below and a few feet aft of the cockpit, were recovered early in the red zone. So early was the departure from the stricken aircraft, and so sensitive was the damage to these parts, that they were excluded from the Supervisor of Salvage list and the NTSB database.

But they did receive A-TAGS. And they were discussed in NTSB Exhibit 18C.[6] This report is a classic example of focusing first on a politically-mandated conclusion, then attempting to explain what caused the damage. Five scenarios were laid out in 18C, all mechanical.

The report concluded, without addressing the issue, that an external blast could not have caused the early loss of these doors. Then the 16-page report describes in detail how the doors were indeed blasted inward, an event that could *only* occur if a missile with a proximity fuse detonated under the nose of Flight 800.

From the earliest moments of the Flight 800 investigation, agents of the United States government engaged in a scheme to alter the debris field. That was not all they would alter from the earliest moments of the investigation.

7

"Justice" at the Scene of the Crime

The United States government had a problem. The FBI was fully prepared to do whatever was necessary to shape the investigative outcome to match whatever policy was finally settled on.

Elements inside the NTSB, however, were not yet fully onboard in the hours after the 747 splashed into the waters south of Long Island. There was a rebellion in the ranks. An NTSB Witness Team had been formed, and it was determined to comply with the law passed by Congress, mandating it as the lead investigative unit on the scene.

There were hundreds of eyewitnesses to a missile rising into the sky in a reddish- orange blaze just prior to Flight 800's demise. The NTSB had a legal obligation to obtain the evidence contained within the brains of these witnesses.

Within the upper reaches of the government, at the decision-making level above Janet Reno and Louis Freeh, a decision was made to begin the process of making the Flight 800 investigation fit whatever policy the bureaucracy would shape over the coming days and weeks. Controlling access to information that would damage the government's ability to first select the cause of the crash, then shape the analysis, was essential. The NTSB Witness Group rebellion would have to be stamped out. James Kallstrom sent an FBI team to lean on the leaders of the rebellion, but the Witness Group resisted.

This called for stronger measures.

The 5'2", 140-pound Justice Department lawyer assigned

the task of putting down the rebellion seemed to have a chip on her shoulder. She walked aggressively, and when talking made a deliberate attempt to speak in a loud, low, almost masculine voice. Shaking hands was a physical contest. Although of diminutive stature, Valerie Caproni was determined to be the biggest, baddest dude inside the Department of Justice. When Janet Reno needed a legal hit-man for less-than-legal assignments, Val Caproni was her (wo)man.

Title 49, section 1131(a)(2), says: "An investigation by the [NTSB] Board ... has *priority* over any investigation by another department, agency or instrumentality of the United States Government." [Emphasis added] In other words, a "parallel" FBI investigation is inferior to the NTSB investigation. "The [NTSB] Board shall provide for appropriate participation,"[1] not the FBI or Justice Department.

Caproni, as an attorney and officer of the court, knew the FBI was the inferior agency at the crash scene. She knew the NTSB could not legally be hindered or restricted in pursuing the cause of the accident.

In spite of the law, she put the full weight of "Justice" and the FBI behind her presence at the meeting with the NTSB Witness Team. They were ordered to cease and desist. The FBI, according to an NTSB document describing the meeting, would not tolerate a second group obtaining evidence of a missile that might conflict with the story the FBI was going to develop.

So the NTSB Witness Group disbanded. The FBI was left as the sole purveyor of the truth.

The FBI missile-witness team would be able to shape the interviews without worrying about a conflicting report from an NTSB Witness Group. Valerie Caproni's first mission within the cover-up of the missile-downed Flight 800 was a success.

It would not be her last mission.

8

HANGAR MAN

Captain Terrell Stacey was a senior manager at TWA. He had flown the 747 into JFK the night before it crashed. He was in charge of all 747 pilot activity within the airline. So it was logical that he would be among the first TWA employees assigned to the NTSB investigation.

Within days of arriving at the Calverton hangar, Stacey was given his first look at the government's plan of action. He was assigned to the NTSB eyewitness team, interviewing those who saw a missile climbing from the area of the ocean and intercepting Flight 800. But the FBI stepped in and ordered the witness team to disband.

Even with exclusive access to the witnesses, a story soon emerged from the interviews of a missile downing TWA Flight 800: "The FBI, by this time (September 22, 1996), had interviewed 154 witnesses to a missile rising into the sky, according to newspaper reports. Thirty-four were judged credible. 'Some of these people were extremely credible,' a top federal official said. ... Struck by the number and confidence of the witnesses, the FBI sat down many of the witnesses with U.S. military experts, who debriefed them and independently confirmed for the FBI that their descriptions matched surface-to-air missile attacks,"[1] Murry Weiss reported in the *New York Post*, September 22, 1996.

Shortly after Stacey and I began our source-to-journalist relationship, Stacey confirmed this story, adding that the 34 most credible witnesses were taken to the sites from where they observed the missile's flight. Surveying equipment was set up. A plot was made of the exact position the missile was first seen, and a second plot established to where it caused an explosion in the sky. According to Stacey, all 34 witnesses saw an object rise from the surface and intercept the flight path of Flight 800.

Shortly after the FBI had military personnel confirm the witnesses were indeed describing an event consistent with a surface-to-air missile shot, David Hendrix broke a story about the military zones near Flight 800's flight path being "hot" that night. He had received a number of FAA documents from a source within the government. These documents reveal multiple warning and restricted zones south of Long Island being activated on July 17, 1996. The first to activate was W-105, and it had remained so the entire day.[2] W-105's northwestern boundary was within miles of the 747's flight path. From 1000 to 1300 hours, July 17, it had been activated for a Cooperative Engagement Capability (CEC) exercise. CEC creates synergistic AEGIS radar coverage for U.S. Naval units. Each AEGIS radar is linked in order to provide comprehensive protection against any approaching hostile threat.

[SEE EXHIBIT A]

Hendrix attempted to get the Navy and FBI on the record about offshore Navy exercises on July 17. Both refused comment. A spokesman for the Joint Chiefs of Staff, in response to a reporter's question, said, "I am not aware that there were any military exercises in the area. I've been told by the Joint Staff that there were not."[3]

9

POWER STRUGGLE

The NTSB/FBI investigation was well into its second month when, in late August, Jim Kallstrom announced his belief that the FBI would have sufficient evidence within 48 hours that a bomb was responsible for the loss of TWA Flight 800, thereby declaring the crash a crime scene. The FBI cannot legally take control of an aircraft crash investigation unless it declares that a crime was responsible for the downing of the plane. Somewhere in the upper reaches of the Clinton administration, this FBI attempt to seize control was thwarted.

Shortly thereafter, *The New York Times* published an article entitled, "Crash Simulation Sets T.W.A. Blast in One Small Area."[1] The subtitle identified the article as having a high probability of being leaked by the FBI's head of the Flight 800 investigation, Jim Kallstrom: "Holes in Seat Backs of Row 23 Also Offer Hints of Bomb, The Investigators Say."

The article, for the first time, revealed that federal investigators had "created a sophisticated computer simulation" of the 747 from the moment the aircraft began to shed parts. The first debris "came from one confined area on the right side" of the plane, "above and ahead of the wing."[2] This describes RF-35, a piece of the right-side fuselage. Also leaving the plane at the same time were seats from rows 17 and 18, seats 8 and 10. These seats landed so early in the red zone that the location they were found was altered, moving them 1,500 feet further east.

Multiple sources said seats on the far right side of row 23

had "several fist-sized holes" through the seat backs, rear to front. This is the area identified by the computer simulation as the site of the initial blast, the article said. I obtained FBI photos under discovery revealing that the damage to the seatbacks in this area suffered much more damage than described in *The Times* article. "The microscopic traces of the plastic explosive PETN, discovered during tests at the Federal Bureau of Investigation laboratory in Washington, were also found in this general area,"[3] according to the article.

This article could not have been written without the co-operation of Kallstrom. Facts were pouring out of the FBI-side of the Flight 800 investigation, from many sources. *The Times* had become the semi-official mouthpiece for the FBI Flight 800 "investigation." The article had all the earmarks of a power struggle within the Clinton administration in which the FBI was aligned against political forces inside the White House.

FBI Director Louis Freeh apparently decided to force the issue. The FBI wanted to take over the investigation, throw the NTSB out, and declare the cause of the crash to be a terrorist act. It would have been a smart move from a law enforcement perspective. Exclusive control of the evidence makes it much easier to come up with a pre-determined cause. Apparently, it was not considered a smart *political* move. Only bureaucratic forces with support from President Clinton could have stopped this power play.

The New York Times article then came within 10 feet of identifying a highly sensitive area that would be tampered with and altered over the coming year in order to remove major evidence of a missile entry point and warhead blast:

In row after row, the tattered seats are burned or ripped or have parts missing. But based on the computer simulation and other evidence, one small area stands out as the likeliest candidate for the initial blast, several investigators said: at the right end of row 23, directly above the center fuel tank and about 15 feet behind the spot where the leading edge of the wing joins the fuselage. This is where the metal backs of two seats are perforated by the fist-size holes.[4]

What *The Times* was not aware of was the presence of a 3 x 4-foot hole in the right side of the center wing tank (RSOB). Row 23 is about five-feet above this hole and perhaps five-feet forward of its center. SWB-2, which is in the center of the hole, is accordioned inward approximately five feet. The right side of SWB-3, debris piece CW-601, just forward of this hole, has many blast-type holes as well as significant heat damage. The front spar six-feet forward of SWB-3 has a distinct right-to-left damage pattern (as does the mid-spar, which is about two feet aft of the hole).

Thirteen pieces of the RSOB fell from the plane too early in the breakup sequence to be allowed into the NTSB computer, failing to conform to the agency's "mechanical" hypothesis.[5] Several pieces of the right wing in the area of this hole tested positive for explosive residue, as did residue from inside the cabin in the area of the RSOB hole. The right wing mid-spar, in the area of the RSOB, was so severely fragmented, according to an NTSB report, that it could not be reconstructed. The Bureau of Alcohol, Tobacco and Firearms (BATF), in writing, identified an external-to-internal hole, beginning inboard of the number-three engine (right wing, inner engine) and culminating at the RSOB hole. NTSB investigators found pieces of the leading edge of the right wing, inboard of the number-three engine, with blast type holes. A five-foot piece of this debris tested positive for explosives and was promptly confiscated by the FBI and flown to Washington, D.C. It then disappeared.

Rows 17, 18 and 19 had a reddish-orange residue, unique to those rows. The residue, when tested, was consistent with a solid-fuel missile exhaust and/or incendiary warhead explosion. Florida State University conducted additional testing that eliminated the 3M glue used by TWA to refurbish the seats as a possible source of the residue.

All of these facts were hidden from *The New York Times*. Only NTSB and FBI personnel at the senior management levels were aware of all the evidence pointing to a missile. The highly compartmentalized nature of the FBI/NTSB investigations precluded anyone outside the senior management levels from gaining a comprehensive picture.

Information from the Calverton hangar computer analysis, leaked to *The Times* in late August 1996, offers a look inside an investigation that would soon have to be prepared to deal with a missile theory or be steered in another direction. Analysis showed the 747 being "shoved sharply left, shifting half a mile out of its original flight path. ..."[6] This is consistent with a missile entering under the right wing, traveling in an upward direction through the number-three fuel tank. Such a damage pattern exists in NTSB photos from early 1997. The critical pieces, however, have been altered and/or concealed.

This first debris included portions of the inner right wing and RSOB—not entered into the NTSB computer because their position in the early debris field precludes a mechanical initiating event.

Almost three-quarters of a second [.73 seconds] before the Cockpit Voice Recorder (CVR) and Flight Data Recorder (FDR) lost electrical power, the CVR detected a "change in the background signal as observed on the Captain's radio channel."[7] A scenario of what occurred during this .73 seconds is consistent with all pre-altered debris.[8]

A missile approached the 747 from below and to the right. It impacted the right wing inboard of the number-three engine, traveling upward in an approximate 30- to 40-degree angle, shattering the right wing mid-spar, punching a hole through the RSOB at SWB-2, exploding just inside the CWT, with the momentum [a Bernoulli effect[9] enhanced by an explosion] of the explosion carrying right to left across the CWT, leaving blast damage and chemical debris, shattering the LSOB, creating a hydraulic effect inside the nearly full left-wing fuel tanks, causing the top of the left wing to blow off, but only directly above the tanks.

The microsecond pause as the blast-wave slammed into the LSOB is consistent with the CWT expanding outward, much like a balloon just prior to bursting. The right-front corner of the CWT split open, causing an upward blast that blew rows 17 and 18, seats 8 and 10, upward and outward to the southeast, along with a large exterior section adjacent to the R-2 door [RF-35].

The port-side potable water bottle, located just in front of the CWT, is believed to have been blown through the left side of the 747, just forward and below the L-2 door,[10] opening up the left side of the 747, allowing CW-504 to exit, carrying a residue stain testing positive for nitrate, a possible explosive signature. The starboard potable water bottle suffered significant damage, probably because it was closest to the initial blast. Color transfer marks on the pre-altered front spar indicate the initiating blast slammed into the front spar right to left, causing the front spar to smash into the starboard bottle, transferring the color marks to the forward side of the front spar. The starboard 1,000-pound bottle may have ascended through the passenger cabin floor and exited through the left top of the 747, approximately above rows 11 through 16.

The passenger cabin, just forward of the CWT, rows 17, 18 and 19, in a general right-to-left pattern, began to exit the stricken 747, along with the "C" Galley, located just in front of row 17. These first seats to leave the plane were blown out with a reddish-orange residue attached to foam rubber padding.

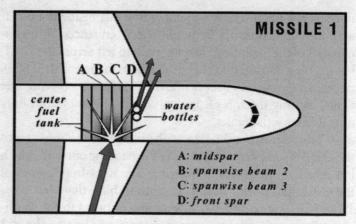

Eyewitnesses observing a missile or flare-like object rise from the area of the ocean fall into two separate groups. One group in aircraft and boats south of Long Island saw missile 1 approach Flight 800 from the south. This is consistent with right-to-left flow of damage charted in the Missile 1 drawing.

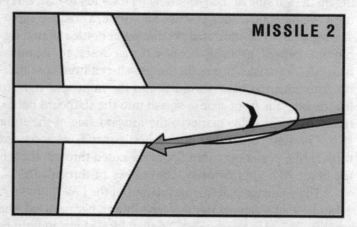

The second group of witnesses observed a missile approach Flight 800 from a location approximately 10 miles north-northeast of Flight 800, which is consistent with the damage path depicted by the Missile 2 drawing.

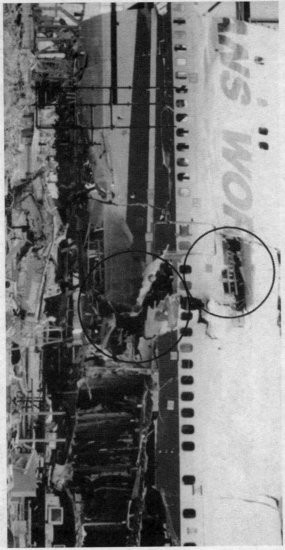

The larger, lower circle is believed to be the port [left potable water bottle exit point. The starboard bottle exit point is the smaller circle.

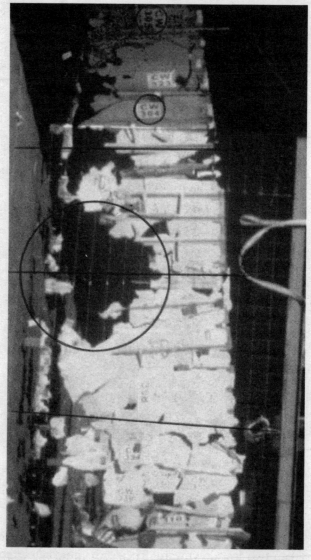

The right-side-of-body (RSOB) is the right side of the center wing tank (CWT). Inside the circle is a 3 x 4-foot hole.

China Lake military experts retained by the FBI said a 3 x 3-foot hole is the necessary starting point for a possible missile penetration. Analysis of the right wing, leading to this hole, and damage pattern spreading in all directions from this hole, indicate an explosive event occurred in this immediate area.

SWB-2, represented by the vertical line in the center of the circle, was accordioned inward approximately five feet. The floor of the CWT was blown downward more than two feet, and the seats directly above this hole, rows 21 to 25, have holes blasted through the backs of the seats.

The interior of the CWT, observed from the right side. The RSOB hole is equidistant between the two circles. The hand-drawn vertical line between the two holes traces the right side of SWB-2 that was accordioned about five feet inward. Directly below SWB-2, the floor of the CWT has been blown more than two feet downward. The seats immediately above SWB-2 have holes blown through the seatbacks. CW-601 is inside the larger circle. In its early iterations, circa 1996-early

1997, many holes could be seen. They are now gone. The exterior shape has undergone several changes over the last three years. Inside the smaller circle is a large hole in the mid-spar. It is not shown in NTSB mid-spar damage diagrams. Portions of the right side of the mid-spar have now been moved into the hole in order to disguise its presence.

Pre-altered front spar (large circle) encompasses an area on the starboard (right) side of the front spar (this photo was shot from front to rear). Because it represents damage from a force that can be traced back to the hole in the RSOB, this area of the front spar has now been stretched toward the starboard side of the fuselage [The Justice Department has blocked publication of the photo showing the altered front spar]. In its current altered form, it represents damage consistent with an initiating event that came from the center of the CWT that caused SWB-3 to topple into the front spar like a falling domino. Circle 2 encompasses additional evidence that a force flowed from the hole in the RSOB, forcing the lower portion of this beam forward and to the port (left). In its current altered form, the beam is bent to the rear, making it appear that SWB-3 toppled forward into the front.

The NTSB released this radar graph alleging that it represented all relevant non-transponder (primary) radar.

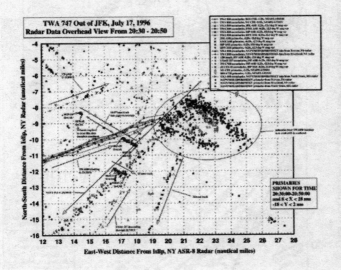

The NTSB radar graph misrepresented surface and air activity in the vicinity of Flight 800. Navy documents and radar data confirm that what you see is the "movement of significant Naval units" that were covered by a national security blanket after TWA Flight 800 crashed.

Shortly after this initiating event, the backstop missile, with a proximity fuse, exploded under the cockpit. The 747 flew through the blast wave, causing extensive damage to the front and right side of Flight 800. The forward part of the 747 broke away from the fuselage. Fuel from the right wing flowed into the center wing tank, expanding rapidly into a fireball.

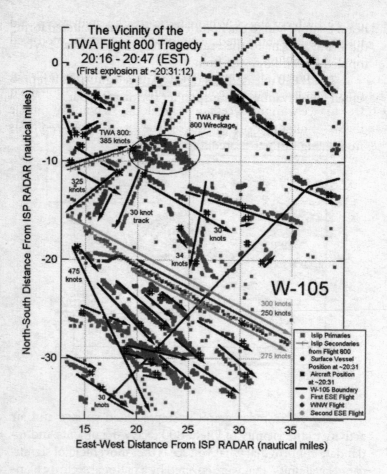

The Vicinity of the
TWA Flight 800 Tragedy
20:16 - 20:47 (EST)
(First explosion at ~20:31:12)

The computer analysis, discussed in *The New York Times*, revealed that about one-mile after the initiating event, "a new mass of wreckage—including the airplane's bulbous nose and the contents of the first-class section"[11] —had entered the ocean in one large pile of debris. This computer analysis, and the remainder of the analysis described in *The Times*, closely parallels the computer analysis I ran in November and December 1996, using NTSB debris printouts removed from Calverton hangar by Terry Stacey. When Stacey saw this analysis, he said the NTSB had completed an "unofficial" study that produced the same results.

Shortly after this newspaper report, the government turned its back on the computer analysis, which brought it face to face with the necessity of developing a bomb or missile theory, or altering evidence to keep the mechanical hypothesis from being further discredited.

10

St. Louis Canine Scheme

You can call it a duck, but if it doesn't quack, waddle or swim, you've got to be suspicious. Especially when it comes to the FBI, NTSB, FAA and St. Louis Airport Police Department's combined analysis of how residue from explosives might have innocently shown up inside *and* outside the Boeing 747 that became TWA Flight 800.

Simply put, investigators tossed away some of the most critical evidence that a bomb or missile might have caused the deaths of 230 innocent people two miles in the air off the shores of Long Island.

To understand the ending, you need to start at the beginning. As investigators pulled crash victims and debris from Boeing 747 No. 17119 from the ocean in the first hours, days and weeks after the mid-air explosion, officials were on high alert, believing they were looking for evidence of a terrorist attack. Indeed, the FBI unit that commandeered the investigation was the New York-based Anti-Terrorism Task Force, a combined group of FBI and New York City police investigators headed by Assistant FBI Director, James Kallstrom.

Five days after the Flight 800 crash investigators found a trace of PETN on a piece of the right wing near the fuselage, *The New York Times* reported. The trace was detected by a field test at Calverton, unnamed investigators reported, but allegedly not confirmed by a later test at the FBI lab in Washington, D.C.

State-of-the-art sampling equipment was available at the

Calverton hangar to quickly perform a non-destructive test for possible explosives. When used at airports for testing luggage, the false positives per sample is much higher than when used on metals such as aluminum. Two NTSB investigators attached to Flight 800 have confirmed that the expected false positive at Calverton would be expected to be in the range of one in 10,000.

On August 23, 1996—five weeks and two days after the unexplained disaster—CNN and *The New York Times* reported that FBI crime-lab chemists had found additional traces of PETN (a chemical in plastic explosives, and found in some missile warheads) in the cabin area between rows 17 and 25 on the right side of the plane, in the same area where the "mysterious" red residue was found. [Patricia Milton's book, *In the Blink of an Eye*, written with the full cooperation of the FBI, places this residue at row 25 or 26.] The area is also near where the right-front wing meets the fuselage, where PETN traces had been detected weeks earlier *outside* the fuselage.

The area is just above the forward fuel cell of the center fuel tank, which exploded at some point in the plane's disintegration. Officials say they may never determine what set off the explosion. But they also say there is no evidence a bomb or missile was the cause.

On August 30, 1996, *Newsday*, the Long Island-based newspaper that won the Pulitzer Prize for its Flight 800 coverage, reported chemical traces of RDX had also been detected in the cabin area where the PETN explosive chemicals were found. RDX and PETN sometimes are combined to create explosives such as Symtex, which was used by terrorists to knock down Pan Am Flight 103 over Lockerbie, Scotland, in 1988. More importantly, RDX/PETN combinations are used in military warheads.

Finding RDX and PETN together diminished the chances that the explosive chemicals "could have been brought on the plane by military troops or someone who works with explosives," *Newsday* reported. RDX is not widely available, while PETN is. RDX is manufactured in the U.S. at one plant, an Army-owned facility in Holston, Virginia.

Inside the center fuel tank, nitrate would be found during scientific testing by NASA. Nitrates are a possible signature for explosives and, when found, require additional testing to determine the source of the nitrate before the sample can be declared to be evidence of an explosive compound from a missile or bomb. When the NTSB was informed of the discovery, an order was given prohibiting further testing to determine the source of the nitrate, and the NASA chemist's report, obtained by the author, officially remains hidden to this day.

The combined PETN/RDX finds were not enough evidence, the FBI said. The twisted metal of Flight 800 allegedly did not show the rending or pitting expected from an exploding bomb or warhead, officials said. Fist-sized holes in the back of seats in row 23 were dismissed because there "were holes all over the place."

Enter the "duck." Only this time it was disguised as a bomb-sniffing police dog, and used to explain away the PETN traces—but not the RDX—that continued to confront investigators.

On September 20, 1996, crash investigators and other federal officials said they had discovered that Boeing 747, No. 17119, was used in a bomb-detection exercise in St. Louis just weeks before the jumbo jet exploded in the sky. Investigators used spills from that exercise to explain away the explosive evidence they found in Flight 800 debris. The bomb-detection exercise took place on June 10, 1996, according to the FBI's Kallstrom.

An exercise may have taken place that day, but evidence overwhelmingly points away from, not to, the plane that became Flight 800. And the evidence that overthrows the FBI and FAA explanation is so simple, it demands an explanation about how it could be ignored, and continues to be ignored to this day.

Crewmembers who flew the 747 on June 10 are mystified by the FBI version of events.

The official story was first offered by Kallstrom in a September 5, 1997, letter to Congressman James A. Trafficant, a member of the House Aviation Subcommittee. Trafficant was the only congressman who openly and vocally challenged the official Flight 800 investigation during its first two years. Trafficant finally concluded a bomb or missile could not have downed the plane because there was no "collateral evidence," such as pitting or explosive residue. The conclusions, however, were based on information from the investigators.

Trafficant had asked Kallstrom if the FBI had "verifiable and concrete evidence" that the plane used for Flight 800 (Boeing 747, No. 17119) was used for a bomb-detection exercise in St. Louis on June 10, 1996. Kallstrom did not answer "yes" or "no," but offered only what investigators pieced together as circumstantial evidence.

Kallstrom said his agents had interviewed a patrolman for the St. Louis Airport Police Department on September 20, 1996, more than three months after the alleged bomb-detection exercise took place. The patrolman, whom Kallstrom did not name, was identified as Herman Burnett in news reports.

The officer, assigned to the department's canine unit, did not write down the identification number of the airplane used because that information was not required, according to the investigators. Neither TWA nor the FAA—which is responsible for such exercises—logged in the officer's activities.

According to the FBI report, the patrolman must maintain daily training for his explosives-sniffing dog, using available aircraft. On June 10, the officer was working a day shift, and called TWA's manager (whose name the patrolman could not recall) to see if an airplane was available for a detection exercise. The officer said he was told a "wide-body" (the term used for a jumbo jet) was available at Gate 50.

But there were two "wide-bodies"—two Boeing 747s— at St. Louis that morning. And they were parked side-by-side.

Gate 50 and 51 at St. Louis Lambert International Airport (now Gates C-36 and C-38, respectively) are at the end of Concourse C. According to TWA records provided by the FBI, Boeing 747, No. 17119—the future Flight 800 aircraft—was parked at Gate 50. Adjacent, at Gate 51, was Boeing 747, No. 17116, the clone sister aircraft. Both aircraft are normally operated out of John F. Kennedy Airport in New York, but were shifted to St. Louis for that day because other 747s were undergoing maintenance work, according to TWA records.

The officer said he was enthused because it was rare that a "wide-body" aircraft was available in St. Louis for such training. However, TWA had a 747 flight to Hawaii from St. Louis daily—sometimes two flights—and L11011 as well as 767 wide-body flights daily. As this author can personally attest, it was a rare event when no wide-body was visible. Absent a verifying statement by the Airport police officer, this must be considered one of Kallstrom's frequent gratuitous, false statements, attached to fictional "facts."

Kallstrom said the officer told agents he went to a police bunker and retrieved four types of explosives used for detection training: water gel, C-4, det cord and ammonia dynamite. He also used smokeless powder, which was stored in the trunk of his patrol car. The officer, with his Belgian Malinois "Carlo" in the car, then drove to Gate 50 where he "found a 747 parked. The patrolman made no notations regarding the tail number of the aircraft, as it was not his policy to do so," Kallstrom said.

The officer boarded the plane and determined no one else was present. He returned to his patrol car to get the explosives, and believes he made two trips to do so, the FBI said. He placed the explosives on the counter in the galley just inside the "main" entry door to the aircraft. He then began placing the explosives around the aircraft.

Had the FBI bothered to ask TWA flight attendants where the "main" door was located for 747s using St. Louis gateways, they would have learned it was "L-1," the first door on the left side of the aircraft. If you turn to the left after entering through L-1, it means you paid a large price for your "First Class" ticket. To the right was Business Class [also called "Ambassador Class" during that time]. Coach Class began at the L-2 door.

It was 10:45 a.m. local time, according to the officer.

The FBI says the patrolman placed the smokeless powder on its side, cap unscrewed, inside the center armrest of row 2, seat 2 [left side of cabin], in the First Class section. The water gel was placed on the floor inside a tall, narrow closet/storage bin upstairs at the rear of the upper-level First Class section, separated from the rest of the plane by a circular stairway. A 1.4-pound block of C-4, covered with a thin covering of clear cellophane-type material, which the patrolman described as being in poor condition, allowing some of the explosive to be exposed, was placed in the pouch on the back of the backrest of row 10, seat 9, the right side of the 747, just to the rear of the R-1 door, far from where residue samples would later test positive for PETN/RDX.

The det (detonation) cord, described as a 30-foot piece "in extremely poor condition," with cracks every few inches, was brought in its container to row 20 of the main cabin. "The patrolman said that he believes he went to the side of the cabin opposite from the side where he placed the C-4, since it was his practice to place the explosives in a zigzag pattern . . ." the FBI reported. "The patrolman placed the container in which the cord was stored on the floor in the aisle, removed the cord and placed it in an overhead compartment in row 20. The patrolman noted that the can containing the det cord contained quite a bit of powder from the cord, and said if one were to "wave it in the air it would create a visible cloud of powder." Patricia Milton, writing her pro-FBI Flight 800 book, suggests the patrolman waved it around, creating a cloud of powder.

One stick of ammonia dynamite was partially concealed in a groove in the flooring near an emergency door.

Smokeless powder, water gel and ammonium nitrate (dynamite) have no PETN or RDX in them, said Dr. Jimmie Oxley, an explosives expert at the University of Rhode Island. She is an FBI, BATF and FAA consultant. Det cord, with its powder-rich container placed somewhere on row 20, is PETN-based. The C-4 packet, placed in row 10, is RDX-based, Oxley said.

The officer said FAA regulations require that he wait 30 minutes after the first placement before beginning his training exercise with the dog. At 11:45 a.m., the patrolman brought the dog into the aircraft and worked the animal through the three areas of the aircraft where the explosives were placed.

"Carlo" found all the explosives.

The exercise lasted 15 minutes, meaning it ended at noon.

After returning the dog to his patrol car, the patrolman removed the explosives and returned them to the car and left. He said he was the only person involved in the exercise. By the time the FBI interviewed him three months after the exercise, new packets had replaced all but the smokeless powder.

Depending on how long it took the officer to re-board the plane (which is like climbing stairs to the second floor of an old building with high ceilings), retrieve the explosives in the same order in which he hid them, return to the car and place them inside; he left the plane well after noon.

Records—including those sent by Kallstrom to Congressman Trafficant—show that the airplane, Flight 1 to Hawaii, backed away from Gate 51 at 12:35 p.m. to begin its flight. Scheduled departure time was 11:50 a.m., just when the officer would have been in the midst of his exercise. The flight had more than 400 passengers aboard.

TWA written regulations in effect in 1996 mandate that the crew of a wide-body report for briefing 90 minutes before *scheduled* takeoff. The crew therefore reported to the TWA airport briefing room no later than 10:20 a.m. They had 30 minutes to complete their briefing *and* get onboard the 747. The TWA manual mandates the crew actually board the 747 one hour before scheduled takeoff. So they were onboard no later than 10:50 a.m.

In the rare circumstance that a "scheduled" delay was known to be in effect during the 10:20 a.m. briefing, *and* the crew knew the length of the delay, they could have delayed boarding until 11:35 a.m., 10 minutes *before* the patrolman is alleged to have brought the dog onboard.

So a crew was onboard the 747 no later than 11:35 a.m., preparing the plane for a full load of passengers—stowing their belongings, performing safety equipment pre-flight, and checking food and beverage supplies. A minimum of three pilots, one flight service manager and 13 flight attendants were onboard. Add to that the maintenance, food service and gate agents coming and going during this extremely busy pre-flight period—yet the patrolman saw no one. And no crewmember saw him.

Records show that Captain Vance Weir of Fallbrook, California, piloted TWA No. 17119 from St. Louis to Hawaii that day and Thomas D. Sheary of Seminole, Florida, was First Officer.

David E. Hendrix, an investigative reporter for the *Press-Enterprise* newspaper in Riverside, California, interviewed Captain Weir personally and F/O Sheary by phone. No dog or patrolman was on that plane that day. How can they be so certain? During each of their 20-plus years flying commercial aircraft, they have never seen a dog and patrolman onboard their plane conducting such an exercise. Nor, they said, have they ever had take-off procedures delayed because of such exercises.

There is one inescapable conclusion that must be drawn from this wealth of evidence: Kallstrom misrepresented the facts, engaged in willful blindness by not checking the obvious airline rules and regulations and crewmember statements that would confirm beyond a reasonable doubt that the patrolman and dog were not on 747 No. 17119.

When you follow major media reporting for August and September 1996, it becomes apparent that a policy decision at the highest levels of the Clinton administration was made mandating a "mechanical" finding.

11

THE SANDERS' GANG EMERGES

Within weeks of major media abandoning an independent Flight 800 investigation in late summer 1996, my wife, Liz Sanders, called Terry Stacey and asked him if he would be willing to talk to me about what was going on inside the TWA Flight 800 investigation. Terry Stacey was a senior TWA Pilot Manager, in charge of all 747 pilots. The night before Flight 800 crashed, he had flown it to JFK Airport from France. When Flight 800 went down, Stacey was one of the first TWA people assigned to the NTSB investigation. He told Liz to give him a couple of weeks to think about it.

I'm a retired California police officer and author of two non-fiction books exposing government wrongdoing, and I wanted to talk to someone inside the Flight 800 investigation in order to determine whether it looked as bad on the inside as it did from the outside. If it did, my intention was to expose it in a book.

The FBI had used *The New York Times* to leak its version of the truth; but that had changed in September 1996 as the FBI moved away from the bomb scenario and continued to run from the missile theory. The NTSB established a close relationship with NBC News as the government began the long arduous task of preparing the American public to passively accept a "mechanical" explanation.

At the end of October, I called Terry Stacey, and we agreed to meet at Newark Airport on October 30. My notes reflect the following:

- There is absolutely no analysis of how each part contributes to the overall picture. The NTSB will seize upon an individual part as a possibility.

- Within a day or two it is on the national media as the latest theory when, in reality, it is nothing more than a guess. [Stacey identified the NTSB's Dr. Merritt Birky, head of the Fire and Explosion Group, as the leader of an NTSB group that periodically met on the hangar floor discussing various hypotheses. When an agreement was reached, it would soon appear on NBC News, presented as the NTSB closing in on the mechanical problem that caused the crash.]

- The FBI does not communicate or share information with the NTSB. The NTSB first heard about possible bomb residue when it was broadcast on national news. Since then, the sides are even further apart. The FBI, at will, can come into the hangar and remove any piece of the aircraft. It is not signed out or otherwise tracked by the NTSB investigation. Prior to a part arriving at the hangar, then tagged and placed into the NTSB computer, there is no control or tracking of evidence, as required in criminal cases.

- The FBI conducts tests without ever sharing the results with the NTSB.

- The center wing tank (CWT) low-level explosion could not produce enough energy to simultaneously put both recorders out of action [Cockpit Voice Recorder and Flight Data Recorder]. This has been an insurmountable problem during the informal discussions at the hangar of the chain of events leading to the large explosion that destroyed the plane.

- FBI teams identified all missile witnesses thought to be credible. Each witness point of observation was established and surveyor equipment was used to establish a flight path for the missile. All trajectories came from an area south of Long Island and intersected the flight path of Flight 800.

- A senior-level FAA person at the Flight 800 crash scene

shortly after the event, flew to the FAA Oklahoma City Training Center the next day and commented to another senior-level FAA person: "You won't believe what brought down Flight 800." [Stacey provided the name of one of the participants in this conversation.]

Terry Stacey was a very cautious individual. He carefully measured each thought before verbalizing it. He was not a missile proponent, or proponent of any other hypothesis. As of the end of October 1966, he was certain of one thing: an honest investigation was not being conducted.

He was in a prime position to formulate that opinion. He had watched the FBI and Justice Department illegally muscle the NTSB to shut down the NTSB Witness Group. Stacey had a front-row seat when the NTSB senior scientist at Calverton hangar, Merritt Birky, and other senior NTSB personnel hypothesized about mechanical causes that had no basis in fact—then watched this idle verbal rambling turn into propaganda spewed across the world by NBC evening news as fact.

Two weeks after the first meeting, Stacey and I met a second time, on November 14, 1996. An NTSB debris-field printout of the red/yellow zone, where the first pieces fell from the plane, was turned over to me.

The printout was dated November 13 [1996]. All debris that made it past the FBI censors was tagged and entered into the NTSB computer the day it arrived at the Calverton hangar and came under NTSB control.

I computerized what appeared to be key pieces of debris in the NTSB red zone database printout. A pattern soon appeared. A narrow damage pattern, centered on rows 17, 18 and 19, with a general right-to-left bias, crossed the 747 in the first seconds after the initiating event. I believed the narrow pattern offered significant evidence that the initiating event was not a catastrophic explosion. Rather, it was a limited event, which produced an initially limited footprint.

Then, a secondary event blew off the front of the 747. [More than two years later I would acquire enough additional documentation to conclude that the secondary event was caused by a second "backstop" missile with a proximity fuse that exploded under the nose of the 747.] At this point I didn't have the green zone debris field, but was able to see that more than 98% of the center wing tank (CWT) remained with the stricken plane after the red and yellow zone. This offered clear evidence the NTSB "mechanical" initiating event deep inside the CWT was nothing more than propaganda.

It was time for another face-to-face meeting with Stacey. On November 24 I flew to Newark Airport, rented a car and drove to Stacey's home in rural New Jersey. In Stacey's den I unfolded my debris-field map and, using 747 schematics as flip-charts, showed Stacey the narrow trail of damage I had found crossing the plane, prior to the secondary event.

At that point, Stacey revealed for the first time the existence of a reddish-orange trail across the cabin interior of the plane in this same area. He said the NTSB had just produced a duplicate of my initiating-event diagram. "They [NTSB] are perplexed," Stacey said. Stacey also said the "coroner [is] supposed to release a report saying it was not the center fuel tank that caused the plane to crash—per analysis of body damage."[1]

The conversation frequently returned to the reddish-orange residue. Terry Stacey provided more detail. The residue was on foam rubber seat-cushion backing attached to the metal frame [Stacey did not know it at the time, but a brownish glue was apparently used to bond the foam rubber to the metal chairbacks. It could not be seen until all the foam rubber was stripped from these seats in March 1997]. The foam rubber was rapidly deteriorating.

I asked Stacey what the NTSB and FBI had to say about the residue trail. Stacey said the FBI had taken several samples in late August but refused to share the test results, blowing off requests by Stacey's team for test results. [Within a month after our meeting, the FBI told inquisitive NTSB people the test results would not be shared because it was evidence of a crime.]

A lengthy dialogue then ensued between Stacey and me, discussing how the government would counter any red residue report. The question could not be answered. No hint had been given when the residue had become a hot topic at the Calverton hangar in September 1996.

The residue was deposited in the same narrow passenger cabin area impacted immediately after the initiating event. It was reddish-orange. The majority of the witnesses to something rising into the air shortly before Flight 800 fell out of the sky said they observed a reddish-orange flare-like object.

No one from the FBI or NTSB had said to Stacey or other NTSB investigators in his section, "Forget it, the red residue is glue commonly found at civil aviation crash scenes." Nor did anyone say FBI chemists had looked at it and were so certain it was glue they were not going to bother testing it. These excuses were offered by the NTSB and FBI only *after* the residue trail was publicly revealed on March 10, 1997.

We both agreed that, without forensic testing, there was no way to know if the residue was from the exhaust of a solid-fuel missile. The residue appeared to have flakes on the surface that would probably fall into a plastic bag with very little help. I was certain I could find a non-government lab to test the flakes.

My contemporaneous notes say Stacey would do the following for the week of December 2, 1996:

1. Confirm R-2 door and damage.
2. Scraping from possible missile residue.
3. Printout of body damage by seat [number].
4. Missing seats.

5. Detailed info on center fuel tank.

It was a very productive meeting. Stacey also told me that Linda Kunz, another TWA employee attached to the NTSB investigation, the Cabin Reconstruction Group, had taken 35mm photos of the cabin mock-up seats. Over an extended period of time, through sources other than Stacey, the question "why" was answered.

Kunz and two New York police officers had taken the photos because the NTSB began to alter the locations where some of the seats were found. Some seats that exited the stricken aircraft had landed too early in the red zone to fit the developing NTSB "mechanical" hypothesis. So senior NTSB personnel at Calverton were assigning longitude and latitude tags, moving some seats further east, away from JFK Airport.

At some point, Linda Kunz' story and photos were forwarded to the NTSB and FBI by TWA, along with a strongly worded letter to the government. The FBI descended upon TWA. Linda Kunz shortly thereafter went out on medical leave, according to two sources, who also said she would have been indicted except that two New York police officers assisted her photographic effort.

No one seems to know what charges could possibly have been brought. It is clear the New York police officers would also have had to be indicted—creating a law enforcement war the FBI would certainly lose.

The second week of December 1996, I received the NTSB green zone printout of the last debris to fall into the ocean. About 98% of the CWT was strewn throughout the green zone, as were the four engines, left and right wing, more than two miles east of the initiating event. For the NTSB "mechanical" hypothesis to be correct, it is necessary to believe that the portion of the 747 in the immediate vicinity of the cataclysmic event was impacted last by the blast, while the parts of the plane furthest from the initiating event were *first* impacted by the blast. It was an Alice in Wonderland scenario.

12

THE CHAIRMAN'S REPORT

A few days later, I received an NTSB document in the mail from Terry Stacey, which began to explain the transparent political manipulation guiding the senior NTSB and FBI investigation managers. Entitled "TWA 800 Chairman's Briefing/Status Report November 15, 1996," it was a summary of NTSB Chairman Jim Hall's briefing by senior NTSB managers at the Calverton hangar. The disingenuous nature of the document's wording becomes apparent when compared to action taken. For instance, the Radar Data section of the report, pp. 3-4, says in part:

> Ron Schleede will write a letter for Bernie Loeb's signature to Ron Morgan for a full explanation of the FAA handling of ATC and radar tapes concerning TWA Flight 800. The letter will reference the technician who did the analysis resulting in conflicting radar tracks that indicated a missile. It will inquire why that information was reported to the White House and sent to the FAA Technical Center before the Safety Board was given access to the data.

From this wording it could easily be inferred that the NTSB wanted more missile details from the FAA to add to its storehouse of knowledge to be called upon as they diligently searched for the truth. And it certainly was legitimate to inquire why the politicians at the White House were first given access to missile information before the primary investigative team was told that a missile appeared to have been the reason

TWA Flight 800 crashed.

But that's not what the wording really means. The NTSB approach to the FAA was to make sure the FAA technicians were going to recant their blasphemous missile testimony:

> The purpose of this letter is to request a written explanation of certain events related to the processing of Federal Aviation Administration air traffic control (ATC) radar data for TWA flight 800 that crashed near Long Island, New York on July 17, 1996. As we have discussed, I would like to clarify the circumstances to alleviate any potential future misunderstandings or inappropriate speculation regarding the results of preliminary radar data analyses.
>
> As you know, during the first few hours after the accident, some FAA personnel made a preliminary assessment that recorded ATC radar data showed primary radar hits that indicated the track of a high-speed target that approached and merged with TWA 800. One of your staff called our office about 0930 on July 18, 1996, to advise us of the preliminary assessment of the radar data by FAA personnel, suggesting that a missile may have hit TWA 800. This preliminary assessment was also passed to other government officials, including White House officials. After the Safety Board received the ATC radar data and reviewed it, it was determined that the preliminary assessment by FAA staff was incorrect. We understand that FAA official[s] now agree with the Safety Board's determination.
>
> I would appreciate it if you could verify that all specialists and/or managers involved in the preliminary radar analyses fully agree that there is no evidence within the FAA ATC radar of a track that would suggest a high-speed target merged with TWA 800. I would also appreciate an explanation about how the preliminary incorrect assessment occurred, so that potential public or media inquiries can be handled in an accurate and consistent manner.
>
> If you have any questions about this matter, please call me or Mr. Ron Schleede. I trust that you appreciate the need to ensure a clear record of these particular events to allay public concern or speculation.

The letter was signed by Bernie Loeb, NTSB Director of Aviation Safety, and sent to David Thomas, Director, FAA Office of Accident Investigation. The letter was as disingenuous as the wording in the November 15, 1996, NTSB Chairman's Report authorizing this Bernie Loeb letter. The letter does nothing more than outline what is expected of the FAA. It is a demand for the entire organization to become a team player. The team leader says it is not a missile, therefore, the entire team will chant the "mechanical" mantra.

But the FAA seemed to want to sit out this particular game. They were not going to become team players. They would genuflect toward the mysterious Team Leader's wishes, but they would not get onboard:

Dear Mr. Loeb,

This is in response to your letter of December 26, 1996, regarding the Federal Aviation Administration's (FAA) processing of preliminary radar data following the TWA Flight 800 accident on July 17, 1996.

During the night of the accident, one of the many concerns of FAA traffic personnel was the possibility of a midair collision between two aircraft. In an attempt to conduct a rapid assessment of this possibility, personnel at the New York Air Route Traffic Control Center (ZNY) replayed the ZNY radar data at the facility using a commercially available radar-replay software program called "Radar Viewpoint." The review of the printout from the program indicated that there were radar tracks, which could not be accounted for by FAA staff. This information was immediately relayed to the appropriate law enforcement organizations with the understanding that it was preliminary and did contain some unexplained data.

Subsequently, after receiving the request for radar data from the National Transportation Safety Board (NTSB), all radar information from every radar site, which had recorded information on TWA 800, was provided to the NTSB. Concurrently, an exhaustive internal review of those data was conducted at the

FAA Technical Center. The assessment by the FAA Technical Center indicated that the likelihood of a missile [being one of the tracks observed by the FAA technicians] was remote. It must be noted, however, that FAA air traffic radar is designed to detect and monitor aircraft, not high-speed missiles, so any conclusions based on this review must consider the technical limits of the radar. Since that time, there has been no other evidence developed from the radar that would indicate the existence of a missile.

Your letter asks the FAA to "verify that all specialists and/or managers involved in the preliminary radar analyses fully agree that there is no evidence within the FAA ATC radar data of a track that would suggest a high-speed target merged with TWA 800." Although we understand and share your desire to allay public concern over this issue, we cannot comply with your request. The ZNY facility personnel in question do not possess the in-depth technical background required to conduct the level of analysis needed to positively reach a conclusion on the significance of the radar data. The preliminary assessment made by ZNY facility personnel on the night of the accident was as thorough as possible, but was, and is, limited by technical factors. Therefore, they would neither agree nor disagree with that assessment.

Regarding the notification of the White House and other government officials, you will recall that immediately after the event there was speculation within the media and other organizations of possible terrorist activity. By alerting law enforcement agencies, air traffic control personnel simply did what was prudent at the time and reported what appeared to them to be a suspicious event. To do less would have been irresponsible.

I trust that this information is responsive to your concerns. If I can be of further service, please let me know.

David F. Thomas, FAA Director of Accident Investigation, signed the letter, reaffirming that the FAA acted in a responsible manner, giving the White House and other government personnel a heads-up that a missile may have been responsible for the demise of TWA Flight 800.

The NTSB November 15, 1996, Chairman's report contains additional evidence permitting an inference of lawlessness within the investigation:

- "… there was a forty-second gap between the last recorded radar hit and the time the explosion was mentioned on any ATC tapes."[1] Comment: An American Airlines pilot who observed TWA Flight 800 as it exploded, placed an ATC call within seconds after the explosion. It can be heard on audiotapes, and read on transcripts released by the FAA. The forty-second gap is due to a NTSB alteration or analysis problem somewhere within the cockpit voice recorder, data recorder, radar tapes and FAA ATC tapes. There is no actual forty-second gap.

- "Fragment evidence found in the CWT was indicative of an explosive event, not necessarily a missile or a bomb but rather associated with the CWT explosion."[2] Comment: After this was written, significant portions of the CWT were altered because the explosive damage that so concerned the NTSB at this point in the investigation could not be explained by an initiating "overpressure" as now alleged by the NTSB. And, no one inside or outside the TWA Flight 800 investigation alleges that fifty gallons of kerosene will create an "explosive event" inside the CWT, which is why the NTSB now uses "overpressure" to describe the mythical initiating event.

- "Merritt [Birky] indicated that to date, his group has seen no evidence of erosion or pitting in any of the wreckage. He also indicated that they have not discovered any static or fuel transfer problems with the center wing tank."[3]

Merritt Birky, or someone with access to his words and thoughts, was officially leaking mechanical myths to NBC evening news; and Robert Hager was authoritatively passing it on to America as the NTSB closing in on the answer for the Flight 800 crash. Static had been the fallback position when the fuel pumps were recovered and found to be functioning normally.

When this Chairman's memo was released to the media in December 1996, NBC news decision-makers had compelling evidence they were being used as shills by the NTSB and were passing factually false information to the American people. But no one at NBC News appears to have assigned an investigative team to get at the reason for the NTSB misrepresentation. Instead, NBC News continued to receive mechanical hypotheses, dress them up and spew them across America as fact.

When I received the 10-page NTSB Chairman's Report from Terry Stacey in December 1996, I was working with "Inside Edition" reporter, Mark Sauter, who immediately recognized the significance of the information contained in multiple areas within the report.

Sauter is an unusual reporter, with a Harvard degree, Columbia School of Journalism Masters, and a tour of duty as a Special Forces officer. That aggressiveness gave him the ability to attack, but not in the usual, disgusting mode seen in today's TV journalist—as a member of the screaming herd who, in mass, stampede from one feeding frenzy to the next. Sauter has an ability to focus on a problem and bring every possible resource to bear.

[The following is reprinted from my first book, *The Downing of TWA Flight 800*:]

According to Mark, the representatives of the federal agency alleged to be hard at work getting at the truth acted suspiciously like they had something to hide. They tried not to say anything on the record or on background. Sauter had faxed the NTSB selected parts of the memo as part of his strategy. They admitted off the record that the document was real, at least the parts Sauter had faxed. The NTSB public affairs officer [Peter Goelz] said 'there were errors' in the document. But he would not say which specific portions of the NTSB memo were incorrect. It was their memo. When written, every word was alleged to be true. Now that they were in a damage-limiting mode, they wanted to imply that nothing in the memo was true.[4]

After a day of maneuvering, the NTSB said one thing wrong with the memo was a reference to the FBI's not returning photos to the NTSB. It was a minor point. But the NTSB left the issue of errors hanging by suggesting this was only one of multiple errors. During this verbal sparring, the NTSB let slip that their Chairman, James Hall, was testifying on Capitol Hill the next day, but they refused to say where.[5]

Normally this type of information is readily available. Perhaps the Chairman was hiding from the *Washington Post*, alleged to be hard at work trying to confirm the NTSB memo written by Hall. Whatever the reason, his upcoming testimony was not part of the public record. But Sauter learned that the Chairman was testifying on air bags in front of a congressional committee. The next morning, Sauter was on a plane headed for D.C. When he arrived at the hearing on Capitol Hill, Sauter sent the film crew into the crowded hearing room for the typical talking-head shots seen on the evening news.[6]

Sauter warned the public affairs staff hovering around the Chairman that he and the film crew would be waiting just outside the door, the only exit. The Public Affairs person was told that Sauter was going to talk to the chairman about the inability of NTSB Public Affairs personnel to answer very simple questions about the accuracy of the chairman's own memo. While Sauter and film crew waited in ambush, an official came out to greet them. "Are you waiting for the chairman?" He asked.[7]

"Yes," Sauter responded.

"He's not going to answer any questions," the man said.[8]

"We'll see," was Sauter's response.

"But maybe you'll talk to me, I'm Peter Goelz, the head of governmental and media relations for the NTSB. Maybe I'll answer some."[9]

"On camera?" Sauter questioned.

"Uh, I guess," was the less than self-assured response.[10]

The camera began to roll. Peter Goelz was Director of Public and Government Affairs at the National Transportation and Safety Board.[11]

"What is this report we're talking about?" Sauter asked.

Goelz replied that it was a draft of "working minutes from a regularly scheduled review of our investigation."[12]

This statement confirmed the report in its entirety. Unless Goelz wanted to confess that everything the Chairman wrote was incorrect, the ambiguous suggestion that Sauter possessed a false document was disproved by the number one NTSB Public Affairs official.[13]

"We hold these kinds of meetings periodically, where we just get caught up on what everybody is doing. We all try to sit down in one room and review where we are. And that was the first draft. From what I can see, it certainly wasn't the final draft."[14]

"So there were other versions of this? Later versions?"

"There were a few inaccuracies in that first draft," Goelz said.[15]

Sauter interrupted with, "Let's go through and tick them off and make sure we're all straight."[16]

"I'm not sure what I know, but certainly one that was indicated, that you raised, was the photo. And the truth on that was shortly before that meeting we did get the photos back. They had been given to somebody in Calverton. It was not a big deal. We just hadn't communicated it to the right person," Goelz concluded.[17]

If it was such a minor incident, why did Goelz, the head of NTSB Public Affairs, not give a simple, direct response the day before? Probably because there were no real inaccuracies on which the NTSB could collectively hang its hat. But they needed something in order to cast a cloud of doubt on the entire 10-page memo.[18]

Goelz was in front of the camera, still trying to pitch the line that, "There were a few inaccuracies in that first draft." But he could only name one.[19]

Sauter asked a question about the FBI and NTSB investigations not cooperating. Specifically, the NTSB report said the FBI turned over redacted interviews of witnesses. The FBI was blacking out portions of records being used inside the investigation before giving them to the NTSB, the lead investigating agency.[20]

Goelz responded: "Even the slightest evidence of a criminal act would have pushed us to treat the investigation as a crime scene," he stated. The truth is, the FBI tried to take over the investigation in the early stages but was ordered not to by the Justice Department.[21]

In true Public Affairs form, by the time Goelz finished answering the question, you would have thought there was an extraordinary level of cooperation between the world's two great investigative agencies. Somehow the redacted portions were forgotten, as was the almost open warfare in the press between the two agencies.[22]

"I can assure you we have had complete cooperation from all federal agencies in this investigation," Goelz concluded.

"What about the missile the FAA technician said was on a collision course with Flight 800?"[23]

"We saw those radar tapes shortly after we got on the scene. Our staff has reviewed those tapes, and they show absolutely no sign of a missile," said Goelz.[24]

The facts expose Goelz as a purveyor of disinformation. Most government public relations spin doctors attempt to make their statements technically accurate while leading the press away from any sensitive areas that would cause the government embarrassment or pain. Not Goelz. He apparently is willing to say anything without regard to his own integrity.

He would demonstrate his moral flexibility on into the future. More than two years later, Robert Davey, a reporter who frequently writes for the *Village Voice*, faxed Goelz a question about nitrate residue being found on center wing tank debris-piece CW-504. Goelz faxed Davey back, saying no nitrate was found on CW-504.

That was factually false, as well. Davey faxed the NASA report to Goelz, who then responded that he had misunderstood the initial question. Goelz apparently thought Davey was using "nitrate" as a code word for "explosive." Goelz, it would seem, was responding to this perceived code word. The alternative is that Peter Goelz lied and was caught in the act by a very good reporter.

13

RED RESIDUE

December 8, 1996, 1312 hours; Terry Stacey was at home in rural New Jersey when he placed a call to my Williamsburg residence. As is my normal practice to ensure the accuracy of my notes, I taped the phone call. Most of the early conversation centered on the NTSB Chairman's Report. I attempted to identify the role each of the NTSB officials identified in the memo played in the investigation. As the conversation begins to wind down:

Sanders: … In any case, I won't keep you anymore here. I wanted to check in with you. So I'll just anxiously await the residue and whatever else. …

Stacey: Whatever else I can scrounge.

Sanders: Yeah. Exactly. Yeah. I can either come up and get it or, whichever is more convenient, I can come up and get it, or mail it. But it's a little easier for me now normally because Liz lands at her apartment this evening. She's driving up there right now.

Stacey: Oh, my.

Sanders: Then she ends up next week going right back to St. Louis for five days. Then from the twentieth through the end of the year she's flying or at least on-call to fly.

Stacey: Does she get the holiday off, or Christmas off?

Sanders: No. No. She's working through the thirtieth.

Stacey: I think this one [TWA flight schedule] ends on the thirty-first.

Sanders: So, if they grab her for one of those, where she's halfway through a flight on the thirty-first, she's working on the first, too. In any case, I'll have easier access to places to stay and cars and that kind of stuff. I also have a forensics expert online to analyze it very quickly so we don't have to stand in line at a crime lab somewhere, probably out on the West Coast, and wait for a month while they get around to it.

Stacey: I'll make that my *top priority*, because that group, like I say, Les and them were talking about finishing up, so that place ought to be fairly secluded in a few days—there won't be a lot of people. [Emphasis added]

Sanders: Oh, outstanding, good.

Stacey: OK.

Sanders: OK. Well, give me a buzz whenever and we'll figure out how to do a handoff on it and go from there.

Stacey: OK. Very good.

Sanders: OK. Talk to you later.

Stacey was firmly committed to obtaining a sample of the residue and having it tested to determine if it contained additional evidence of a missile striking Flight 800—and additional evidence of lawlessness within the FBI and NTSB investigation. Notice that, although my wife is going to be living in New York, within miles of the Calverton hangar, no conversation occurs suggesting she take custody of the residue or participate in the ongoing Sanders/Stacey investigation.

Terry Stacey called me two days later and said his effort to scrape off some residue failed because a VIP tour walked through the hangar as he prepared to remove the sample. At this point Stacey told me the hangar was going to shut down for the holidays, and that he would probably not get back inside until sometime in January.

Notes taken from this tape-recorded conversation[1] reveal the following:

• Bob Swain [NTSB investigator] and Merritt Birky [NTSB], Fire & Explosion pushed mechanical early on. When nothing obvious showed up—bomb/missile—and fuel tank obviously exploded, these two ran with the theory [mechanical] and it was continually leaked to the press, until piece after piece was recovered and the theory fell apart. Shortly after 11/15/96 "big change in NTSB attitude."

• Stacey reconfirmed that the residue is only on the backs of the seats.

• Stacey is checking for a missile hit directly below rows 17 and 18 and exit below rows 18 and 19.

Sometime between December 15 and 19, TWA held its company Christmas party in St. Louis. To my wife's surprise, Terry Stacey showed up. In the middle of a few hundred TWA employees and spouses, they exchanged "chit-chat," according to FBI field notes obtained under pre-trial discovery. The FBI field notes are a synopsis of what Terry Stacey is alleged to have told the FBI agents during their more than 30 hours of meetings.

FBI agents know that such field notes may be turned over under discovery if the case is not resolved pre-trial. Statements that will obviously cause the FBI problems are not recorded. But the agent must be able to look into the future and recognize what will and will not cause problems. In this case the FBI agent was Jim Kinsley, whose capabilities along those lines were always kept well hidden.

So "chit-chat" was recorded in his notes, effectively eliminating December as a month in which TWA's own Mata-Hari, *aka* Liz Sanders, could use her feminine wiles to literally force Terry Stacey, the senior TWA manager, into doing something he did not want to do—remove the residue to have it tested.

A more perfect setting cannot be imagined. Face-to-face

communication is much more effective than telephone, particularly when it is male-to-female conversation meant to force a reluctant male to do something he otherwise would not.

So the lovely 5'3", 110-pound flight attendant stood face-to-face with her conspiratorial target. If the government is to be believed, she was, at this very moment, focused on using her very considerable charm to force Terry Stacey to do what he did not want to do. This was to become the government theory of the "crime" in the months to come.

The Justice Department knew, from phone records and sign-out logs, that this was the only place and time the government could establish probable cause with which to legally carry out their promise to indict Liz Sanders. These records said Liz and Terry spoke in October 1996. Their next telephone conversation was January 9, 1997. Records in the Justice Department's possession prove beyond any doubt that Terry Stacey had already removed the residue when this telephone conversation occurred.

But all Terry and Liz did was chit-chat when face-to-face at that TWA Christmas party.

On December 20, "Inside Edition" ran a segment based on the [NTSB] Chairman's November 15, 1996, memo Stacey had mailed to me. Mark Sauter of "Inside Edition" asked me for Terry Stacey's comments on the program, so I called Stacey on December 21. An 18-minute conversation ensued. Stacey was disappointed that only the conflict between the FBI and NTSB was to be featured.

The next communication between Terry Stacey and a member of the Sanders' Gang was on January 9, 1997, 2024 hours, East Coast time. My wife called Terry Stacey from St. Louis to tell him she had been transferred back to the St. Louis Training Center. If he came through town they could hook up for dinner.

Terry, who had logged out of the hangar four hours earlier, told Liz he was about to call me—he had removed two residue samples from the hangar that day and FedEx'd them to me. He was concerned that they were too small.

After a 20-minute conversation, they signed off. One minute later, according to phone records, Stacey called and told me two residue samples were en route to Williamsburg by overnight Federal Express.

As Stacey would state two years later in federal court, I was surprised. Notes from this Sanders/Stacey tape-recorded telephone conversation indicate:

• New York Air National Guard pilot Christian Bauer, who saw a missile strike Flight 800, had been hypnotized in an attempt to gain more precise information on the projectile he observed strike Flight 800. Less information was available under hypnosis.
• Cal Tech had been hired to assist Birky—"fuel air mixture explosions, small and large."
• The wing structures both show shear and tension.
• Span-wise beam #2 also discussed.

The next day, January 10, about 3:20 P.M., I received the Federal Express package. Within the hour, I sent an e-mail to California stating that I had just received two samples of residue.

I soon learned the testing process would be more difficult than anticipated. After talking to chemists at the University of Virginia and UCLA, it became apparent that no one outside of government could test the residue *and* provide an analysis of what the residue elements represented.

So I made arrangements with a commercial laboratory in the Los Angeles, California, area to determine what elements were found in the reddish-orange residue. Step two was to give one copy of the elements to David Hendrix, a reporter at the *Press-Enterprise* newspaper in Riverside, California.

Hendrix and I had worked on various investigative projects for more than 10 years, and he had excellent sources within the federal government that fed him documents and information related to Flight 800.

We went our separate ways to interview people within the missile industry who could answer the question: "Are these elements consistent with what would be expected to be found in the exhaust residue of a solid-fuel missile?" Hendrix and I received the same answer: the elements *are* consistent. No other explanation for the residue was apparent.

Months later, a retired missile-industry scientist would confirm the same conclusion, adding that these elements would also indicate an incendiary warhead explosion. The scientist added that incendiary warheads were current-generation warhead technology only. The high amounts of magnesium, calcium, aluminum, iron and antimony were all key ingredients of incendiary devices and would not be legally allowed in any "glue" associated with an airplane cabin interior.

Additional research revealed that "energized explosives" used in warheads create much more heat when magnesium, boron, aluminum and zinc are added to RDX and/or PETN.[2] These elements are a significant percentage of the residue I received from Terry Stacey. Several RDX and PETN samples were found on Flight 800 debris, including parts of the right wing near the RSOB hole and altered portions of the center wing tank. Calcium, representing 12% of the reddish-orange residue, is used when extreme heat is desired. Almost 99% of the elements, by volume, in my residue samples are consistent with elements expected to be found in an incendiary warhead.

Polymer-bonded explosives [PBX] combine PETN,[3] RDX[4] and other explosives in a "rubber-like polymeric matrix"[5] during the manufacturing process, to promote stability. I learned that PETN is sometimes inserted into silicone rubber during the manufacturing process. Silicone is in a significant percentage of the residue I received from Stacey. Other explosive binders include polyester, polyamide, latex, vinylidine chloride and polyurethane.[6]

These binders are quite similar in composition to adhesives such as the 3M 1357 HP adhesive the FBI and NTSB would, a few short months later, allege was the residue. This is the reason Kallstrom used "glue" as the government explanation for the residue. Non-intrusive microscopic analysis could safely conclude such substances were consistent with adhesive. Left unsaid is that such substances are equally consistent with explosive "binders." Intrusive testing is required to resolve the issue. But the government stripped all reddish-orange foam rubber from the hangar in order to prevent further testing of the reddish-orange residue—compelling evidence the residue is *not* glue.

During the same December 1996 timeframe,[7] Stacey briefed me on the latest from inside the Calverton hangar:

• Coroner says no lower-leg damage, therefore the initiating event was NOT the major explosion in the CWT that blew off the nose of the plane. CW-504[8] does not fit NTSB mechanical.

• New York Air National Guard Captain Chris Bauer's tape-recorded statement has been heard. Bauer says 'burning object' going east to west hit another object and caused it to explode. Stacey believes Bauer's superiors ordered him not to say missile.

• Alcoa metallurgists working with the FBI.

• NTSB side has asked many times for residue test results. "No response."

• Two-man FBI missile team "feel strongly it was a missile." This team gave a presentation to NTSB side November 1996. Said shoulder-fired missiles capable of hitting Flight 800. Probably wasn't radar guided because it was not picked up on radar. Infrared guidance is their best guess. Third-generation infrared goes for "center of the heat," per FBI missile team.

The only missile that was politically correct for the FBI to investigate was shoulder-fired. At this point in the investigation a missile could, in an emergency, still be admitted to, as long as it could be blamed on terrorists. Anything larger than shoulder-fired became very difficult not to blame on "friendly-fire"—a taboo subject, in spite of the fact that the "projectile[s]" described by witnesses, with a reddish-orange exhaust and 10-mile trajectory, was consistent with a larger missile and highly inconsistent with shoulder-fired.

On February 3, 1997, Stacey called me with the row and seat number where the FBI had lifted reddish-orange residue in early September 1996: Row 18, seats 6, 7 and 8; row 19, seat 7; row 27, seat 2. And on February 12, Stacey and I had our final face-to-face meeting. I briefed Stacey on the residue elements; and Stacey briefed me on what had just transpired at an NTSB meeting he had, only moments before, attended.

At that meeting senior members of the NTSB said the Flight 800 Cockpit Voice Recorder revealed a vibration traveling through the frame of the plane at over 2,000 feet per second. The NTSB had access to data, establishing that a bomb vibration travels through an airplane frame at about 340 fps. A low-order overpressure/explosion caused by kerosene-like jet fuel would result in a vibration no greater than 340 fps. This gave the NTSB yet another compelling piece of evidence that a missile caused the downing of TWA Flight 800. But the NTSB decided against retaining one of only two firms in the world with the expertise to analyze the vibration and pinpoint its origin.

The next time Terry Stacey and I saw each other was on April 7, 1999, inside the federal courtroom at Uniondale, Long Island, New York.

14

PRELUDE TO WAR

On February 21, 1997, a CBS producer contacted me, saying CBS sources had confirmed that part of a Navy Seal team was at Fort Monmouth, New Jersey, when Flight 800 went down. "Sunday, [the Seal Team] dived alone and would not allow NYPD divers in certain areas"[1] of the early red zone. [I was preparing to meet with a government official who claimed to have first-hand knowledge that this Seal Team operation found and removed missile parts from the red zone. But before this meeting came about, in December 1997, I was arrested. Understandably, no further communication with that source has been possible since then.]

By early March 1997 a decision was made to publish a series of newspaper articles describing my investigation of the government's Flight 800 cover-up. At the time, I, along with a First Amendment lawyer and senior members of the *Press-Enterprise* newspaper staff, believed that the rule of law would contain an excessive government reaction.

On March 5, I interviewed Stacey for the last time by phone. Notes from this conversation say: "Hangar Man conversation (1) Brookhaven residue test [this was a sample from hold area of the plane that had reddish-orange residue. The first sample did not produce results to the government's liking, so a second sample was lifted and sent to Brookhaven], (2) entry/exit holes." Stacey went into fairly extensive detail. The left side reconstruction was complete, and there was definitely space for a missile to have emerged. Reconstruction of the right side was not yet complete toward the front. Stacey noted considerable speculation about the damage in the area of the R-3 door. He then observed: "Left side L/2 door aft 'large hole' several feet."

The next day Terry Stacey had two hour-long telephone conversations with David Hendrix, as the Riverside *Press-Enterprise* newspaper prepared for the launch of the articles exposing the reddish-orange residue. Hendrix typed questions into his office computer prior to the interview, which was his normal practice. During the interview, Hendrix wore a headset in order to type in contemporaneous notes. Stacey was a fully cooperating, forthcoming source.

It is important to read and get a feel for the nature of the interview. Three months later, when the interview was relatively fresh in his mind, Stacey would present a dramatically different story to the FBI as he struggled to shape a scenario that would please his new masters. They had the power to permanently remove him from gainful employment as a senior 747 pilot, and a life of comfort developed over a 30-plus-year career as a pilot at TWA.

David Hendrix, and David Hendrix alone, interviewed Terry Stacey. Travel and phone records prove I was preparing for the flight to California and was en route from Williamsburg, Virginia, to the Riverside *Press-Enterprise* when this interview occurred:

Hendrix: What made you suspicious that maybe something other than a bomb or mechanical failure were involved?

Stacey: Very early in the investigation, with some of the reports of things in the sky and after reading some of the FBI summaries of witnesses, plus the fact that mechanical failure would have [developed relatively slowly and] most likely indicated something on one of the recorders. [There is] nothing to indicate that all of [the] flight recorder data is not there[,] or cockpit voice recorder [although Stacey was not aware of any scientific testing of the data and voice recorder to eliminate the possibility of tampering].

Hendrix: I understand you do not want any of this attributed to you personally, is that correct?

Stacey: That must be the case.

Hendrix: Is there a characterization we can use about you? Like an investigative source or person with detailed information about the investigation?

Stacey: [I do] not have a problem with those.

Hendrix: Can you tell me about the red residue? When did you notice it?

Stacey: Noticed back in August of last year. It was brought to my attention by somebody else. It was a color that was different from anything else on seatbacks, primarily. This guy looking at it was looking at possibilities of [a] missile going through. [He was] another investigator [at Calverton]. Residue is [in a] fairly uniform area. Just a little residue in row 27; primarily [on] row 17, 18, 19; on all the seats; this is not on the [front of the seats], this is on the panels on [the] back of [the seats]; residue is reddish-orange. Not sure to call [it] residue; looks like glue that [is] holding seatback on, that changed color. [It is] not like residue that would scrape off. [Stacey learned this through his attempt to scrape some of the flake-like residue into a plastic bag less than two months before this interview.] It is like a coating that has changed colors due to [a] reaction; epoxy appearing. Has bonded [to the foam rubber]. If that is what happened (missile residue), it [the foam rubber] had epoxy-type material [attached to portions of the foam rubber before the missile impacted Flight 800] and [the foam rubber] absorbed the [reddish-orange] residue.

Hendrix: Is it anywhere else in the plane, other than on the rows [17, 18, 19]?

Stacey: None on any other area, other than seats [in rows 17, 18, 19].

Hendrix: Has anybody else seen or commented about the red residue?

Stacey: Everybody in [the] investigation team has seen and commented about it. [I] don't expect to see FBI info. [The] FBI [is] conducting [a] criminal investigation. Could be that the FBI exchanges info with [the] NTSB at [a] higher level. That's the frustrating thing, those samples were taken in August and no results have been shared (at this level). Everybody has seen the residue. I don't know (why anybody hasn't talked); it was a hot issue for awhile, and they (investigation) moved on to something else, and we heard nothing else from it. It was an anomaly being looked into[,] is how it was described.

Hendrix: Anybody we can call who will tell us about the red residue, with or without their name being used?

Stacey: Don't know of anybody I would want to [have interviewed].

Hendrix: Have FBI investigators commented about it, even in passing?

Stacey: Recorded as samples being taken, but no results. That's just something that never made the news.

Hendrix: Some other anomalies?

Stacey: The way [there] is fractur[ing] and curling, and the fact that there's some titanium in [the] center wing tank that heated [and affixed itself] to [the] center wing tank—something drastically happened. There's nothing on the plane that says missile in large letters, but it may all be there in small pieces. There may be large letters there but nobody knows about it except the FBI. A lot of tests and interviews but no idea about the results. There are things on the record—holes, damage—that are unexplained strictly by mechanical failure and [the] plane going through [the] windstream and hitting the water. Each scenario—mechanical, bomb, and explosion—eventually does not fit.

Hendrix: Why doesn't [the] metallurgy report talk about

[the] nose falling off and what might have caused it to?

Stacey: They don't know. All they can say is what happened from a certain time. Those red zone pieces that came off the plane (front spars, doors, rows 17, 18 and 19). FBI says [the investigators inside the hangar] can't let that be known (red stuff) because of the criminal aspect of the investigation.

Hendrix: What would happen if [a] large group got together and said, this is what we think's happening, somebody do something about it.

Stacey: That's been done in meetings of investigators, in a large group wanting information: they [FBI] say they can't do it because of the investigation.

Hendrix: Any bodies have red residue on it?

Stacey: No info of that happening.

Hendrix: Where are the residue seats in relationship to the dog-sniffing bomb tests?

Stacey: Don't know where; will try to find out.

Hendrix: How long were the seats on the ocean bottom?

Stacey: Don't know; will be on the log.

Hendrix: Any other clues to the missile?

Stacey: (Puzzling about how residue bonded to [the foam rubber]). [The foam rubber may have] held or absorbed the residue from [the missile]. China Lake [Naval Weapons testing area in California]. Lots of experts from missiles [section], been here, but nobody's said anything.

Hendrix: How about the exit hole in the schematic? Where do I locate it?

Stacey: There are entry and exit holes all over this plane. [There is a] hole on [the] other side of C galley, that [is] a hole. Have to understand in reconstruction, that you're putting [the] plane back together. Hard to tell when [a] certain hole [aligns with another hole]. There is that large hole there, just forward of the wing area. [We are] Looking in reconstruction for line-of-site areas. If there was a hole that said missile on it we would be home; you certainly can say in that area where the residue was found, there certainly are plenty of holes both in and out. Other places like [the] L-3 door [left side of plane, third door back], is [a] very heavy structure [that is] bent in and [pieces are] missing.

Hendrix: Do you believe it was a missile?

Stacey: Yeah, I'd have to say I do. Eyewitness accounts, interviews I've conducted, the ANG [New York Air National Guard] pilot. He said [an] object traveled and hit [Flight 800] and exploded. His superiors have told him to quit using the word missile. The immediate nature of what happened; voice recording stopped—there has been a lot of interest by the FBI in the missile theory. Lots of people have studied missiles.

Hendrix: I understand the FBI missile team believes it is a missile.

Stacey: Yes. I know at least two on [the missile team]. They're trying to prove their theory. [They have] given briefings and explored all the area . . . are actively pursuing it.

Hendrix: Any other FBI think it [is] a missile?

Stacey: Can't speak to that. They don't say anything outside what they publicly believe. [I] can't say they've said they are convinced. Others on the investigation team believe it was a missile.

Hendrix: They [FBI missile team] ever said that in a meeting or is it only chat?

Stacey: Both—some official briefings; in briefing they talk about missile capabilities—hand-held, shoulder-fired; [a missile shot is] certainly within [the] capabilities [of shoulder-fired]; Kallstrom has vociferously denied friendly-fire. [The FBI missile] team in briefing says missiles capable of hitting [planes] at that altitude. [There is] talk [within the hangar] about work[ing] with eyewitnesses and triangulation, where [the missile] might have come from. Primarily [w]hat they talked about were Stinger-type and Russian [missiles] and others.

Hendrix: [Do] people on investigation team think friendly fire possible?

Stacey: Oh, yes.

Hendrix: Suspicious or belief?

Stacey: Belief among some and suspicion among others.

Terry Stacey was a cautious, methodical person, not prone to speculate or attempt to shape answers to fit a scenario—at least up to this point in his life, when he had not yet been threatened by the government.

The residue had been a "hot" topic within the investigation that had not been reported on by *The New York Times* or NBC evening news. One can infer, from the prominence the residue had within the investigation over a period of time, that major media was made aware of its presence, but elected not to pursue it because of the obvious "missile" implication, which was politically incorrect from the earliest days of the investigation.

The FBI did not come back and tell Terry Stacey's team it was glue. The NTSB scientists did not come back and say it was glue, that they knew it was glue because they saw it in virtually all crashed planes. "It was an anomaly being looked into," the senior crash investigators said. The FBI told the NTSB investigators not to reveal the residue trail to the media because it was part of their criminal investigation.

That is how the residue issue was being handled inside the Calverton hangar before it became known that some of the residue had escaped.

One day after interviewing Terry Stacey, David Hendrix placed a call to the New York City FBI headquarters. He identified himself and gave the FBI press person a general description of the questions he wanted the FBI to answer prior to publishing an article exposing the reddish-orange residue trail for the first time.

Hendrix placed the call shortly after 0600 hours West Coast time. I had arrived from Virginia via TWA about five hours earlier, and Hendrix had picked me up at Ontario airport. Now I sat in Hendrix's office, prepared to listen to the FBI response. It would be a long wait. The FBI press person said they would have to get back to Hendrix with a response.

Twelve hours later, Kallstrom personally returned Hendrix's call. After the opening pleasantries, when Kallstrom attempted to sound like the reporter's long-lost best friend, Hendrix asked the first question:

Hendrix: I'm doing a story saying there is an apparent residue trail through TWA Flight 800 that tests out as missile propellant. I have confirmation that you had residue in your possession no later than August 3, and that the trail across the fuselage was completed at Calverton no later than the end of August.

Kallstrom: It's not true. … I don't plan to talk about the evidence. … There is a red residue trail. It has no connection to a missile. I'm not going to get into it. There's a logical explanation, but I'm not going to get into it. That is a non-starter. I wish we had something that was definitive of any theory. The notion that you would run an article saying this is proof of a missile. There's no basis in fact. To my knowledge that is not factual.

Hendrix: The FBI took [samples] from seats in rows 17, 18 and 19. What were the results of those tests?

Kallstrom: We're not in the habit of discussing lab tests.

Then Hendrix began to read some of the elements and the percentages of each. At this point Kallstrom turned on an office speaker so unknown persons in his office could hear Hendrix revealing one of two things: (1) Residue had escaped from the hangar; or (2) someone at the FBI lab had leaked highly sensitive information from tests conducted off the books in September. There was not supposed to be a paper trail to these tests.

It is difficult to know what story to tell when you do not know precisely how much of the truth has escaped from your control. So Kallstrom stonewalled, blustered, huffed and puffed. The one thing he did not say was: "Hendrix, are you nuts? It's glue. Check it out. It's 3M 1357 HP glue." He did not say that because he did not know what the official line was going to be.

Glue was certainly the explanation that had been prepared in the summer of 1996, when the FBI saw the reddish-orange trail begin to march across the cabin interior as more and more seats were recovered. Glue is used on airplane seats, although in much smaller amounts than the government alleges. And, as long as you carefully select the scientific testing to be performed, an FBI lab technician could look at the residue and say it was a "chlorinated polymeric material consistent with glue." The binding agents in explosives and solid fuel are made of material similar to many glues and paints. So this was a great cover story, but only as long as the FBI had exclusive possession of the residue.

Forensic evidence, however, was a possibility the FBI did not contemplate. They dealt with major media reporters who did not have a clue how to spell forensics, much less understand what powerful evidence it was if the FBI was engaged in criminal activity within the Flight 800 investigation. But I was a retired police officer. During a career in law enforcement I personally observed how scientific evidence time after time carried the day in court against the most carefully thought-out lies.

My investigation of criminal activity within the government Flight 800 investigation seriously threatened the government's carefully crafted scheme.

The FBI and NTSB investigations had one primary purpose: to keep the decision-makers informed of any problem within the investigation requiring a change in the politically-contrived answer for the loss of Flight 800.

Within minutes of ending the interview with Hendrix, Kallstrom sent a message out telling the decision-makers that a major threat had surfaced.[2] It would be dealt with in a manner designed to protect those within the government placed at risk by my investigation.

Janet Reno's Justice Department sprang into action. Using the power of the grand jury, they began the process of recovering incriminating evidence that had escaped FBI control at the Calverton hangar.

Calls were certainly placed, and meetings held, with key people that control major media's agenda. Would they continue to play the role of government shill so finely honed over the previous months? Or, would the smell of blood create a media feeding frenzy, forcing the Clinton administration's strongest media supporters to run for cover?

The government had from Friday evening, March 7, 1997, until Monday morning, March 10, to make a final decision about what line to use and how best to orchestrate and manipulate the media.

A game plan to regain any untested residue that could be used in future tests to debunk the scheme being hatched was formulated over the weekend and readied for action. The Justice Department took the lead.

It would be necessary to violate any number of federal criminal statutes, case law and the Justice Department's own internal rules and regulations in order to subvert the rule of law. But this particular Justice Department had a long, sorry history of subverting the rule of law to protect the Clinton administration. They would not disappoint this time.

15

THE *PRESS-ENTERPRISE* ARTICLE

"New Data Show Missile May Have Nailed TWA 800," screamed the 1.5-inch headlines across the top of the Riverside *Press-Enterprise* March 10, 1997, front page. For almost three days the government had been preparing for this moment. It was time to circle the wagons.

A damage-control team had been assembled. The Justice Department obtained a subpoena for radar tapes believed to be in the possession of a retired commercial airline pilot who lived in Florida, Dick Russell. Getting these tapes back while simultaneously planning and implementing a disinformation campaign to vilify and discredit a *Paris Match* magazine article being released in Europe at the same time the new threat in California was emerging, was the opening salvo. Seldom had a cover-up experienced simultaneous highly damaging leaks of hard evidence. It was going to be a tough week for "Justice."

There was nothing the government could immediately do against the residue threat until they obtained the article due to be published the morning of March 10, 1997. They did have a predetermined plan of action in case knowledge of the residue trail leaked from the Calverton hangar. Government agents responsible for neutralizing such media flare-ups had an explanation at hand: it was glue.

There was indeed glue in the area. It was used to hold the tray tables to the backs of the seats, fastening the plastic to the metal seatbacks. This was not the residue in question, but it was a brownish color. Close enough for disinformation agents to work with.

The page-one, column-one subtitle: "Debris Pattern Provides Key to Mystery," provided information critical for the Justice Department and FBI taskforce developing a plan of action to get in front of this story.

"The answer to the mystery of what happened to TWA Flight 800, which last July crashed in the Atlantic Ocean, killing all 230 onboard, lies clearly written on the ocean floor, according to an ex-accident investigator who says a missile downed the airliner," the page-one story began.[1] Written by a young *Press-Enterprise* reporter, Loren Fleckenstein, the 30-column-inch story identified me as an "investigative reporter," provided information on my previous non-fiction books, and described my investigation of the FBI and NTSB Flight 800 investigation over the preceding five months:

> The pattern of the first wreckage to hit the water, combined with evidence of missile-propellant residue in the Boeing 747, clearly indicates that a missile carrying an inert warhead smashed through the airliner, author and *investigative reporter* James Sanders has concluded." [Emphasis added]

The National Transportation Safety Board disputed that assertion.

> We will be testifying before Congress on Tuesday that as of today there is no physical evidence of a bomb or a missile in any of the records (evidence) that we have recovered," NTSB spokesman Peter Goelz said Sunday.

Sanders and reporter Mark Sauter co-authored two books, *Soldiers of Misfortune* and *The Men We Left Behind*, about America's prisoners of war from World War I, World War II, Korea, the Cold War and Vietnam. Using documents and officials' memos from the National Archives and U.S. intelligence agencies, they alleged that evidence showed thousands of U.S., French, British and Canadian prisoners of war were left in enemies hands at the end of each conflict.

Sanders and Sauter have appeared as expert witnesses at Senate hearings about the American POW-MIA issue. Their early assertions that many allied POWs with sensitive military knowledge were sent to China or the Soviet Union were discounted until former Soviet intelligence agents and declassified KGB documents attested otherwise. U.S. officials have since discounted those Soviet documents and testimony.

"As for TWA Flight 800, analysis of the wreckage also disproves the most widespread version of the cause of the tragedy, an explosion of the airliner's center wing tank," Sanders said.

He used classified documents obtained from confidential sources inside the official investigation to reconstruct the plane's final moments and called on his own skills as a former auto accident investigator and officer in the Seal Beach [California] Police Department.

Sanders said he believes high officials at the FBI and National Transportation Safety Board, the two principal agencies investigating the crash, must have already reached the conclusion that a missile caused the crash. For reasons Sanders say he does not know, he says the government is attempting to cover up the true cause of the crash.

James Kallstrom, the FBI's assistant director in charge of the investigation, bristled at the suggestion he or his agents were covering up anything. "I wish we had something that was definitive of any theory, but the FBI does not," he said. "You could walk in there (reconstruction area) and have 50 theories … and to the amateur mind and novice … conclude that something specific happened."

Sanders said the government's documents paint the trail, not him. "I would love to say I'm a genius, but any accident investigator in the United States would take this same information and come up with the same answer in two to three weeks," Sanders said.

A Federal Aviation Administration crash analyst who reviewed the NTSB Flight 800 crash documents said they made him believe some outside object pierced the jumbo jet right to left and started the catastrophic sequence that eventually dismembered the plane. The analyst spoke on the condition his name not be used.

TWA Flight 800 took off from John F. Kennedy Airport in New York at 8:19 P.M., July 17 (1996), on a nonstop flight to Paris. At 8:31 P.M., the jet was about 12 miles south of the Long Island coastline, over the Atlantic Ocean, when it lit up the sky in a blaze and plunged into the ocean. Everyone on board died.

About 150 eyewitnesses from the ground reported seeing what they thought to be a missile, climbing to meet the 747 seconds before seeing the jet erupt into flames. The FBI lists 34 witnesses it considers "credible."

Government officials, including the vice chairman of the National Transportation Safety Board and the White House press secretary, since have made statements all but dismissing a missile or "friendly fire" from U.S. military forces as the culprit.

Sanders said his quest for the answer to the fate of TWA Flight 800 got off to a real start last November. Someone whom Sanders declined to identify passed him a 104-page printout of the FBI-NTSB catalog of every article recovered from the undersea crash site.

The tragic tally, thousands of items long, includes clothing, luggage, food trays, a woman's purse, passenger seats, aluminum wing fragments, beams and struts, human bodies and body parts.

Each entry lists the latitude and longitude of the resting place on the ocean floor of an item or group of items, pinpointed within a few feet by Navy and police scuba divers using satellite-assisted position-finding electronics.

Sanders punched that information into a personal computer and produced a diagram of the debris pattern. The resulting map reveals a west-to-east swath of wreckage scattered across 2.5 miles of ocean floor.

"It's like skid marks on the bottom of the ocean," Sanders said. "The diagram tells you a story of what happened."

His experience reconstructing auto accidents led him to home in on the first 4,700-foot stretch of undersea debris.

"It is generally recognized that whatever was impacted first falls off first. That principal applies whether you're in the air or on the ground, moving slowly or moving fast," Sanders said.

"It's like the crash of a Corvette moving more than 120 miles an hour. I've seen a Corvette engine more than three-tenths of a mile from the road, but that's not where the impact occurred. To find the cause, you trace the skid marks back to the point of impact."

A January NTSB report describing the order in which the plane fell apart states that the point at which items left the plane was among the more critical criteria needed to establish the cause.

Two of the first aircraft parts to fall into the ocean, according to the FBI-NTSB log, were the R-2 door, a door on the right side of the forward cabin, and a leading edge of the right wing where the wing joins the fuselage, or body of the aircraft.

The area between the door and the wing fragment corresponds exactly to a "gouge" that investigators discovered on the right side of the fuselage, Sanders said. That hole, Sanders said, was where a speeding missile punched into the airliner.

Investigators also discovered a second, larger hole on the opposite or left-hand side of the fuselage, one of Sanders' inside sources said. Sanders said he believes the missile, which he thinks contained no explosive warhead, created the second hole exiting the airliner.

Sanders said the official government statements and news reports on theories into the cause of the crash have given short shrift to that first, critical 4,700-foot portion of the crash site. Instead, the government has focused its analysis on the far-less revealing wreckage that fell into the ocean afterward, he said.

More missile evidence reached Sanders in a December conversation with an investigator who had access to the facility in Suffolk County, Long Island, where the National Transportation Safety Board was identifying and piecing together the recovered parts of the aircraft, Sanders said. The investigator, who Sanders declined to identify, said some of the passenger seats were coated with an orange-red residue, Sanders said.

Sanders said he later obtained samples of the residue and sent one to a commercial laboratory for analysis.

The analysis by West Coast Analytical Service, Inc. in Santa Fe Springs, California, found the residue contained, among other elements, silicon, calcium and aluminum. Those elements, Sanders said, are consistent with emissions from the burning of solid rocket fuel.

Sanders dismissed a different theory for what caused the crash.

NBC News, citing sources at the National Transportation Safety Board, has reported the most likely cause of the disaster was an explosion of the aircraft's center wing tank. Sanders said analysis of the undersea wreckage "completely eliminates" that theory.

Sanders agrees that a fire did occur in the fuel tank. However, that event did not occur until well after the aircraft already was in trouble, he said. The NTSB Metallurgy/Structures Sequencing Group Report, signed by its nine members on January 22 (1997), reached the same official conclusion.

According to Sanders' version, the missile's impact led to a fire in the center wing tank, located underneath the cabin floor and just behind, or aft, of the missile's path through the aircraft. The tank exploded 4,700 feet after the missile impact, causing the already weakened forward cabin to break free from the rest of the airplane, Sanders said.

The forward cabin—including the cockpit, all first-class seats and the most forward-placed coach-class seats—plunged into the ocean, Sanders said. By this point, most of the crew and forward passengers had been ejected from the plane or went down with the forward cabin, Sanders said.

Meanwhile, the remaining part of the aircraft—most of the fuselage, including the remaining passenger sections, both wings, all four engines and the tail section—stayed airborne a few seconds longer, Sanders said. According to the FBI-NTSB logs, almost all of the center wing tank ended up on the ocean floor, 12,000 feet east of the first fall of debris. It defies the science of accident reconstruction, Sanders said, that something located virtually at the end of such a long debris trail could have caused a disaster like TWA Flight 800.

"Things fall generally in the order in which they are impacted," Sanders said. "The center wing tank, if it were the initiating event (of the crash), would be among the first debris, not the last."

This story created an enormous legal obstacle for the Justice Department. I was clearly identified as an "investigative reporter." The article's words confirmed I was indeed an investigative reporter on the trail of criminal activity within the Flight 800 investigation.

The article was just as clear to major media: An investigative journalist was alleging a cover-up within the investigation that, if correct, reached to the top of the Clinton administration. Major media had been leaned on for the three days prior to publication. They had a choice: balanced journalism telling both sides of the story, providing he-said, she-said journalism to the American public as the two sides in the Flight 800 controversy slugged it out—or major media could protect the President from yet another scandal that promised to turn into a media feeding frenzy threatening the Administration's existence.

16

GLUE REPELS MISSILES

The FBI and Justice Department had failed in their mission to make the evidence fit the predetermined outcome. Debris with blast damage had been altered. Explosive residue had been stripped from seats and removed from the Calverton hangar. Phony NTSB diagrams of the damaged CWT, spanwise beams and front spar had been created for dissemination to working groups within the investigation.

The aircraft's right wing was not rebuilt because the damage to its mid-spar near the fuselage offered additional evidence of a missile strike in the area. Portions of the right wing in the area of the mid-spar had blast holes and tested positive for explosive residue. They were removed from the hangar.

Now, the government's worst nightmare had occurred. Forensic evidence had been removed from the hangar and tested. The elements found in the reddish-orange residue were consistent with exhaust from a solid-fuel missile. But an even more telling explanation of the residue had not yet been uncovered by me or the *Press-Enterprise*—more than 98% of the volume of the residue was commonly found in incendiary warheads.

Compounding government hysteria was the certainty that additional residue was poised for testing as soon as the government's disinformation campaign locked onto an alternate explanation for the reddish-orange residue.

I arrived in New York City early Monday morning, March 10, 1997, making the rounds of New York City's major publishers, conveniently congregated a short distance from Jim Kallstrom's office and Associated Press (AP) headquarters on Manhattan Island.

After each publishing-world interview I stopped by the AP offices to visit with reporter Richard Pyle. The government was going to issue a statement on the residue by 12 noon, I was initially told. The time of release was gradually set back by some faceless bureaucrat, then cancelled as of 3:00 p.m. The government resorted to its more traditional means of vilifying the messenger—anonymous leaks. In this case, a steady drumbeat of shrill statements that the residue was glue, with nothing to back it up except more, shrill words. But that was enough for major media in New York. They began to report the missile theory had once again been "shot down."

The next day, March 11, NTSB Chairman Jim Hall was scheduled to testify before the House Aviation Subcommittee. The focus turned to the reddish-orange residue:

Congressman Wolf: ... These articles report that a trail of reddish-brown residue was found embedded in seats [sic] 17 through 19, which contained chemical elements consistent with [a] solid-fuel missile. Although your accident investigation into this crash is still ongoing, can you give us some explanation for the residue?

Dr. Loeb (NTSB): ... One thing I can say categorically is there is no such thing as a red residue trail in that airplane. There is a reddish-orange substance that is on virtually all of the seats in the forward part of the airplane. For that matter, I am sure it is on all of the seats in the airplane because we believe that that red residue material is an adhesive. I cannot say for certain that that is what these folks are talking about, but it is the only reddish or orange material that we are aware of that exists inside that airplane in the seats. We took seven samples yesterday from Calverton and had them brought to our headquarters. We are now testing them in our laboratory, and we will do some testing in the FBI laboratory. If need be, we will do testing in outside laboratories just to make certain that they are, in fact, consistent with the manufacturer's descriptions of those products. Adhesive is the only substance that we know of that is reddish or orange in that airplane.[1]

When he made that statement on March 11, Dr. Loeb was technically telling the truth. If he had been under oath before Congress the previous Friday, his testimony would have been false.

Multiple sources inside the Calverton hangar verified Terry Stacey's claim that a red residue trail existed across the passenger cabin in rows 17, 18 and 19. The government, by arresting Terry Stacey and my wife and I, confirmed the residue given to me for testing represented legitimate foam-rubber samples from the Calverton hangar.

Kallstrom knew, as of 1530 hours East Coast time, March 7, 1997, that the reddish-orange residue was outside his control.[2] We know from multiple sources and the samples Stacey removed from the hangar, that the reddish-orange trail was on foam rubber. We know the foam rubber laden with residue was stripped from the seats at the Calverton hangar sometime after 1530 hours March 7, 1997,[3] when the FBI learned the residue was outside their control.

Four days later an NTSB representative confidently stated that no foam rubber unique to rows 17, 18 and 19 would be found inside the Calverton hangar. So we can reasonably place the time of removal of the foam rubber between Friday afternoon, March 7, 1997, and Tuesday morning, March 11, 1997.

After the act of removal was complete, no reddish-orange foam rubber could be found in the hangar.[4] All that remained was rust-colored bare metal and some hard plastic panels glued to the backs of some of the seats.

Dr. Loeb's testimony before Congress on March 11 changed the public debate. If they could produce any glue from the plane, it *prima facie* meant there could be no residue from the exhaust of a missile inside the Calverton hangar. In other words, the government's position was that glue repels missiles.

It was a stupid argument that was immediately and enthusiastically embraced by major media as the truth.

The senior NTSB scientist at Calverton, Doctor Merritt Birky, Chairman of the Flight 800 Fire and Explosion Group, said the "brown to reddish-brown-colored material"[5] he sent to NASA for testing was "consistent with a polychloroprene 3M Scotch-Grip 1357 High Performance contact adhesive."[6] The NTSB then circulated this report among the major media, alleging this was independent proof that my residue was glue; another easily debunked argument that was instead immediately and enthusiastically embraced by major media as the truth.

The NTSB did not connect my residue samples with the samples sent to NASA. They merely adopted the "glue repels missiles" hypothesis. Major media, in turn, embraced this buffoonish hypothesis.

One phone call to NASA chemist Charles Bassett, the man who performed the test for Birky, would have exposed the fraudulent NTSB claim. Bassett's name and phone number could be found in the Fire and Explosion Group Report available to all journalists.

But no one within major media picked up the phone and made a call to confirm the story being handed out by the NTSB—a story that, if true, destroyed my credibility. The opposite side of the argument was, if the government was found to be lying, their shrill denials would be *prima facie* false, and they would stand convicted in the court of public opinion: guilty of a cover-up, criminals under the law.

As usual, major media filed their stories, exclusively using government propaganda as fact, with no attempt to fact-check or balance the story.

But I did pick up the phone and call Charles Bassett.[7] He then provided me with an affidavit which said, in part: "The tests performed by me at NASA-KSC on samples Dr. Birky said were from rows 17, 19, 24 and 27 of the Flight 800 cabin interior did not address the issue of the origin of any reddish-orange residue [James Sanders had tested by West Coast Analytical Services (WCAS).][8] The tests I performed for the NTSB cannot answer such a question."[9]

In a tape-recorded telephone conversation, Merritt Birky obliquely confessed to having lied in his Fire and Explosion Report and to the media:

Question: So Sanders did an elemental analysis and the whole world was shocked that [he] thought it was a missile fuel. You at the NTSB went ahead and got what you thought was the same residue and did an analysis yourself.

Birky: A different analysis.

Question: A different analysis, right. And concluded that this residue was, in fact, not missile residue, it was 3M adhesive. And I think it would have been good if you did an elemental analysis, not to prove whether it was adhesive or not, but to prove if it was the same stuff. To make sure that you and Sanders had the same stuff. Therefore, when you say the residue is adhesive, you mean it is the same residue that Sanders is talking about.

Birky: No. Because you see the problem is, before we even got that far, we knew that 3M had already changed their formula. They had represented that to us when we tried to get some reference samples. Well, that's old material. We haven't the foggiest notion what that formula is, nor do we have any of the old formulation; we don't know what was used at that time on those seats. So, in trying to prove that we have the same samples as Sanders, I'm not sure it gets us very far. Supposing Sanders' comes out differently?

Question: Right, right.

Birky: Then what are you going to say? Well, you're not going to put the thing to bed.

Contrary to sworn testimony before Congress and dozens of leaks to major media alleging the residue was glue, the truth from Merritt Birky's lips exposed the government position. The residue was not glue. The government never had reason to believe it *was* glue.

The truth is that within days after the March 10, 1997, *Press-Enterprise* story revealed the residue, both the NTSB and FBI came into possession of what remained of the samples sent to me by Terry Stacey. The FBI and NTSB did not need to go to the hangar for additional samples. They had them in their possession. The NTSB sample came from CBS News and the FBI sample was seized under subpoena from West Coast Analytical Services.

If theirs was an honest investigation, all the NTSB and FBI had to do was have Charles Bassett at NASA test my samples while keeping the media and Congress fully informed. Dr. Birky admitted the NTSB did not take this path because they were afraid the results would confirm my missile theory and debunk their mechanical hypothesis.

One can only be afraid of such results if "mechanical" failure was predetermined at the highest levels of the United States government to be responsible for the loss of 230 lives.

17

DYSLEXIC FOG

Anonymous leaks from within the government and perjured testimony before the House Aviation Subcommittee would not be enough to stop the political hemorrhaging. The cover-up was threatening to unravel. Major media was asleep, but regional news, talk radio and the emerging power of Internet news continued to be a threat. So Valerie Caproni, the aggressive Justice Department lawyer previously tasked with ordering the NTSB Witness Team to violate its congressional mandate, once again lead an illegal Justice Department operation. She was tasked with using the power of a federal grand jury to shut down the journalistic investigation threatening the predetermined outcome of the Flight 800 "investigation."

A series of legal barriers stood in her way. The Justice Department's own rules and regulations, CFR 50.10, prohibit harassment, intimidation and persecution of journalists. The preamble states: "Because freedom of the press can be no broader than the freedom of reporters to investigate and report the news, the prosecutorial power of the government should not be used in such a way that it impairs a reporter's responsibility to cover as broadly as possible controversial issues." Moving words, indeed. Important words in a society where the governed are determined to maintain control over those who govern.

The First Amendment Freedom of the Press guarantee, enforced by 18 U.S.C., sections 241 and 242, is supposed to protect journalists from lawlessness on the part of government officials: "If two or more persons conspire to injure[1] , oppress, threaten, or intimidate any person in any State ... in the free exercise or enjoyment of any right or privilege secured to him by the Constitution or laws of the United States, or because of his having exercised the same. ... They shall be fined under this title or imprisoned not more than ten years, or both. ..."

"He who defies a decision interpreting the Constitution knows precisely what he is doing ..." the Supreme Court warned in *Screws v. United States*. The warning is specific to government officials, such as Valerie Caproni, who engaged in violating the constitutional and civil rights of journalists.[2] "Indeed, the important social interests in the free flow of information that are protected by the reporter's qualified privilege are particularly compelling in criminal cases," the Second Circuit stated in *Burke*.[3] "Reporters are to be encouraged to investigate and expose, free from unnecessary government intrusion, evidence of criminal wrongdoing," the court concluded.

In 1987, four years after *Burke,* the Second Circuit Court stated in *Von Bulow:* "... the process of newsgathering is a protected right under the First Amendment, albeit a qualified one. This qualified right, which results in the journalist's privilege, emanates from the strong public policy supporting the unfettered communication of information by the journalist to the public. ... The underlying policies served by the New York Shield Law and federal law are congruent. Both 'reflect a paramount public interest in the maintenance of a vigorous, aggressive and independent press capable of participating in robust, unfettered debate over controversial matters, an interest which has always been a principal concern of the First Amendment.'"[4]

In a society where the governed are determined to control those who govern, these words represent sacred concepts. But they are mere words, without force or meaning when those who are governed lose the power to control those who govern.

Von Bulow provided Caproni with a statement of what a journalist could possess and the means used to obtain the evidence. Also included in the mandate is the procedure the Justice Department must follow if it wishes to question the *prima facie* "investigative reporter" definition attached to my name in the March 10, 1997, *Press-Enterprise* article: "It is axiomatic that the burden is on a party claiming the protection of a privilege to establish those facts that are essential elements of the privileged relationship. ... We hold that the individual claiming the privilege must demonstrate, through competent evidence, the intent to use *material*—sought, gathered or received—to disseminate information to the public and that such intent existed at the inception of the newsgathering process. This requires an intent-based factual inquiry to be made by the district court."[5] [Emphasis added]

So Caproni knew she had no chance of legally using the federal court system to go after me, forcing me to reveal my informant inside the Flight 800 investigation. Since the Second Circuit court had declined to place limits on what a journalist could ask for and obtain from a source, it was equally doubtful the court would have allowed Caproni to use the grand jury to seize the residue samples I continued to possess. She knew the lawful approach was doomed to failure.

Von Bulow presented Caproni with a legal prohibition to "injure, oppress, threaten, or intimidate" me in my journalistic pursuit of government wrongdoing. "Material" comfortably includes the reddish-orange residue obtained four months into my investigation of government wrongdoing, after evidence was first obtained tying the residue to the first seats to exit the 747 at the onset of the plane's demise.

Von Bulow defines a journalist as much more than a passive gatherer of whatever magically falls from the sky. Journalists are encouraged to aggressively seek out evidence of government wrongdoing. Asking is not just tolerated, the court encourages it.

Nor is this some quaint Second Circuit opinion. It is based on more than 200 years of experience as the unique spirit that is America has struggled to keep the government under control.

Almost 30 years earlier, the Supreme Court had severely chastised the Nixon Administration in the Pentagon Papers case. The Court, in its written decision, created clear language to guide the government in future confrontations with journalists: "Madison and the other framers of the First Amendment, able men that they were, wrote in language they earnestly believed could never be misunderstood: 'Congress shall make no law abridging the freedom of the press.' Both the history and language of the First Amendment support the view that the press must be left free to publish news, whatever the source, without censorship, injunctions, or prior restraints. In the First Amendment the Founding Fathers gave the free press the protection it must have to fulfill its essential role in our democracy. The press was to serve the governed, not the governors. The government's power to censor the press was abolished so that the press would remain forever free to censure the government. The press was protected so that it could bare the secrets of government and inform the people. Only a free and unrestrained press can effectively expose deception in government. And paramount among the responsibilities of a free press is the duty to prevent any part of the government from deceiving the people."[6]

Justice Douglas, concurring with Justice Black and the majority, further outlined the compelling national interest in a free press unfettered by an arrogant, vindictive government: "… the administration of government has become more complex, the opportunities for malfeasance and corruption have multiplied, crime has grown to most serious proportions, and the danger of its protection by unfaithful officials and of the impairment of the fundamental security by criminal alliances and official neglect, emphasizes the primary need of a vigilant and courageous press. ... The dominant purpose of the First Amendment was to prohibit the widespread practice of government suppression of embarrassing information."

The Supreme Court was analyzing the Pentagon Papers case and acknowledged that the papers would damage national security. It was also acknowledged that they had been stolen by a government official and received by *The New York Times* and *Washington Post*. The federal law covering theft of federal documents, including Xerox copies, is 18 U.S.C., section 641: "Whoever embezzles, steals, purloins, or knowingly converts to his use or the use of another, or without authority, sells, conveys or disposes of any record, voucher, money, or thing of value of the United States ... or Whoever receives, conceals, or retains the same with intent to convert it to his use or gain, knowing it to have been embezzled, stolen, purloined or converted. ..."

On its face, the Pentagon Papers case presented the government with an airtight reason to indict senior *New York Times* and *Washington Post* reporters. But no one was indicted, even though additional "national security" laws had also apparently been violated.

This federal law should result in the indictment of every journalist who ever received a government document without the government's permission. But it does not because the First Amendment's Freedom of the Press provides a "protected" right for journalists in pursuit of government lawlessness. The First Amendment provides a journalistic exemption from laws of general applicability.

So the government schemers were in a box from which they could not legally extricate themselves without abandoning the mission for which they had volunteered. By their actions, they demonstrated a willingness to move beyond the pale of legality.

A dyslexic fog settled within their collective gray matter, creating a willful blindness. Justice Department attorneys Valerie Caproni and Ben Campbell, along with FBI agents Jim Kallstrom, Jim Kinsley, et al, could not see "investigative reporter" to the left of "James Sanders" in the March 10, 1997, *Press-Enterprise* article.

Nor could they see the description of my two previous non-fiction books. Also invisible to the bureaucratically-induced dyslexic fog was page after page of printed words in the *Press-Enterprise* newspaper dealing with what my investigation had uncovered. If they did not know I was a journalist, their otherwise lawless acts magically became lawful.

"We can find no support for the assertion that Mr. Sanders is a member of the media," Caproni and Campbell declared in an April 1, 1997, message to my attorney, Jeff Schlanger. So I became nothing more than a "source" of information for the *Press-Enterprise* in this contrived dyslexic fog: "All indications from the article are that Mr. Sanders was simply a source of information—not a colleague," they declared in the letter. A source cannot be shielded by the First Amendment as a news gatherer, Caproni and Campbell declared; unilaterally voiding carefully crafted Second Circuit Court case law.

Amazingly, the Caproni/Campbell team concluded this infarcted diatribe with: "… we believe that we are proceeding in a responsible, lawful manner."

Perhaps their conduct passes for responsible and lawful in the twilight hours of the 20th century, during the final years of one of the most lawless administrations in the history of this country. "Responsible" and "lawful" as defined by Attorney General Janet Reno.

Lurking in the background inside *Von Bulow* were even more stringent rules that Caproni/Campbell must follow to avoid being "visited with punishment" if a lawful administration should appear on the horizon before the statute of limitations runs out. "In examining the boundaries of the journalist's privilege," the Second Circuit *Von Bulow* decision continued, "we may consider also the applicable state law, in this case New York's so-called 'Shield Law', N.Y. CivRights Law, 79-h et seq. Although we are not bound to follow New York law, neither should we ignore New York's policy of giving protection to professional journalists. The Shield Law provides that a professional journalist shall not be held in contempt by any court for 'refusing or failing to disclose any news or the source of any such news coming into his possession in the course of gathering or obtaining news for publication ... by which he is professionally employed or associated in a newsgathering capacity.'"

This makes it apparent why the Caproni/Campbell/ Kallstrom team elected to resort to actions proscribed by federal civil rights law. A court-ordered debate could not be tolerated. Disclosure of the source would in all probability be judicially blocked. Government assertions that the residue was glue, both public pronouncements and statements before Congress, were put at risk in any legal setting. The ability to use the power of the government to continue to squelch the debate and "injure, oppress, threaten (and) intimidate" would end. In such a legal setting, my source would be protected. The residue would come under the definition of "material" used by the Second Circuit Court since 1987. And, most important, the FBI could not seize the remaining residue, which was to be used to determine the veracity of whatever story the government issued in response to the March 10, 1997, *Press-Enterprise* article's statement that the elements in the residue were consistent with solid-fuel missile exhaust.

The government had no choice: a multi-agency coordinated effort had to be mounted to neutralize the messenger. Caproni used the grand jury process to improperly obtain a summons for me, demanding my appearance before a grand jury process controlled by those who conspired to violate my civil rights.

She also used the power of the grand jury to seize my phone records. My computer hard drive was also seized without a warrant. The schemers had to have as much intelligence as possible as they pursued and harassed me. They could not go before a judge and hope to get lawful permission, so they resorted to an unending string of lawless acts to achieve their goal. This lawlessness would extend to rifling though my police personnel file without a warrant, a warrant they could not legally obtain under California law.

As these events began to unfold, my wife Elizabeth believed that the wife of a journalist could not be made to reveal information about his investigations. All wives know their husband's work. So when the FBI began their pursuit, it was overwhelming.

Liz was appalled at the crass bullying tactics of the FBI. They stomped throughout TWA, interrogating her friends and co-workers. They stomped through her neighborhood in Williamsburg, Virginia, intimidating her friends and neighbors. Then they stomped through the Norfolk, Virginia, airport attempting to intercept and drag her off a TWA flight. They seized records without a search warrant and then seized my computer without a warrant.

They were trying to use Liz to get to me. Was this really America? As a journalist, they could not legally subpoena me, but the government would now target my wife to "encourage" me to cooperate.

The FBI continually harassed her—trying to get her to "talk" to them. She knew what they wanted—the name of Hangar Man—and she would never give it up.

To avoid any more harassment to reveal Terry's name, Liz was forced to leave TWA, her home, or anywhere else they could show themselves. Because of high ethical standards and commitment, Liz endured great personal sacrifice. For eight months in 1997, she was cut off from her career at TWA, at which she excelled and enjoyed; but was also away from her husband and son, family and friends. Liz' life had been turned upside down because the government was out of control. The stress was unbearable. She suffered from depression, which continues to this day.

As the wife of a journalist, she would protect his source. As a TWA employee, she would protect her friend.

The Justice Department would allege at trial that removing one's self from government bullying is "consciousness of guilt," even though a lawyer was immediately retained to contact the Department with specific instructions to be a communication conduit between the government and us. She was not hiding to avoid the legal process, she was hiding to avoid government harassment while remaining available for any legal process.

Except for David Hendrix at the Riverside *Press-Enterprise*, all print journalists distanced themselves from me. Nor could contact with Terry Stacey, *aka* Hangar Man, be reestablished. Another NTSB source with first-hand information and documents related to FBI removal of parts from the Calverton hangar, refused further communication with me. A military source, alleged to be an eyewitness to the removal of missile parts from the ocean in the first days after Flight 800 went down, also disappeared, as did two additional sources with information that, if true, went to the heart of the government motive for conspiring to violate our constitutional and civil rights.

18

CIA DISINFORMATION

The Calverton hangar was never declared a crime scene. The FBI stopped leaking bomb stories to *The New York Times* in August 1996, and in September began a concerted campaign to remove "missile" and "bomb" from major media thought processes. This campaign is easily tracked through the pages of *The New York Times*, the favored FBI outlet when manipulation of the public mind was the goal.

The NTSB assumed almost exclusive control over the propaganda offensive designed to rewrite the history of TWA Flight 800. "Mechanical" was the only hypothesis allowed to officially leak from the hangar. The NTSB investigators were warned daily not to leak to the press—that was to be the exclusive domain of those in control of the "investigation." It was their divine right to shape the message leaving Calverton. Competing views would not be tolerated. The mechanical hypothesis was so preposterous it could not withstand scrutiny or competing ideas.

The government spent $40 million looking for any scientific thread that could conceivably provide a basis for the government's hypothesis, but could not uncover even one identifiable scientific fact to back it.

As Kallstrom, Caproni, Reno, et al, were frantically trying to shore up the bleeding cover-up, the BATF, trying to be helpful, attempted to provide Kallstrom with what they proudly thought was the answer to the attack on the integrity of the FBI investigation by the *Press-Enterprise* newspaper. But

Kallstrom responded in a very strange manner, refusing to see or take possession of the report on March 11, 1997.[1] He was "upset w/report—locks him into eliminating missile—refuses to see report," according to handwritten BATF investigator notes unearthed by a Senate subcommittee.

The entire government investigative process used official leaks to major media, particularly *The New York Times* and NBC, to eliminate a missile. Major media demonstrated a strong willingness to disburse government leaks without attempting to offer balanced journalism. Everything was going the government's way until March 10, 1997. Now, 24 hours later, Kallstrom was complaining that he would be "locked into eliminating missile," a clear propaganda goal for many months.

The residue forced him to pretend his criminal investigation was vigorously pursuing a possible terrorist shootdown of Flight 800, therefore the "crime scene" had been contaminated by the residue's escape from FBI control. The BATF report effectively dated the demise of any serious criminal investigation to before the date the residue was removed from the Calverton hangar.[2]

One cannot allege a violation of the sanctity of a crime scene unless the façade of a crime scene remains. This was to become the focal point of the Justice Department assault on me. Therefore the BATF's well-intentioned effort was met with a seemingly irrational Kallstrom response. Significant damage control would have to be performed.

On March 14, 1997, Kallstrom sent a rather shrill message to Louis Freeh:

> … The publication of this unsolicited, premature report violates the agreement made by ATF regarding their participation in the TWA investigation.[3] ADIC, NY believes ATF's preparation of a report providing an opinion regarding the cause of this tragedy while knowing full well, among other things, that the investigation is continuing; that parts of the aircraft are still

being recovered; that substantial parts of the side walls of the center fuel tank have not been recovered or identified and potentially significant pieces, i.e., the scavenger [sic] pump, have not been recovered; that the reconstruction of the aircraft is ongoing; and that other testing, i.e., metallurgical examinations, China Lake missile testing, is planned or ongoing is unprofessional and reprehensible.

The only parts still being searched for were parts from a missile within a 2.75-mile radius of where the plane began to shed debris. This was a sensitive operation that began in early November 1996 and concluded abruptly in early April 1997.

The scavenge pump had long since been removed as a possible suspect because of the lack of damage around its location at the rear of the center fuel tank; but it was listed as a priority item to be recovered during the trawling operation, along with missile parts.

Kallstrom complained about the BATF not waiting for the China Lake testing to conclude. Then he went before the press and declared the FBI was exiting the Flight 800 investigation before the China Lake analysis was completed.

In contrast to the shrill attack on the BATF when it attempted to get its Flight 800 report distributed to the NTSB and leaked to the major media, the CIA quietly forwarded Kallstrom a four-page "analytic assessment" of the possibility that a missile brought down Flight 800.

The CIA report hit Kallstrom's desk 15 days after the BATF report. Both reports said the same thing: no missile was involved. Yet Kallstrom was only upset about the BATF report. The BATF had a history of leaking Flight 800 information to the press. But Kallstrom needed to maintain the "sanctity of the crime scene" façade.

Perhaps most interesting is the inference that the CIA possesses "weapons analysts" with an expertise that somehow makes them uniquely qualified to assess whether a 747 was shot down by a missile. No evidence of this alleged institutional expertise has been placed before the public. This is in sharp contrast to military missile experts brought in early in the investigation to interview the eyewitnesses to a missile shot. They culled the witnesses to a core group of 36 who, the military experts determined, had seen a missile shoot down Flight 800.

The FBI needed a more controllable group of "experts" to come up with the correct answer, so the CIA volunteered, declaring in a March 28, 1997, cover letter that: "Our analysis, combined with the total absence of physical evidence to a missile attack, leads CIA analysts to conclude that no such attack occurred."[4] The Analytic Assessment was attached:

> ... Of particular concern to FBI investigators and CIA analysts are accounts from dozens of eyewitnesses who reported seeing an object—usually described as a "flare" or "firework"—ascend and culminate in an explosion. Many people postulated that these eyewitnesses saw a missile destroy the aircraft.
>
> At the request of the FBI, CIA weapons analysts were asked to look into this possibility. The CIA conclusion: A missile was *not* involved. The eyewitness sightings of greatest concern— the ones originally interpreted to be of a possible missile attack—took place after the first of several explosions aboard the aircraft. What these eyewitnesses saw was in fact the *crippled aircraft after the first explosion had already taken place*. [Emphasis added]

A major complication in determining what happened to Flight 800 was the fact that the flight data recorder and cockpit voice recorder ceased operating just after the initial explosion aboard the aircraft. The data recorder registered no unusual activity prior to the end of its operation. But the voice recorder registered a fraction of a second "loud noise" just before it ceased operating. National Transportation Safety Board analysts concluded that this was sound from the first explosion—the one that initiated the destruction of the aircraft.

Based on flight recorder data and airport radar tracking, the aircraft's location, altitude, speed and heading at the instant its recorders ceased operating are known. This information was used to determine the distance and direction of travel of the aircraft with respect to each eyewitness at the instant the aircraft exploded. This, in turn, made it possible to calculate how long it took sound from the explosion to reach each eyewitness, and to associate what eyewitnesses heard with what they saw.

The concept used here is similar to a technique a person can use to determine how far away a lightning strike is—by estimating how long it takes to hear thunder after the lightning is seen. Because sound in air travels about 1,100 feet per second, an observer who hears thunder five seconds after seeing a lightning strike knows that the lightning is about 1 mile away.

On the evening of 17 July, many eyewitnesses reported hearing a loud "boom" as part of their observations, often followed at varying intervals by one or two smaller "booms." Knowing that the first of these sounds originated when the recorders ceased operating (831:07.5 PM [sic]), it is possible to synchronize many eyewitnesses' visual observations with activity aboard Flight 800 by calculating how long it took sound to travel from the known location of the aircraft when it exploded to each of these eyewitnesses.

We can be confident that no sound from the aircraft audible to eyewitnesses was produced *before* the sound heard at the end of the cockpit voice recording. The closest eyewitness hearing such sounds was more than 8 miles away. Any sound heard at this distance and produced near the aircraft before the recording ended would have been recorded. [Emphasis added]

Using the eyewitnesses' visual and sound observations—combined with tracking data from the radar [sic] and infrared data from an intelligence sensor—CIA analysts were able to reconstruct the approximate path of Flight 800 from the instant its recordings ended until it hit the water. The following postulated sequence of events is based on that analysis: Just after the initial explosion at 831:07.5 PM [sic], the aircraft pitched up abruptly and climbed several thousand feet from its cruise altitude of 13,800 feet to a maximum altitude of about 17,000 feet. This is consistent with information provided by National Transportation Safety Board and Boeing engineers indicating that the front third of the aircraft, including the cockpit, separated from the fuselage just two to four seconds after the initial explosion. This significant sudden loss of mass from the front of the aircraft caused the rapid pitch-up. The initial explosion was not seen by any known eyewitness. But the subsequent fire trailing from the aircraft was clearly visible to many of the closest eyewitnesses on the land and sea, and some of the eyewitnesses in other aircraft. The rising, burning aircraft is consistent with what some eyewitnesses described as "an ascending, bright white light resembling a flare or firework." Shortly after Flight 800 reached the apex of its ascent—about 15 seconds or so after the initial explosion—a *second* explosion on the aircraft occurred. This explosion was clearly visible to many eyewitnesses, and often was described as "a small fireball." It was not as loud as the initial explosion, but was clearly audible more than 10 miles away. Following this second explosion, the aircraft went into a very rapid descent, falling 2 miles and traveling horizontally almost 2 miles in less than 25 seconds. As the aircraft descended, it produced an increasingly visible fire trail. When it reached an altitude of about 1 mile—42 seconds after the initial onboard explosion—the aircraft's left wing separated from the fuselage, releasing the unburned fuel in the left wing's fuel tanks. The fuel's subsequent ignition and burning produced a dramatic fireball visible to eyewitnesses more than 40 miles away, and detected by an infrared sensor aboard the US Defense Support Program [DSP] missile warning satellite. About 50 seconds after the initial explosion—eight seconds after the left wing detached—the aircraft and detached wing hit the water.

CIA analysts developed the characterization above using technical data and accounts from the few eyewitnesses who were relatively close to the disaster, and who provided detailed descriptions of what they saw and heard. This portrayal then was evaluated against descriptions provided by almost 200 additional eyewitnesses.

Not surprisingly, most eyewitnesses saw only the most conspicuous segment of the disaster—the ignition of the fuel and resulting fireball in the 10 seconds or so just before the aircraft hit the water. There are three distinctive characteristics analysts used to conclude that these eyewitnesses saw only the end of the aircraft's descent and *not* a missile.

First, sound from the initial explosion took from 42 to 102 seconds to reach each of the eyewitnesses claiming to have heard sounds associated with the disaster. Therefore, things eyewitnesses reported seeing at about the time when they heard the first sound are known to have taken place well after the first explosion occurred.

Second, many eyewitnesses described only things happening within 10 seconds of the time that the left wing detached from the fuselage. This was a very well-defined event, resulting in two distinct fireballs falling to the ocean. The left wing is known to have detached about 42 seconds after the initial explosion.

And third, many eyewitnesses described only things happening within about 10 seconds of the time that they observed a large fire or "cascading" flames. These flames could only be from the burning fuel released and ignited after the left wing detached.

Using the above process of elimination, the majority of observations can be demonstrated to have occurred well after the initial explosion. Consequently, none of these observations can be of a missile which caused this explosion.

The remaining eyewitness accounts describe events fully consistent with observations expected if only the aircraft in various stages of crippled flight were being observed. There is nothing in this last category of eyewitness statements that provides any evidence that a missile was used to shoot down Flight 800.

Indeed, several eyewitnesses, confident that they had seen a missile destroy an aircraft, were puzzled that they hadn't actually *seen* the aircraft before the missile hit it. Only a few eyewitnesses described seeing the aircraft at all, even though it should have been illuminated by the setting sun and clearly visible to any observer witnessing a missile approach and destroy it. The fact that only a few eyewitnesses *reported* seeing the aircraft—which should have been readily visible—suggests that many eyewitnesses may have seen *only* the crippled aircraft without realizing it.

Conclusions. CIA analysts do not believe that a missile was used to shoot down TWA Flight 800. To date, there is absolutely no evidence, physical or otherwise, that a missile was employed.

Speculation that a missile was involved originally was put forward based <u>totally</u> on the testimony of eyewitnesses who were attempting to assist the Federal Bureau of Investigation and National Transportation Safety Board as these agencies probed into the possible causes of the tragedy. Without the assistance of these eyewitnesses, the accounting given here would not have been possible.[5]

The CIA does not have aircraft crash experts. It does have experts in propaganda, disinformation and other artful forms of lying. The above is a mediocre example. Considering how little they had to work with, perhaps history will judge it to have been a good effort. One must always remember the propaganda exercise is not to convince the American people. Rather, it is to dissuade major media from crossing a line that places them with "conspiracy theorists" should they dare analyze this CIA work product and find it fraudulent.

All that is required to cross that line is to read the NTSB's Flight 800 Meteorological Factual Report. Page eight says that sunset, July 17, 1996, at 15,000 feet, was 2031 hours. The Sun's altitude was 0.9 degrees. In other words, Flight 800 was not "illuminated by the setting sun and clearly visible to any observer witnessing a missile approach and destroy it." The

CIA lied about a fact readily available to it and major media but not the American people. The CIA propagandists knew they did not have to worry about major media fact-checking the CIA's work.

Westhampton Beach, about 12 nautical miles north of the crash site, reported "visibility 4 miles; haze; 6,000 scattered (clouds) ... total sky cover 3/8."[6] No one on the south side of Long Island could see Flight 800 through the haze, according to this weather report. The CIA lied about a fact readily available to it and major media.

The NTSB had also investigated the question of witness visibility in the days following the crash. This written summation was readily available to the CIA, but was ignored because it was seriously in conflict with the "spin" the CIA was attempting to provide the FBI:

> During the initial stage of the investigation, as part of the Operations Group functions, several visits to the areas along the south shore of Long Island were made by the Operations Group chairman for the purpose of estimating the visibility environment. The visits were made at times when light and weather conditions were similar to the conditions present at the time of the accident. They were made on July 20, and July 21, 1996. Based on those observations, visibility was ascertained to be limited insofar as being able to see a transport category aircraft climbing out the departure corridor used by TWA Flight 800. When an aircraft was visually tracked from shortly after departure from JFK, visual tracking was possible. When an aircraft was not visually tracked as explained above, visual acquisition was difficult.[7]

When propagandists have limited material with which to work, they massage what they have into the best form possible. Major media spread the CIA story across America without fact-checking, without opposing view—in cartoon form.

The CIA argument hinges on one statement: "The initial explosion was not seen by any known eyewitness." In fact, they had at least three government employees—two New York Air National Guard pilots and a Navy officer—who had seen a projectile [ordnance] approach Flight 800, and then seen the series of explosions. Many civilians, including an engineer who wrote detailed notes, drew diagrams and made speed calculations, also witnessed a missile rise into the air and impact Flight 800.[8]

So the CIA's thesis statement is easily demonstrated to be false. But major media accepted it at face value, presenting it to America and the world as a story known to be factual rather than the obvious propaganda it would have been demonstrated to be if fact-checking and balanced reporting was the criteria used when formulating the story.

More importantly, the CIA report was not revealed for another eight months—far enough removed from the date Stacey took the two samples from the Calverton hangar that the Justice Department "crime scene" scheme would not be threatened.

Only 15 days separated the BATF report from the CIA report. Both offered the same conclusion: no missile. But Kallstrom reacted negatively only to the BATF report, which seems highly irrational until the "crime scene" scheme is factored in.

19

THE THIRD PIECE OF RESIDUE

On March 11, 1997, the same day Kallstrom refused to receive the BATF report, about 31 hours after the *Press-Enterprise* March 10 article hit the streets, the FBI showed up at West Coast Analytical Service (WCAS), subpoena in-hand for "documents and material ... relating to laboratory analysis checks conducted at WCAS in behalf of JAMES SANDERS from Williamsburg, Virginia."[1] Buried in this report is an explosive admission never intended to be made public: "In order to conduct this test [at WCAS], the material was cut by employee GRANDA into four 3/4 " by 1/4" segments. Two of the segments were utilized in the perchlorate tests. A third segment was placed back in the plastic bag provided by SANDERS then stored in the previously described plastic bag provided by WCAS—this piece was never tested or altered."

The FBI had an untested piece of the residue identified in the *Press-Enterprise* story as having reddish-orange residue consistent with solid-fuel missile exhaust. The FBI could test and analyze this piece to definitively determine if my conclusions were valid. But instead they hid the sample away without testing it. They continued to rely on the shrill chorus of unnamed government leakers insisting the residue was glue.

Just as suspect actions create a "consciousness of guilt" to be used to convict and imprison, government consciousness of guilt is established when they literally run from a unique opportunity to destroy the person whose allegations threaten them. Just test the residue obtained from WCAS in a responsible, documented manner and provide that analysis to Congress and the press. Case closed. The government is vindicated—unless, of course, the government can't test the residue without being pronounced "guilty as charged."

20

EXPERT OPINION?

Jack Northington, president of WCAS, provided the FBI agent the history of his dealing with me. It began around January 20, 1997, when WCAS received an e-mail from me inquiring "about WCAS' ability to identify possible solid rocket fuel exhaust he believed was on certain materials he had in his possession. In response, NORTHINGTON e-mailed SANDERS to inform him that WCAS could probably conduct the analysis he (SANDERS) desired, but would need to first ascertain what elements were normally present in solid missile propellant prior to their testing."

In other words, WCAS had no prior experience testing solid-fuel missile exhaust, no institutional knowledge or experience to formulate an expert opinion of what the test results meant. They could test it, but someone else would have to provide an analysis. The FBI and Justice Department knew this as soon as the FBI agent filed this 302 form. They knew they would need an expert's analysis of the elements found in the WCAS test if they intended to provide honest information to the press and American public.

Just as they ran away from using the fresh residue recovered from WCAS to scientifically, honestly, answer the glue-versus-missile-exhaust residue debate, the Department of Justice declined to use the dozens of scientists around the nation, paid by U.S. tax dollars to continually test missile-exhaust residue as part of the vast U. S. military defense program to develop ever more efficient missiles.

The government knew the honest answer, but that answer promised a lengthy prison term and disgrace attached to the names of too many powerful people inside the government. Instead, they turned to a man who had just admitted to them that he was not an expert, not even knowledgeable: "NORTHINGTON advised (the FBI agent) that after getting SANDER's [sic] request, he did some personal research regarding rocket propellant on the internet and was able to learn from the THIOKOL COMPANY web site what components were commonly found in solid rocket fuel propellant."

By this time, Northington had already strayed far from what I had requested, namely to test for possible solid-fuel missile-exhaust residue. The exhaust of a solid-fuel missile, I had learned from interviewing scientists within the missile industry, should be expected to contain trace elements from the rocket motor and metals used to form the chambers through which the flames flowed, as well as higher percentages of the material making up the solid fuel.

Northington missed a second extremely important point: solid fuels are not all the same. Perchlorate is not always present. It is *an* oxidizer, not *the* oxidizer.

Northington told the FBI agent that he had, "recommended to SANDERS that three specific tests be conducted to accomplish this [indication that the reddish-orange residue was from the exhaust of a solid fuel missile]. One of the tests would be to detect the presence of 'perchlorate,' a common substance in rocket propellant. A second test would be to detect the presence of aluminum, another common substance in solid-fuel propellant, and perhaps other key metals in the reddish substance visible in the material. A third infrared test could be conducted which would establish the presence of a certain type of rubber.

"NORTHINGTON explained to SANDERS that the infrared test could not actually confirm that a substance was rocket propellant since this type of rubber is used in so many varying applications, i.e. paint, plastics, etc. After considering his options, SANDERS agreed to tests number one and two and decided against the third infrared test," the FBI field notes stated.

No perchlorate was found in the first test. The elemental test, however, provided 15 elements that were consistent with residue from solid-fuel missile exhaust, and no elements that were inconsistent:

Magnesium (%)	18.000
Silicon	15.000
Calcium	12.000
Zinc	3.600
Iron	3.100
Aluminum	2.800
Lead	2.400
Titanium	1.700
Antimony	0.530
Nickel	0.380
Manganese	0.210
Boron	0.081
Copper	0.530
Silver	0.032
Chromium	0.032

In the months to come, sources within the scientific community would point out that 98% of the elemental volume was consistent with incendiary/pyrotechnic devices. Magnesium is used as a warhead igniter and also in current-technology incendiary warheads, along with calcium, lead, aluminum, iron and antimony.

"NORTHINGTON specifically informed SANDERS that, in his opinion, there was no conclusive evidence the materials conveyed to WCAS contained rocket propellant," the FBI 302 report correctly stated. A basic elemental analysis could not provide "conclusive" evidence. But the test provided elements that were "consistent with" residue from a solid-fuel missile.

"NORTHINGTON then prepared and sent a final report to SANDERS which contained the scientific results of their analysis. The reports made no specific conclusion about the significance of any substances found," the FBI 302 again correctly summarized. Jack Northington and WCAS did not have the expertise to offer expert or even knowledgeable analysis of the elements and wisely elected not to do so in writing. Northington's verbal comments to me were carefully worded to avoid the appearance of expert/knowledgeable opinion.

Nine months later, however, the head of the FBI's Flight 800 investigation, Jim Kallstrom, would lie to the press about Jack Northington and WCAS. Kallstrom would infer that WCAS and Northington were experts capable of providing accurate opinion based on the institutional solid fuel/explosives expertise of WCAS.

But this was not enough to create a story that could be used to vilify and destroy my reputation as an investigator. So Kallstrom told the national media in a press release that I had alleged the WCAS elemental test provided "conclusive" evidence that a missile brought down Flight 800.

NBC News would report this Jim Kallstrom missive as fact. A journalism intern with five minutes to spare would have uncovered the real story: My book and articles had all said the elements were "consistent with" a solid-fuel missile.

The real story was that Jim Kallstrom committed a number of felonies when he lied to NBC News and the national media. But that was not the story that would go out across America and the world.

21

FACE TO FACE WITH THE JUSTICE DEPARTMENT

April 14, 1997: As the government scrambled to alter the Calverton mock-up, a face-to-face meeting occurred between the two warring parties: I was on one side, accompanied by my attorney at that time, Jeff Schlanger—versus the government, represented by Valerie Caproni, Chief of the New York Justice Department Criminal Division, Ben Campbell, her assistant, FBI agent Jim Kinsley, and two other government officials.

The meeting took place at the Brooklyn Federal Building in a large conference room, with a video camera and large screen filling one corner. Caproni went to great lengths to point out the camera and large screen were used for video teleconferences with her superiors in Washington, D.C. All the while, I couldn't help noticing that someone had neglected to remove the light bulb from the video camera, indicating a recording was in progress—no doubt sending beautiful real-time pictures back to senior FBI and Justice Department personnel who were monitoring this confrontation, creating a psychological profile on their "target."[1]

Caproni had been pushing Schlanger for this meeting with me since mid-March. "Justice" had repeatedly pressed for the meeting because "we want to get the material back."[2] The second reason was to intimidate me in an effort to get me to give up my source.

Two years later, Schlanger recounted this meeting, under oath, at the trial, under direct examination by my trial attorney, Bruce Maffeo:

Q: Could you tell the members of the jury, could you summarize for the members of the jury what took place at that meeting?

A: Essentially we outlined, or I outlined for Mr. Sanders, our position, which was essentially that Mr. Sanders had a constitutional imperative, which in my view was as high as the government's constitutional imperative, in protecting his source. And in investigating the workings of the government. In this case with respect to the crash of Flight 800. That he was not prepared to give up his source. That he believed he had done nothing wrong. And we would sit and listen to everything the government had to say to us.

Q: What did the government then proceed to say?

A: ... [T]here was some back and forth. At least talk from the government about why Mr. Sanders should cooperate. And ultimately it ended up with the statement that if he didn't cooperate, they would not subpoena him before the grand jury, but would rather seek an indictment against him. And the next time that we saw them [he] would be on the wrong side of an indictment.

Q: Did the government indicate at that meeting what, if any, actions they were prepared to take with respect to Liz Sanders?

A: At the very end of that meeting there was a change in the status of Mrs. Sanders from being just a subject in the investigation, to a possible target in the investigation. And that was communicated directly to myself and Mr. Sanders.

Q: And when you say [it] was communicated directly to you, what was your understanding if she did not cooperate?

A: That the government would at least attempt to seek an indictment against her as well.

Q: Now ...

A: It wasn't if she didn't cooperate. It was if Mr. Sanders did not cooperate.

Q: Now, after this meeting did you meet with both or discuss this matter with both your clients?

A: Yes.

Q: And did they subsequently change their position with respect to cooperating with the government?

A: No ...[3]

Jeremy Gutman, my wife's attorney, then cross-examined Schlanger:

Q: Mr. Schlanger, you were referring earlier to the April 14 meeting you attended along with Mr. Sanders at the United States Attorney's Office?

A: Yes.

Q: And did there come a time during that meeting, if you recall, that there was any discussion about Elizabeth Sanders cooperating—in which you were asked to communicate anything to Mrs. Sanders independent of Mr. Sanders?

A: Yes. At the end of the meeting Mr. Campbell again asked me to find out separately from Liz whether or not she would cooperate.

Q: And by cooperate you mean provide information regarding her husband's activities?

A: I assumed that was the case. Although I don't think Mr. Campbell specifically outlined what the cooperation would be.

Q: Did you communicate that message to Mrs. Sanders?

A: I did. And I had before that time communicated the same message. But I did communicate it again, and the response was still the same.

Q: You communicated a response back to the United States Attorney's Office?

A: Yes.

Q: What was that?

A: That Mrs. Sanders did not wish to cooperate with the government.

Q: Did the government's request for cooperation imply or contain any reference to consequences that might follow if she—depending on the course she took?

A: Again, in the April 14 meeting it became clear that the government, after Mr. Sanders had refused to cooperate, was going to treat her as a target as well …[4]

My wife and I placed ourselves at risk in order to protect my source inside the NTSB investigation, Terry Stacey. We had been offered complete immunity. All we had to do was turn in the person who had provided me with the reddish-orange residue.

We refused and became targets of the Justice Department.

Liz Sanders had been made a target in the absence of any evidence, real or imagined. The Justice Department would not interrogate Terry Stacey, the sole source of alleged incriminatory evidence, for another two months.

This was the classic definition of vindictive prosecution, retaliating for standing up to the government.

22

Scrupulous Detail?

Within weeks after my meeting with the Justice Department, the NTSB went on a public relations media offensive. A willing major media awaited.

Newsday published an NTSB media offensive piece on June 6, 1997, entitled "NTSB Report Reveals Anatomy of Explosion." Written by Sylvia Adcock and Bob Kessler, it is probably the best example of a commentary piece presented to the public as balanced journalism.

I knew Kessler and was surprised to see a "news" report with such easily debunked "facts." Had Kessler merely picked up the phone and called me, some semblance of objectivity could have been inserted in the article with insignificant effort. But, as Kessler would obliquely admit in a telephone conversation with me, balance was never a consideration. The singular intent of the article was to extol the virtuous NTSB investigation.

During an approximate 15-minute telephone conversation, Kessler admitted that *Newsday* did not have a copy of the "150 page draft report" the article focused on. An NTSB representative Kessler would not name had read portions of the report to Kessler over the phone. I had possessed a copy of the NTSB report for months.

Kessler's article alleged:

A key to determining the initial breakup sequence was this fact: Only three parts of the center fuel tank were found in the westernmost debris field, the area along the flight path closest to Kennedy airport. That area held the parts that came off the plane first.

In that field was the access door from deep within the tank, a piece of the beam still attached. It was notable for its unusual damage and because it was very lightly sooted, in direct contrast to the rest of the beam, which had been in contact with more fire and was found in a debris field to the east. In other words, the access door left the plane before it erupted into a fireball.

I told Kessler the basic premise of the report was, charitably, foolish. The debris in question, A-TAG 490, was recovered 6,000 feet east of the first debris to fall from the stricken 747. More than 600 significant pieces of the plane fell closer to JFK airport than A-TAG 490, I advised Kessler.

Kessler asked me to forward a copy of the NTSB report along with the NTSB red zone. Kessler said he was going on vacation and wanted to "digest" the material before returning to work.

In the months and years to follow, *Newsday* never investigated and reported on the questionable conclusions the NTSB reached, never told its readers that this article, subtitled "In Scrupulous Detail, Anatomy of Blast," was factually false.

Newsday's inability to get at and issue balanced, factual stories about Flight 800, continues to this day. But *Newsday* is not unique. It is the norm within major media.

23

GUESS WHO'S COMING TO DINNER

Terry Stacey had a decision to make that fateful day in June 1997 when the FBI showed up, unannounced, at his home in rural New Jersey. It was not a decision that could be made calmly and rationally. There were two FBI agents bearing down on him. Their job was to intimidate, create a feeling of terror and helplessness—to get Stacey to roll over before he regained his composure and developed the presence of mind to refuse to talk to them without an attorney present. Terry Stacey succumbed to the mental terror and spent seven hours talking to the FBI without an attorney present.

He could have refused to talk and hired a lawyer. Because of the government's pursuit of both my wife and I, Stacey knew this route would require significant financial sacrifice, probably including the loss of his job as a senior pilot for TWA. He instantly faced a multimillion-dollar decision. His final five-year income and benefits represented about one million dollars. The retirement and 401(K) package, medical, dental, insurance, were all on the line. How long could he keep his daughter in college? Make the monthly payments on his beautiful home? Continue the lease payments on three cars? And pay for a defense team capable of opposing the awesome power of the Justice Department?

The only alternative was to cooperate, ingratiating himself with those who held the power to destroy him. Telling the truth, that he was involved in an investigation of government corruption, would not sell well with the intimidating agents sitting across from him inside his home. So a story began to be weaved. Stacey would learn from the FBI and Justice Department agents who confronted him over the following months, what they wanted to hear. He began to deliver a portion of that message—enough to avoid felony indictment.

The destruction of an honorable man by agents of the United States government was accomplished. He became the tool whereby the Justice Department would indict Elizabeth Sanders, even though the government possessed evidence exonerating her.

Kinsley's handwritten notes, taken during the interview, reveal Stacey to have been reasonably forthcoming. He told Kinsley of the meetings with me, what transpired, and listed the documents he had turned over to me.

Kinsley's notes state that Stacey: "FedEx piece of plane to Sanders because Sanders said he could test it." Putting aside the self-serving "piece of the plane" to describe residue, this statement did not, under any circumstance, rise to the level of conspiracy, so Kinsley changed the meaning when he typed his report three days later: "… STACEY had discussions with (James) SANDERS regarding the residue. At that time SANDERS had requested a sample of the orange residue." There is no hint of such a statement by Stacey in Kinsley's field notes. Such a statement would have been instantly recognized as something that needed to be contemporaneously recorded. But Terry Stacey did not make such a statement and it was not placed in the notes because it was not stated.

This is why the FBI does not tape record its field notes. Sometimes it is necessary to manufacture statements.

Kinsley had written me into conspiracy territory, but only if a journalist/source relationship could be kept out of the equation. Since the founding of the country, a journalist engaged in investigating federal crimes could freely talk to a source without fear of it being a chargeable felony offense.

Kinsley's field notes from this first interrogation also contained information about contact between Terry Stacey and Elizabeth Sanders: "(Stacey) at Xmas party week before Xmas, Liz chit chat. Subsequent phone call Liz called Stacey pressing issue for Stacey to get residue." Within two-weeks Kinsley and the Justice Department would know, beyond a reasonable doubt, that this was not accurate information, assuming of course, Kinsley did not fabricate this statement as well.

On June 26, 1997, Terry Stacey and his attorney, John McDonald, met Justice Department lawyers Valerie Caproni and Ben Campbell. Kinsley also attended the meeting, taking several pages of field notes. Kinsley's notes state; "Liz call, (after) > holidays, normal pleasantries, then asked me to get samples. This call convinced me to get the samples." The Justice Department now had a statement from Terry Stacey implicating Elizabeth in a conspiracy with Terry Stacey to remove the residue, but only if the massive documentation already in their possession—phone records, hangar sign-out logs, credit card statements and TWA travel logs—did not directly contradict the implicating statement. It was a statement Terry Stacey would repudiate in court when face to face with Liz Sanders.

When Stacey fixed the date of the call from Liz after New Year's, a call of sufficient length to "exchange normal pleasantries," the Justice Department had facts in its possession to, beyond a reasonable doubt, identify the date of the call as January 9, 1997. Liz and Terry spoke on the phone at 8:30 p.m., four hours after he signed out of the Calverton hangar with the residue.

Stacey's opening comment during that conversation was that he was about to call me because he had Federal Expressed the residue to me at our Williamsburg address earlier that day. Per Kinsley's notes: "on way back to Hol(iday) Inn that day (Stacey) went to Fedex—pd cash—to Arena Dr." We lived on Arena Street, Williamsburg, Virginia.

We don't have to take Elizabeth Sanders' word for what Terry Stacey said during their 20-minute conversation the evening of January 9, 1997. Documents in the possession of the Justice Department and FBI proved beyond a reasonable doubt at this point in the government investigation that Terry Stacey had removed the residue on January 9 prior to 1630 hours, four hours before the conversation took place.

The government had the Calverton sign-out log. It knew precisely when Stacey left the building for the final time that day. The government had Stacey's and our phone records. The government also had an e-mail from me to a California e-mail address, dated January 10, 1997, and electronically time-stamped 1612 hours. My e-mail message said I had two pieces of residue in my possession.

Kinsley's notes reveal that Terry Stacey called me after dropping off the samples at FedEx: "He didn't know I got it so I told him (it was) in (the) mail. He (Sanders) was excited." Kinsley's notes also revealed that I did not know Stacey was going to obtain two samples: "He (Sanders) wanted him (Stacey) to scrap [sic] off (residue) but (the residue) wouldn't scrap [sic] off so S(tacey) took two strips. Then Fedex that day (to Sanders in Williamsburg)."

The phone records prove there was only one phone call to or from Terry Stacey at the Ronkonkoma Holiday Inn, or any other phone on Long Island, during a 45-day period surrounding January 9, 1997—compelling evidence Terry Stacey was providing the Justice Department with inaccurate information.

"Justice" did not allow this second interrogation of Terry Stacey to take place until the normal investigative process gave them the information they needed to reasonably know if the informant was telling the truth—not that truth was what they were looking for; it was merely a baseline from which to proceed. So all records were placed in order and studied. Possible inferences developed.

What quickly developed during the second interrogation was that Kinsley's notes about Liz making a January phone call "pressing issue for Stacey to get residue"[1] are factually false. No phone record existed of Liz Sanders' phone calls to Terry Stacey (or Stacey's to Liz) where she could have had the opportunity to make a call "pressing issue for Stacey to get residue."

FBI field notes indicate Stacey told them he and Liz were at a TWA Christmas party in St. Louis, the week before Christmas. What did they talk about? the FBI wanted to know. The answer did not please them. "Chit chat" is recorded.

This was the logical place-in-time for Stacey to be badgered into remembering something, anything that gave the schemers inside the government the ability to draw an "inference" of guilt. The Department of Justice wouldn't do anything so crude as to overtly demand that Stacey lie, but their goal would be obvious, as well as the fallout from failing to heed it.

By the evidence in the possession of the Justice Department and FBI as of June 26, 1997, when Valerie Caproni, Benton Campbell and Jim Kinsley sat across the table from Terry Stacey and his lawyer, the government side of the table knew Liz Sanders was not involved. They had the phone records, sign-out logs and e-mail fixing my knowledge of the two pieces of residue being removed from the Calverton hangar no later than the evening of January 9, 1997.

But Caproni, Campbell and Kinsley were not there to obtain the truth. The truth would be an unmitigated disaster placing them in jeopardy.

Terry Stacey testified under oath that the Justice Department and FBI never used phone records to refresh his memory to ensure the most factual statements possible. Caproni and the others were not interested in factual statements, they were only interested in shaping Stacey's testimony to meet their needs.

At the second meeting on June 26, 1997, Terry Stacey said "he was concerned that himself or TWA might get thrown off the investigation if he was caught handing over documentation to SANDERS. He stated that he didn't think he was breaking the law but he was concerned about his image." This statement, and the documentary evidence held by the Justice Department, constituted a prohibition from further "targeting" and harassment of my wife and I.

Stacey and I had discussed the legality of taking residue from the hangar. I had questioned Stacey about the volume of residue remaining after a residue sample was removed. Stacey assured me that enough residue remained for at least hundreds of samples. This eliminated obstruction of justice as a possible legal problem.

Stacey told me he would not be committing a crime if he took the residue. He explained that he was an authorized investigator with significant discretionary power. When I asked him what would happen if he was caught removing documents and/or residue and giving them to a journalist, Stacey said he would be thrown off the investigation and TWA would be embarrassed.

I then used the William and Mary Law School Library in Williamsburg, Virginia, to look at federal statutes and case law. Title 49 makes the NTSB the senior investigative agency at all aircraft crash scenes. The FBI is an inferior investigative agency. If involved, the FBI is to promptly share all tests with the NTSB. All NTSB investigators have the statutory authority to "test." If the NTSB leadership find fault with the actions of an individual, including the FBI, the NTSB has the statutory authority under Title 49 to impose a civil fine—this is the congressionally-mandated procedure within any NTSB crash-scene investigation. Terry Stacey faced a civil liability as an authorized investigator, not a criminal liability.

I knew that where the rule of law existed, I, as a journalist, was on firm ground. Terry Stacey, sitting in front of Caproni, Campbell and Kinsley, knew the rule of law did not exist. He had choices to make each time a question was asked. He had a comfortable lifestyle to protect. He also had a wife and daughter to protect—they had been inside the Stacey' home when Terry Stacey told me about the reddish-orange trail across the plane. Any hint of involvement by a family member, an opinion expressed, encouragement, or even a strong statement about the lawlessness of the FBI, could be construed by the Department of Justice to be conspiracy within the Stacey family. So Terry Stacey wisely moved the scene of divulging this information from his home to some vaguely remembered conversation:

> Stacey advised that sometime after the meeting at his home and before the holidays he got a call from SANDERS regarding the residue found on the seats at the hanger [sic]. Sanders asked Stacey if it would be possible for him to obtain a sample of the residue so it could be tested. STACEY advised that he had trouble deciding whether [sic] or not to get the samples for SANDERS. He recalls thinking it over for a two or three-week period which included the holiday break. STACEY advised that sometime after the holidays he received a call from LIZ SANDERS asking him to obtain the samples for her husband. STACEY advised that this convinced him to obtain the samples for SANDERS.[2]

At trial, I would produce a [legally] tape-recorded December 8, 1997, telephone conversation with Terry Stacey, in the middle of the time frame Terry was supposedly struggling to make a decision. The truth, revealed by the tape, is that Stacey, without being asked, volunteered to make obtaining the residue his "top priority." His enthusiasm was such that he volunteered to remove anything else he could "scrounge."

The Justice Department knew that "sometime after the

holidays" pointed to one, and only one, phone call: January 9, 1997. They knew that call occurred four hours after Stacey removed the residue and overnighted it to me. They knew my wife did not ask Terry Stacey to remove residue, because he had already taken it.

Each step along the way, when Liz would have been in contact with Stacey if she was indeed involved in my investigation of Justice Department and FBI actions, no contact occurred. She was in New York the entire month of December 1996. Terry Stacey had documents critical to my investigation. He frequently drove within a mile of Liz's Howard Beach apartment. The documents would have been dropped there if she were involved. What safer way to transfer documents without leaving a paper trail?

Liz Sanders and Terry Stacey would have met in December 1996 when they both were in New York, if she was part of the journalistic investigation. That didn't happen.

FBI field notes at the June 26 meeting say Terry Stacey removed the two strips of foam rubber of his own volition:

> He [James Sanders] wanted me to scrap [sic] off [flakes of residue] but [the flakes] wouldn't scrap [sic] off so I took 2 strips, then Fedex that day.

The Justice Department and FBI had a serious problem with that statement. Stacey admitted the heinous act of removing less than one ounce of foam rubber from the plane was his decision, and his alone.

The government's scheme would unravel if Terry Stacey's statement was not altered. Why? Because the only criminal section the Justice Department had to work with was Title 49, section 1155(b):

A person that knowingly and without authority removes, conceals, or withholds a part of a civil aircraft involved in an accident, or property on the aircraft at the time of the accident, shall be fined under Title 18, imprisoned for not more than 10 years, or both.

If the flakes of residue "he wanted me to scrape off" were from a missile's exhaust or the byproduct of a warhead detonation, the flakes did not come under the definition of Title 49, section 1155(b). They were not "part of a civil aircraft," nor were they "property on the aircraft" [i.e., luggage or cargo].

The government would have to prove by scientific testing that would stand up under cross-examination in court, that the flakes of residue I had tested were glue from the seats. Putting aside the incredible pettiness of such a prosecution effort, the FBI already knew the residue was not 3M glue as alleged.

And Stacey clearly said it was he, on his own, who made the decision to remove two pieces of foam rubber. There was no aiding, abetting or conspiracy. He was motivated to give a journalist forensic evidence that might provide compelling evidence of the cover-up he was certain was occurring inside the investigation.

Allowing our prosecution to descend into such dangerous territory was simply not allowable. The government schemers would essentially be writing their own indictments if the truth continued to flow from Stacey's lips.

The Justice Department knew Stacey was firmly under their control. They also knew the Supreme Court had removed a defendant's right to challenge their culpability prior to or during trial. "Interlocutory appeals," the right not to be tried, was abolished as a tool to control federal lawlessness, in the early 1990s.

24

THE HOUSE AVIATION SUBCOMMITTEE

The House of Representatives Transportation Committee, Subcommittee on Aviation, held a hearing on July 10, 1997, to look into the "Status of the Investigation of the Crash of TWA 800. ..." "The purpose of [the] hearing [was] to ... review the efforts of the FBI and NTSB to discover the cause of the TWA 800 crash one year after the accident."

Surprisingly, the Subcommittee, in its "Written Explanations for the Crash," presented a balanced view of the opposing arguments:

Investigators have apparently concluded that the plane crashed because its center fuel tank exploded. But they are still not sure why. They have generally stated that there are three possible explanations—a missile, a bomb, or mechanical failure.

Missile theory. The proponents of the missile theory suggest that a missile fired either by the U.S. Navy or a terrorist[,] hit the plane. This theory remains under consideration because of the number of eyewitness accounts from people who said they saw something in the sky. For example, Captain Chris Baur, a civilian pilot for U. S. Customs, repeatedly told investigators that he saw a missile strike the plane. Because of his clear view from his helicopter and his military training, Baur's account is one of the most credible.

Proponents allege that radar tapes show a projectile heading toward the TWA aircraft. Also, they point to red residue on a section of seats which could be rocket fuel [sic]. Proponents suggest that in the reconstruction of the aircraft there is an opening on the right side of the fuselage which is caused by a missile.

Opponents of the missile theory, including NTSB officials, have provided the following arguments against the missile theory:

- The radar tapes showing a projectile might not be authentic;
- The dot on the authentic radar tapes thought to be a missile is in fact a Navy P-3 plane in the area at the time;
- The red residue on the seats is glue;
- The red residue is not rocket propellant because chemicals found in rocket propellant that would be there are missing;
- What witnesses believed to be a missile was actually parts of the falling plane or a stream of flaming jet fuel from a ruptured fuel tank on the plane's right wing. According to investigators, the initial explosion in the center fuel tank caused the fuselage of the plane to separate, but the rest of the plane continued to fly with all four engines running, spewing a trail of flaming jet fuel. The head FBI investigator James Kallstrom and other government officials have vigorously refuted the theory that "friendly fire" downed the aircraft. *In a closed briefing*[1] of our subcommittee last March [shortly after the *Press-Enterprise* article was published], the FBI, NTSB, and the Navy argued that—while a Navy P-3 plane and a submarine were *near the flight path*[2] on a practice mission, neither were armed with missiles; [Emphasis added]
- The only U.S. military equipment capable of launching a missile at Flight 800 was the cruiser USS Normandy, and after being inventoried, it was found to still have all its missiles.

While the Subcommittee made a good effort to present a balanced pre-hearing report outlining the controversy, the witness list presents compelling evidence the Subcommittee lacked the courage to gather facts placing the government version of reality in dispute:

PANEL 1

Mr. James Hall, Chairman
National Transportation Safety Board
Accompanied by:
Dr. Bernard Loeb, Director
Office of Aviation Safety

PANEL 2

Mr. James K. Kallstrom
Assistant Director in Charge
New York Office
Federal Bureau of Investigation

The usual suspects testified on the government's behalf, but no forum was provided to tell the other side of the debate. Congress seemed to be mimicking major media.

On March 11, 1997, unidentified government sources spread the line that the radar tapes obtained by retired commercial aviation pilot Richard Russell, were not authentic. Except for faceless government sources, no hard information ever surfaced from within the government calling the two tapes into question. Today they are considered to be authentic.

At least 11 radar tapes are in the possession of the government. One of these tapes, RP44, from a Navy radar, may have been tampered with. Four lines of data, each representing one radar hit, 2.8 seconds before TWA Flight 800's transponder lost power, were expunged from RP44.

This is not a unique event when radar may have captured events the government wants removed from the record. In 1980, 22 minutes of NATO radar data disappeared. A Libyan MiG and Italian DC-9 were shot down that day by American or other NATO fighters, according to an indictment recently handed down within the Italian judicial system.[3] The 22 minutes covered the time both planes went down. Eighty-one civilians perished.

At the time Jim Kallstrom was assuring Congress "The red residue on the seats is glue," he had compelling evidence it was not glue. The government alleged it was 3M 1357 High Performance Contact Adhesive.[4] The National High Magnetic Field Laboratory operated by Florida State University and Los Alamos National Laboratory, analyzed a sample of the 3M adhesive to compare against the elements found in the sample I had tested at WCAS.[5] This is the same test the government can be presumed to have used if they were looking for an honest answer to the basic question: is the residue I had tested 3M 1357 HP Adhesive? The side-by-side elemental analysis:

	3M	WCAS
Aluminum [Al] (%)	0.0082	2.800
Antimony [Sb]	none detected	0.530
Boron	0.0053	0.081
Calcium [Ca]	0.0820	12.000
Chromium [Cr]	0.0002	0.032
Iron [Fe]	0.0108	3.100
Lead [Pb]	0.0000	12.400
Magnesium [Mg]	0.9657	18.000
Manganese [Mn]	0.0013	0.210
Nickel [Ni]	0.0001	0.210
Silicon [Si]	0.0266	15.000
Silver [Ag]	none detected	0.032
Sodium [Na]	0.0157	none detected
Titanium [Ti]	0.0007	1.700
Zinc [Zn]	0.2125	3.600

The 3M adhesive flunks the elemental analysis test. The above comparison provides compelling evidence the residue I received from Terry Stacey is *not* 3M glue. So Kallstrom gave the Aviation Subcommittee a factually false statement, saying the reddish-orange residue *was* glue.

The government allegation that the residue is not rocket propellant because chemicals found in the rocket propellant that would be there are missing[6], is equally without logic or merit. The government has not, and cannot provide any test or series of tests proving that all elements found in missile-exhaust residue, then soaked for days in salt water, will always be found in a given sample. Simple logic defeats such an assertion.

Unfortunately for the government, Jim Kallstrom, Jim Hall, Bernie Loeb, et al, had scientific evidence in their possession at the time that two elements, chlorine and oxygen, not found in my sample but normally present in solid fuel, had been found during tests performed at NASA-KSC.[7] Also found in the NASA tests was a significant presence of carbon. Carbon is a byproduct of some explosives.

But that does not end the bad news received from NASA-KSC. Three additional elements in moderate to high quantity were found in the passenger cabin of Flight 800:

• Sodium. Combined with chlorine, is an oxidizing agent in matches and explosives. When combined with nitrates, also found in NASA testing, sodium nitrate is used in explosives.

• Phosphorous. "Unites easily with oxygen so that it ignites spontaneously at room temperature."

• Sulfur. Is used, among other things, in making matches and[8] gunpowder. It is also combined with explosives such as RDX and PETN [Semtex when used in combination] to increase the heat from an explosion.

These three additional elements were found in residue tested by NASA-KSC's Charles Bassett.[9] His report indicates that:

Elemental analysis by EDS (Energy Dispersive Spectroscopy) of the lighter side of the foam indicated the material was high in carbon and oxygen, with trace amounts of sodium, magnesium, aluminum, silicon, sulfur, chlorine and nickel present. The EDS overview analysis of the darker side was found to contain high concentrations of carbon and oxygen. The concentrations of sodium and chlorine (probably in the form of salts) were higher in the darker side of the foam material than in the lighter side. Finally, trace amounts of magnesium, aluminum, silicon, phosphorous and sulfur was also found.

All of these elements point toward an explosion. But NTSB requested no further testing when they received the results.

Even this does not end the scientific testing performed by NASA-KFC that should have resulted in extensive additional testing for explosive and missile residue. On May 19, 1997, NASA's Charles Bassett reported another test result to Merritt Birky. Its findings so disturbed the government that the report has not been released to this day. Therefore, the brief narrative from the withheld report is now provided:

The samples were submitted by the NTSB for the on-going investigation of TWA's flight 800 accident. The objective of the analysis was to characterize the chemical nature of the unknown material.

Samples identified as MB-1 and MB-2 were "splatter like" material scraped from the center wing tank pieces labeled as CW-114 and CW-504, respectively. The samples were collected on January 17, 1997.

The analyses were accomplished using Infrared (IR) microscope spectroscopy and Ion Chromatography (IC).

The material in the sample bottle labeled MB-1 Z-3028 CW-114 (MB-1) was optically examined under a microscope and organic appearing materials isolated for preparation and IR analysis. The sample consisted of a dark-looking material and some translucent material, closer examination of which revealed a fibrous texture.

The material in the sample bottle labeled MB-2 CW-504 Inside Top (MB-2) was optically examined under a microscope. Samples of a dark material, a translucent-looking fibrous material and a discolored fiber (which may have been red at one time), were isolated and examined with IR microscopy spectroscopy.

Subsequent to information obtained from a separate analysis of a related accident sample, IC was conducted on both samples. Information obtained from the IC analysis indicated the presence of 7.5 micrograms nitrate, 70 micrograms sulfate, and greater than 400 micrograms chloride anions for the sample Z-3028 CW-114 (MB-1), and 10 micrograms nitrate, 70 micrograms sulfate and greater than 200 micrograms chloride anions for the sample CW-504 Inside Top (MB-2). The related accident sample analysis previously mentioned, will be addressed separately and will reference this report.

CONCLUSIONS: *Polyurethane* was the major component of the dark material from both samples. ... An attempt to determine the origin of the [nitrate] present in both samples was not conducted at this time but is of concern and is under further investigation.[10] [Emphasis added]

Polyurethane is a commonly used explosive "binder" and should have been a flashing neon sign, particularly when found in combination with a lengthy lists of elements, such as sulfur, expected to be found in an incendiary warhead explosion.

Charles Bassett called NTSB's Merritt Birky when he saw the nitrate and asked permission to conduct further tests.[11] Birky told him to desist. Birky later told Bassett the NTSB had developed a "plausible" explanation for the nitrate. It was cigarette smoke from the air conditioning ducts that somehow transferred to the inside of the center-fuel-tank during the explosion.

Further testing was critical because of the presence of

"chloride anions" mixed with nitrate. Sodium is a chlorate and is commonly mixed with nitrate in explosives. Sulfate, also found in this sample, is also used in explosives. But Merritt Birky, senior scientist inside the NTSB's Flight 800 "investigation," said no more testing.

25

CONGRESSMAN TRAFFICANT

Simultaneous with the FBI/Justice Department 1997 efforts to neutralize my investigation, Congressman James A. Trafficant was making one, brief effort to demand an accounting from the FBI.

Trafficant had sent a number of written questions to Kallstom in April 1997 when Flight 800 was on the front pages of America's newspapers. Three months later, on July 27, the FBI responded in writing:

Trafficant: In its analysis of radar tapes, has the FBI been able to positively identify every single aircraft and surface vessel that was in the proximity of TWA Flight 800 at the time of the accident?

FBI: No. Following extensive analysis of raw radar returns by the FBI, the NTSB, and an outside expert, in January 1997 the FBI *first* noted the presence of a surface vessel, which, because of its speed of between 25 and 35 knots, is believed to be at least 25-30 feet in length[1] [a specious assertion. The FAA radar did not pick up the dozens of 25- to 35-foot civilian boats that raced to the crash sight to assist with search and rescue. It can be inferred from the evidence that the 30-knot target was a ship of substantial size], approximately 2.9 nautical miles from the position of Flight 800 at the time of the initial explosion. The analysis first noted the boat's presence at approximately 8:11 p.m., traveling in a south-southwesterly direction. The last radar contact was noted at approximately

8:45 p.m. Despite extensive efforts, the FBI has been unable to identify this vessel. However, based on our investigative efforts, *we are confident it was not a military vessel.* [Emphasis added]

Trafficant: [C]an the FBI positively match every surface vessel and aircraft with an individual or individuals? Has the FBI interviewed every one of these individuals?

FBI: With the exception of the vessel discussed in response to question two, all other vessels and aircraft *noted on radar* have been identified and appropriate interviews conducted. [Emphasis added]

Trafficant: Can the FBI share with my office the results of its radar analysis, specifically, the identities of all surface vessels and aircraft in the proximity of TWA Flight 800?

FBI: No, for the reasons stated in question number one, above.

The FBI was dodging giving up radar information to a congressman who was making life uncomfortable for them. The FBI's carefully crafted answer says they did not know until January 1997 that a ship was in the area, when this (by inference) vague radar track was finally noticed by the "experts" who were analyzing the data. No mention was made of the military-like formation of ships or other activity commonly seen during naval maneuvers.

The FBI's answer expunged from the record two additional ships and a high-speed jet in the immediate proximity of Flight 800. The two ships were about 10 miles north-northeast of Flight 800, and the jet, flying in a southerly direction, passed a few miles behind Flight 800.

Trafficant was fishing in troubled waters. The FBI admitted that a high-speed ship was within three miles of Flight 800 when it went down. It had been tracked for 21 minutes prior to the hundreds of eyewitnesses seeing a reddish-orange flare-like object ascend from the ocean and bring down the 747. FAA technicians had observed the same event on their radar screens and so advised the White House.

Left unsaid by the FBI is that the high-speed ship they described to Trafficant was headed directly toward a large number of ships steaming in the same approximate easterly direction. The vanguard of this formation was inside military warning zone W-105, already activated for naval exercises.

The FBI's failure to acknowledge the 30-knot target's approach to this military-like formation must be considered part of a disinformation campaign waged against the congressional Aviation Subcommittee, timidly performing the role of "watchdog."

Now it was the FBI's responsibility to neutralize Congressman Trafficant, a job the highly politicized FBI was well prepared to do.

In the coming months Trafficant's top aide would be indicted by the federal government for racketeering charges that came perilously close to allegations that had at one time swirled around the Congressman himself. Trafficant's enthusiasm for taking on the federal government would disappear in this new environment.

26

FINAL RESPONSE

On September 5, 1997, the FBI made its final written response to Trafficant's questions before the Congressman began to scurry for cover:

Trafficant: You (Kallstrom) noted in your written testimony that "… over 100 individuals reported seeing events in the sky associated with the TWA Flight 800 disaster." Has the FBI interviewed all these witnesses? How many of these witnesses reported seeing an object ascending toward TWA Flight 800 or ascending in the sky?

Kallstrom: The FBI interviewed over 400 individuals who reported seeing something in the sky in the vicinity of the crash of TWA Flight 800. Of these, 115 reported seeing something ascend into the sky, and of these 115, only three reported seeing something ascend toward a second object.

Trafficant: Did the FBI and National Transportation Safety Board (NTSB) make a coordinated effort to canvass and interview witnesses in the days and weeks following the crash?

Kallstrom: At their initial meeting on the morning of July 18, 1996, at the Center Moriches Coast Guard Station, which was the forward command post for the search, rescue and salvage operation, ADIC James K. Kallstrom and Bob Francis, Vice-Chairman of the NTSB, agreed to conduct simultaneous investigations and that all information developed would be shared between the two agencies. The FBI's role was to be the lead criminal investigative agency seeking to determine if the crash of Flight 800 was the result of a criminal act.

In the first four weeks following the crash of TWA Flight 800, the FBI and the law enforcement team conducted approximately 860 interviews. Among those interviewed were witnesses who called in to report that they had observed events in the sky, air crews that reported seeing something in the sky, witnesses identified from news media interviews, individuals developed in canvasses of neighborhoods and apartment complexes for potential witnesses, and occupants of boats and shipping vessels in the area. To date approximately 7,000 law enforcement interviews have been conducted in connection with the TWA Flight 800 investigation. *The NTSB did not participate in most of these interviews because they did not have the personnel resources available.* However, all interview/witness statements have been *shared* with the NTSB and, after reviewing the results of initial interviews, the FBI and NTSB created a Witness Group Panel. The purpose of the witness group was to conduct joint interviews of individuals who previously provided information to the FBI about mechanical-related issues and events observed in the sky on 7/17/96.[1] [Emphasis added]

While much of Kallstrom's response to Trafficant can be evaluated as vague and non-responsive, the answers to the two questions above are factually false. An NTSB report was filed exposing much of Kallstrom's mendacity:

> On July 19, 1997, National Transportation Safety Board (NTSB) investigator, Mr. Bruce Magladry, formed a witness group which was to include representatives from TWA, ALPA, and FAA. The group was to have begun work on July 20, 1996.
>
> Following this initial group formation, on July 19, 1996, FBI agent Robert Knapp informed Mr. Magladry that the FBI was not prepared to share any information outside the NTSB, so parties could not be involved with this group. In addition, Mr. Magladry was informed that he would not be permitted to

conduct any interviews because the FBI did not want conflicting information. The parties were notified and the formation of the Witness Group was not continued.

On July 21, 1996, at the NTSB evening progress meeting, Mr. Magladry and Mr. Wiemeyer, the NTSB Operations Group Chairman, met with assistant United States Attorney Valerie Caproni. In that meeting, Ms. Caproni reiterated that no interviews were to be conducted by the NTSB, but the NTSB could review FBI-supplied documents provided no notes were taken and no copies made.

On July 22, 1996, an agreement was reached with the FBI, that interviews could be conducted by the NTSB, but would be done under the direction and in the company of the FBI, and all information would be kept private, with no notes being taken by Mr. Magladry. According to Mr. Magladry, this caused him concern, because in his view, the NTSB is mandated to make information collected during an investigation part of the public record. The FBI has no such mandate.

On July 24, 1996, Mr. Magladry ended his witness information gathering efforts.[2]

No agreement had been reached between the NTSB and FBI to share all information, as alleged in Kallstrom's letter to Congressman Trafficant. The NTSB did not participate in missile eyewitness interviews because the FBI and the Department of Justice teamed up and forced the NTSB out "because the FBI did not want conflicting information."

27

KALLSTROM'S LAST PRESS CONFERENCE

By November 18, 1997, when Jim Kallstrom held his last press conference prior to retiring from the FBI—rumored to be a forced retirement because of his dismal performance as head of the FBI Flight 800 "investigation"—he knew my wife and I were going to be arrested. Orders to perform a drive-by surveillance of our Williamsburg residence had already been given in order to catch us at home and drag us out in chains before our neighbors and media cameras, to throw us into the federal prison transportation system as a means to intimidate and terrorize us into copping a plea before our attorney could find us.

The FBI and Justice Department had given its word to our attorney that such tactics would not be used. In detecting the FBI surveillance, I knew something nefarious was in the works. "Justice" had broken every felony law and virtually all case law on the books designed to protect journalists when confronting wrongdoing within the federal government, so I was certain further illegalities were about to begin. My wife and I quietly left in order to spend the rapidly approaching Thanksgiving and Christmas holidays free from federal harassment.

As we were on the road to California, Kallstrom, for the last time as a FBI official, misrepresented the reddish-orange residue I had obtained and had tested:

The seat cushion residue, reported in the Riverside, California, press, of the red residue that someone said was rocket fuel. The truth is the material is contact adhesive. We know the manufactured formula, which is patented, and we know without a doubt—without any doubt whatsoever—that it's the adhesive that holds the back of the seats together. It's not rocket fuel. It's not residue of a rocket, never was, never will be.[1]

28

THE ARREST WARRANTS

In the early morning hours of December 5, 1997, the FBI released the arrest warrant for James and Elizabeth Sanders to the press. The FBI's New York office Internet site had "conspiracy theorist and wife charged with theft of parts from airplane" emblazoned across the top of the page.

We were not charged with theft of parts from an airplane. Nor would we ever be. We were charged with conspiracy, aiding and abetting. But major media was comfortable reporting theft. It was a comfortable lie designed to make it easy for major media to continue to exclusively print what was fed to it by government propagandists. If a journalist has stooped to the level of a common thief, it is easy to turn your back on his plight, and that of his wife—particularly if his views are diametrically opposed to major media's.

If a journalist is charged with conspiring to obtain additional evidence of lawlessness within a federal investigation, and have that evidence tested, it presents major media with a real quandary. To accurately report the battle in Sanders v. Government would require major media to cease being government shills on the issue. It would require balanced reporting. The slippery slope to siding with a "conspiracy theorist" was to be avoided regardless of the facts.

Attached to the arrest warrant written by Jim Kinsley, was a Jim Kallstrom press release alleging we had been involved in a "scheme." Putting aside the criminal implications of Kallstrom's actions on and before December 5, the "scheme" allegation places him squarely within the definition of "advocate" in a public debate. As the federal Second Circuit has noted: "Advocates have a right to a full opportunity to appeal to reason, interest, policy, or morals, but they have no right to seek to alter the mind or conduct of the audience by coercion or obstruction. ...."[1] American citizens "need not tolerate coercive or obstructionist conduct merely because it serves some passionate ideology or interest. The First Amendment protects peaceful communication, not self-indulgence. Nor need we tolerate such conduct because it makes the advocate feel good. ... The notion of a marketplace of ideas gives primacy to the right to persuade largely for two reasons. First we justifiably fear that those who govern will be relentlessly tempted to censor their critics. ... Second, we want citizens to have exposure to competing ideas in the faith that truth and humane values will have the best chance of prevailing under such a system."[2]

Noble words, but words without meaning if the aggressor party is the Justice Department. Literally thousands of equally noble words can be found throughout Second Circuit and Supreme Court case law. These noble words were given prosecutorial teeth more than 50 years ago when Congress enacted Title 18, sections 241 and 242, which made it a felony civil rights violation for Jim Kallstrom, Jim Kinsley, Valerie Caproni, Janet Reno, et al, to carry out a vendetta against us. Under any conceivable rule of law, Justice Department conduct was not merely obnoxious; it fell outside the law.

The FBI had abused its power to obtain an arrest warrant for a journalist and his wife, for journalistic actions protected by the First Amendment Freedom of the Press and more than 200 years of case law. The scheme would fail if this became the public perception. Even the most pliant of grand juries would rebel against such blatant government lawlessness. So the cabal stoked the vilification flames in order to manipulate the grand jury with the assertion that my journalistic efforts constituted a "scheme" and "plot to rewrite the history of TWA 800."

My wife and I surrendered at the FBI field office, Uniondale, Long Island, on December 9, 1997. Jim Kinsley was in charge of the arrest detail.

Kinsley personally handled my booking procedure, while two young FBI agents went through the booking procedure with Elizabeth in another area of the FBI offices. In response to Elizabeth's question, the female agent said that all transport decisions were up to the senior agent, Kinsley, including whether handcuffs would be used.

Later, when Kinsley entered the room where we were seated, the young male agent suggested that we remain at the FBI office until it was time to go to court, because it would be more comfortable. Kinsley rejected the suggestion. The same agent then suggested that handcuffs not be used. Again Kinsley said no. The young agent then suggested handcuffing us in the front. Kinsley said no. The young agent suggested that the transport cars be moved to the ramp, away from the large media presence. Kinsley also refused that suggestion. We were then told to stand. We were bound with our hands behind our backs, and paraded through the throng of reporters and photographers to FBI vehicles in the parking lot. Kinsley escorted me to one vehicle, while the two young agents escorted Elizabeth to a second vehicle.

I marveled that the collective genius of the New York media herd we had just been dragged through could not articulate one First Amendment question to Jim Kinsley or the other FBI agents. Perhaps MIT professor Noam Chomsky was correct: "Far from performing a watchdog role, the 'free press' serves the needs of those in power."[3]

Upon arrival at the Federal Eastern District Court at Uniondale, Kinsley ordered the cars to stop in front of the courthouse, adjacent to where a large number of cameramen and "journalists" were gathered. The driver said he thought they were supposed to use a ramp in the rear of the building. Kinsley insisted on stopping by the gathered media, with the clear intent of subjecting us to a second "perp walk," which has been declared unconstitutional in the Second Circuit. As soon as we were removed from our respective vehicles, a bailiff approached Kinsley and advised him that the proper procedure was to drive to the ramp in the rear. Kinsley declined to take the advice, saying they would use the front entrance. The bailiff repeated the suggestion that the ramp was the appropriate choice. Kinsley again said they would use the front entrance. The bailiff repeated what he had already twice said. At this point Kinsley gave up the attempt to parade us through the crowd of "reporters" and ordered us returned to our respective vehicles. We were then driven to the ramp and entered the Marshal's area through the rear of the courthouse, away from the press. Elizabeth was deliberately placed in a cell adjacent to a male suspected of counterfeiting and parole violation, when another cell away from any male prisoner was available.

Three hours later we were taken from our cells and again bound with hands behind the back. Kinsley again personally escorted me. We were taken up a flight of stairs to the main courthouse hall. Kinsley then paraded us on our third unconstitutional "perp walk" through the courthouse, past the designated courtroom and into the main reception area immediately adjacent to the courthouse front door.

Kinsley then turned us around and walked us toward the courtroom door with the apparent intent of taking us inside the crowded courtroom with our hands bound behind our backs. Just before being paraded through the courtroom door by Kinsley, I heard a male voice say, "I've had enough of this B.S." This FBI agent then took control away from Kinsley and removed the handcuffs before my wife and I entered the courtroom.

A not-guilty plea was entered for each of us, and a $50,000 bail requirement announced by the magistrate. Shortly thereafter the legal proceeding ended and the journalistic herd filed out the front door to await our exit.

At the press gathering outside the court house, the collective New York media continued to fail to frame even one First Amendment question designed to investigate the possibility of Justice Department lawlessness. When Jeff Schlanger, our lawyer at that time, attempted to bring this issue into the questioning, Bob Kessler, *Newsday's* representative, began to argue the government line, insisting that the Justice Department, in spite of its best efforts, was never able to find sufficient evidence to discern that I was a journalist entitled to First Amendment protection. Another reporter asked Schlanger why his client did not immediately return the residue and turn Terry Stacey in to the FBI. These questions were not the exception, they were the rule. As I stood there listening to this sad exercise of seeming mass journalistic incompetence, whatever doubt I had about Professor Chomsky's basic theory evaporated.

29

ARREST WARRANTS AS PROPAGANDA

Jim Kinsley wrote and signed the Affidavit in Support of Application for an Arrest Warrant, used to bring my wife and me into custody in New York on December 9, 1997. It was little more than a propaganda tool.

Residue was an issue that could not be allowed to become a focal point of the judicial proceedings, but the arrest warrant language was being spewed across America by major media, so the FBI and NTSB glue story had to be included in the warrant:

> From Row 17 to Row 28 of the seating area there is a reddish residue on the metallic frame and backs of the passenger seats. The residue is manifested most strongly on seats from Rows 17 through 19. According to TWA maintenance records, the seats on which the residue can be seen had been refurbished, and glue was used to affix fabric and plastic to the metallic frames of the seats. Other rows of the airplane were not similarly refurbished, or were made by different manufacturers, and a similar residue cannot be seen on them.

Kinsley continued the disinformation campaign, on page 5-6:

> On March 10, 1997, the *Press-Enterprise*, a newspaper in Riverside, California, published a series of articles asserting that a U.S. Navy missile was responsible for the crash of TWA 800. In those articles, the newspaper extensively quoted the defen-

dant JAMES SANDERS. SANDERS was identified in the articles as a former police officer, accident investigator, and Virginia-based writer. The articles indicated that the defendant JAMES SANDERS was conducting an independent investigation into the cause of the crash and had concluded that a U.S. Navy missile had shot down the plane.

In fact, the U. S. Navy is not mentioned in any of the articles published by the *Press-Enterprise* on March 10, 1997.

More importantly, Kinsley misrepresented how I was identified in the article. I was "identified" on page one, above the fold, as an "investigative reporter." More than 30 column inches were then devoted to Investigative Reporter James Sanders' analysis, opinions and conclusions. This page-one story precluded the Justice Department and FBI from legally harassing us. But they did it anyway, and Kinsley placed this disinformation in the warrant to provide "facts" with which to mislead the grand jury.

Keep in mind that the grand jury is a captive audience of the prosecution, Justice Department lawyers Valerie Caproni and Ben Campbell. They alone decide what information goes to the grand jury.

The arrest warrant carried the factually false allegation that the Justice Department and FBI simply did not know I was a journalist until many months later, after they had fortuitously obtained all the documents they needed to identify my source.

Kinsley continued:

In support of his claim, the newspaper reported that the defendant JAMES SANDERS had obtained fabric from passenger seats from TWA 800 from a source connected to the NTSB/FBI investigation. According to the articles, the defendant JAMES SANDERS told reporters from the *Press-Enterprise* that, after he received the parts in January 1997, he took them to a laboratory for analysis. The defendant JAMES SANDERS stated that the seat parts from TWA 800 were covered with a "red residue" and that chemical analysis of the residue was consistent with solid rocket fuel. The defendant JAMES SANDERS concluded that the test results, coupled with a "residue trail" which his source allegedly told him traveled from one side of the cabin to the other along the seats inside the aircraft, confirmed that a missile had punched through TWA 800 and caused it to explode.[1]

I did not tell reporters from the *Press-Enterprise* that the elements detected in the chemical test were "consistent with" solid rocket fuel. I gave the newspaper a copy of the WCAS elemental test. The *Press-Enterprise* found its own sources who said the residue was consistent with exhaust from a solid-fuel rocket. I found additional sources, independent of the newspaper, who gave the same analysis.

The *Press-Enterprise* also sent my written analysis and documents to a former government crash expert who concurred with my conclusions. All of this was, in detail, presented in the March 10 articles Kinsley so grossly misrepresented in the arrest warrant.

Perhaps the most outrageous misrepresentation is Kinsley's factually false statement that I relied exclusively on the "test results" and "residue trail" to conclude that "a missile had punched through TWA 800 and caused it to explode." What the *Press-Enterprise* actually wrote was:

> The pattern of the first wreckage to hit the water, combined with evidence of missile-propellant residue in the Boeing 747, clearly indicates that a missile carrying an inert warhead smashed through the airliner, author and investigative reporter James Sanders has concluded.

The residue elements and residue trail across the first three rows of seats to exit the aircraft were part of a much broader picture painted by the NTSB debris-field document Terry Stacey removed from the Calverton hangar and gave me to analyze. That 140-page document so incriminates the NTSB "mechanical" hypothesis that the government has never released it.

The *Press-Enterprise* also located an independent source who confirmed the residue trail across rows 17, 18 and 19. In fact, the newspaper independently confirmed my entire analysis and added considerably to what I had uncovered.

But Kinsley had to write this section alleging that I was feeding information to *Press-Enterprise* reporters who obediently passed it on to the public. The FBI arrest-day vilification program depended on Kallstrom pointing to the arrest warrant as his proof that I "misrepresented" the residue elements, saying the elements, and the elements alone, provided "conclusive" proof that Flight 800 was brought down by a missile. I never made such a statement, but without such misrepresentation, the Department of Justice and the FBI were left with explaining away their arrest of a journalist who had indeed developed scientific evidence that the residue was "consistent with" the exhaust from a solid-fuel missile. That was an argument certain to begin a media feeding frenzy, placing the government scheme in serious jeopardy.

Kinsley wasn't clever enough to build a misrepresentation of facts, carefully crafting prose that misinforms without being false. On page eight of the arrest warrant, he alleged the head of West Coast Analytical Services (WCAS): "[Jack Northington] indicated that he told JAMES SANDERS that the tests were *not conclusive* that solid rocket propellant was present. … [Northington] stated that the laboratory later sent the defendant JAMES SANDERS a written report summarizing the conclusions of the tests. …" [Emphasis added]

Here is what Jack Northington actually told a Los Angeles-based FBI agent, who wrote his report as if he had no personal animus toward me: "Northington then prepared and sent a final report to SANDERS which contained the scientific results of their analysis. *The reports made no specific conclusion about the significance of any of the substances found.*"[2] [Emphasis added]

Kallstrom attached a press release to the arrest warrants, which state in part: "According to the criminal complaint, despite the laboratory test results, JAMES SANDERS misrepresented those results in media reports for which he was a source." From the evidence it can be inferred that Kallstrom and Kinsley conspired to create false statements in an arrest warrant, with the specific intent to further violate our civil rights[3] and maliciously vilify us.

The *Press-Enterprise* articles clearly stated that the elemental analysis was "consistent with" a solid fuel missile—not "conclusive" proof. My book, *The Downing of TWA Flight 800*, page 136, presents the reader with a list of the elements detected in the WCAS test, and provides the percentage of each element. The next sentence says: "All these elements are *consistent with* a list of the residue from a solid-fuel missile." Terry Stacey's 3500 file, obtained under discovery, has multiple references where he expressed his irritation with me and *Press-Enterprise* reporter David Hendrix because we always used *"consistent with"* when talking about the WCAS test results. And he repeated that frustration when testifying before the grand jury:

> [Stacey]: At some point [Sanders] indicated that he had the results from the lab and that someone had indicated that it was *consistent with* rocket propellant.
>
> Q: What was your reaction to that?
>
> A: I was somewhat skeptical and wanted more definitive information. It didn't have a lab report and I was skeptical of the term *"consistent with"*[4]. ...
>
> Q: Was there any discussion again about the results of the laboratory analysis?

A: At that time? I believe again we talked about the term *"consistent with"* rather than fact, you know.

Q: And what did you tell him about that?

A: Well, that again I didn't like that term *"consistent with."* A lot of things could be consistent with other things. [Emphasis added]

So I got hammered inside the grand jury room for not developing forensic evidence strong enough to conclusively state the residue was from a solid-fuel missile exhaust, while Jim Kallstrom was outside the grand jury room claiming I had said the residue was *conclusive* proof of solid-fuel missile exhaust.

The Kallstrom press release built Jack Northington up as an expert, whose knowledge of missile exhaust residue was so significant that the FBI could rely solely on his expertise to discredit me.

The truth is that Jack Northington's opinion is no more credible than any citizen on the street when it comes to residue from a solid-fuel missile. Here is what Jack Northington wrote to me about his personal knowledge of missile-exhaust residue, and the institutional knowledge level of WCAS: "We could probably detect residues from rocket propellant if we knew what the rocket propellant contained. ..." This is not the statement of a man who is qualified to render any opinion, expert or otherwise, on any scientific observation related to solid-fuel residue.

The above written statement by Northington is precisely why I never questioned him about what the elements meant. Northington didn't have a clue. The FBI had obtained this e-mail on March 11, 1997, from WCAS. The Bureau knew Jack Northington was literally clueless when it came to analysis of what the elements detected in the testing meant.

As of December 5, 1997, the FBI was still hiding the

fact they had recovered an untested piece of the residue I had received from Terry Stacey. Kinsley's narrative continued:

> During the interview, [Northington] provided the FBI agent with two bottles containing segments of the material he received from the defendant JAMES SANDERS.

Once again Kinsley had lied in the arrest warrant. My attorney and I expected the FBI to recover two used pieces of residue because two tests had been performed by WCAS. The FBI was hiding the fact they had also recovered an unused piece.

Almost 16 months later, at trial, I discovered the truth. The FBI had the ability to test the residue I had received from Stacey—but the FBI ran away from the opportunity. Instead, they lied on the arrest warrant in order avoid admitting they had the ability to determine, without any doubt, who was telling the truth about the origin of the residue—glue or missile exhaust residue.

With sufficient notice, my legal team could have pursued a judicial order allowing this sample to be tested. But that requires significant lead-time.

The Justice Department withheld this information—and the FBI lied—in order to eliminate a Court-ordered test exposing their culpability.

30

THE GOVERNMENT LEANS ON TWA

In August 1997, the FBI had gone to the movie company holding the option to produce a movie based on my book, *The Downing of TWA Flight 800*, and asked if the company wanted to remain involved in a project that would undoubtedly result in the arrest of individuals for conspiracy. The president of the movie company immediately called to advise me that his company was in the entertainment business, not the confrontation business. The FBI's actions cut me off from a source of revenue needed to continue the extraordinarily expensive fight against the government. It also cut off a means by which views opposed to the government could be transmitted to the American public.

Then, in December 1997, shortly after my wife and I were arrested, the government approached TWA and demanded that Elizabeth be immediately fired. The government strategy was to neutralize us publicly and financially.

TWA senior management attempted to fully comply with the government demand through the use of chicanery. On December 17, 1997, Chris Rhoads, General Manager, TWA In-flight Services, Eastern Region, oversaw the writing of the following letter to Liz:

> This letter will serve as a directive to meet with me at 1100 on Monday, December 22, 1997, room 215, Hangar 12, JFK, to discuss your suspected theft and unauthorized possession of company and/or government property. Due to the status of

this matter, you have been suspended from flight and pay status.

Failure to attend this meeting will result in the investigation being concluded without benefit of your input. In addition, your failure to abide by this directive will be considered insubordination, which is a terminable offense.

Terry Stacey had been removed from flight status but remained on the payroll. He plead guilty to theft. Liz Sanders plead not guilty and was removed from the payroll. Later, she was removed from medical benefits as well.

This letter gave Liz only five days from the instant the letter was written to receive it and fly to New York. TWA mailed it to our home address, knowing Liz was not at that location. No certified mail or signature required. They really didn't want Liz to know about the meeting. They were going to summarily fire her when she did not show up.

The "copy to" portion of the letter said it was also forwarded to Jeff Schlanger, our attorney in New York at that time. He never received the letter. Liz found out about it when she just happened to call the TWA Flight Attendant union about another matter on the afternoon of December 17, and they immediately put her in touch with the union attorney. Liz advised the union attorney she was not involved in the investigation of TWA Flight 800, that she had been framed, and was going to fight the injustice in court.

The IAM attorney escorted Liz to the hearing, which lasted all of two minutes. TWA's Chris Rhoads handed Liz and the union attorney a written statement from TWA's Legal Department:

This hearing involves the theft of fabric swatches from a passenger seat and NTSB written reports from the Calverton F800 wreckage-recovery site, and the subsequent unauthorized testing of that fabric and printing of the report to publicize

your theory that a trail of missile propellant was found in the
F800 aircraft. The laboratory analysis from that testing as well
as the report appeared in the book, *The Downing of TWA Flight
800,* by your husband, James Sanders. According to the FBI,
your husband's book erroneously reported the results of those
lab tests and caused the victims families' additional anguish
and grief.

As you know, the F.B.I. conducted an investigation into the
unauthorized removal of these fabric swatches as well as the
NTSB reports, from the Calverton Hanger [sic]. TWA cooperated fully in that investigation and many TWA employees voluntarily came forward to tell the F.B.I. what they knew.

As a result of the unauthorized actions of yourself and others, TWA's status as a party to the NTSB investigation into F800
was and remains under the threat of expulsion and the relationship between NTSB investigators and TWA staff investigators is now seriously strained. The theft of this material has
only served to make TWA's job in the investigation more difficult to fulfill. ...

We also suspect that your actions were motivated not out of
a desire to seek the truth, but were instead motivated by the
financial gain and notoriety you and your husband stood to
gain by publication of the book.

Accordingly we are holding this hearing to determine what
role you played in these events.

Both the union attorney and Liz told the TWA representative that she was not involved in my investigation and had
never seen the residue. If Terry Stacey had said anything to the
contrary, he was in error.

TWA attempted to immediately level additional internal
charges against her, but the union attorney went on the offensive. Soon, Chris Rhoads' hands were noticeably quivering.
The union attorney was a very intimidating female who took
justifiable pride in eating the Chris Rhoads of the world for
lunch.

The TWA Legal Department statement was astounding. I had met with an intermediary of TWA's legal department shortly before the March 10, 1997, newspaper article revealing my findings on the FBI and NTSB investigation at Calverton. In a multi-hour meeting, I laid out my case, described all documents in detail, then went into the reddish-orange residue, its removal from the hangar, elemental testing, and what the test results meant. The intermediary was told an additional sample was available to counter any government disinformation.

Within days I received a message that the head of TWA's Legal Department at St. Louis Corporate Headquarters had been briefed and was confidentially preparing a civil suit against the federal government, to be filed if my allegations placed the government on the defensive.

31

PRE-TRIAL DISCOVERY

The first step in any federal case is for the defense to attempt to obtain from the government as much documentation as possible related to the case. When the unlawful actions of the government is the central issue on which the defense wants to focus its attack, discovery is the only means available to get at memos, e-mail and other documents to establish who the real criminals in the case are.

In most state courts the defense automatically receives all such documentation. The prosecution, in most state courts, must offer full disclosure of documents that may be relevant to illegalities committed within law enforcement or prosecution ranks. But not in federal court. Congress and the Supreme Court have gone to extreme lengths to ensure that federal agents are protected from scrutiny.

The Federal Second Circuit Court, which includes New York, where our indictments were handed down, previously ensured a defendant the right not to be tried if government agents were acting in an outrageous or vindictive manner. But the Supreme Court struck down decades of carefully crafted Second Circuit case law. No one, the Supreme Court says, has the right not to be tried.[1] Without this ruling by the Supreme Court, the Department of Justice and FBI could not seriously consider resorting to rampant lawlessness.

The only protection we had was District Court Judge Joanna Seybert. But she seemed to have been adversely affected by the barrage of government vilification directed against us.

Government conduct would not be questioned in this judge's court.

The legal maneuvering began with the defense motion for discovery.[2]

Jeremy Gutman's specialty is appellate law; i.e., writing appeals for presentation to the Second Circuit Court. Gutman has an unusual ability to write legal briefs in a way that can actually be understood:

> The present indictment, charging Mr. and Mrs. Sanders with aiding and abetting the removal of property from an aircraft involved in an accident ... and with conspiring to do so, arose from an investigation that commenced immediately after a newspaper reported that Mr. Sanders, who was identified as an investigative reporter and the author of two non-fiction books, had gathered and reviewed evidence from which he concluded that the tragic crash of TWA Flight 800, in which all 230 individuals on board were killed, was the result of a collision with a missile. The Sanders were arrested and indicted only after Mr. Sanders published a book detailing his findings regarding the cause of the crash, and accusing participants in the highly-publicized investigation conducted by the Federal Bureau of Investigation ("FBI") and National Transportation Safety Board ("NTSB") of a "cover-up"—and only after he and his wife, in the face of express threats of prosecution, resisted government demands to reveal a confidential source.
>
> The indictment is based on the allegation that Mr. Sanders asked Terrell Stacey, a TWA pilot assigned to participate in the crash investigation, to remove two tiny swatches of material from a seat recovered from the plane's wreckage so that a laboratory could analyze the chemical composition of a reddish-orange residue trail that appeared in the section of the reconstructed passenger compartment where that seat was located. The charges against Mrs. Sanders, who was a TWA flight attendant supervisor, are based on the allegation that, on one occa-

sion, she communicated her husband's interest in a residue sample to Mr. Stacey.

The defense contends that the determination to bring criminal charges against Mr. and Mrs. Sanders for their alleged accessorial roles in the removal of an inconsequential quantity of material was motivated by an improper desire to retaliate against them for the exercise of rights protected under the First Amendment to the United States Constitution, and to chill the exercise of those rights. Based on this contention, we intend to move for dismissal of the indictment on the ground of vindictive or selective prosecution.

Because claims of vindictive or selective prosecution revolve around the internal decision-making process of governmental agencies, access to discovery is critical to a defendant's ability to establish such a claim. … Weighing the defense's need against the burden that discovery imposes on the government, the Supreme Court has held that, to obtain discovery, a defendant must present 'some evidence' tending to establish the essential elements of the defense. … Although this standard is "rigorous" … it does not require the defendant to persuade the Court that his claim should ultimately be upheld; rather it requires that the defendant establish what has been described variously as a "colorable basis," a "substantial and concrete basis," a "substantial threshold showing," or a "reasonable likelihood."

Dismissal is warranted where a defendant demonstrates (1) that the prosecutor harbored an animus against the defendant for his exercise of a protected statutory or constitutional right, and (2) but for this animus, the defendant would not have been prosecuted. … A claim of "selective" prosecution may be based on a showing (1) that others similarly situated have not generally been proceeded against because of conduct of the type underlying the charge against the defendant, and (2) that the government's discriminatory selection of the defendant for prosecution was based on such impermissible considerations as race, religion, or "the desire to prevent his exercise of constitutional rights." … Where the second element concerns a defendant's exercise of First Amendment rights, the permissibility of the prosecutor's conduct must be assessed on the basis of a heightened standard, recognizing that government regulation is justified only

If it is within the constitutional power of the Government; if it furthers an important or substantial government interest; if the governmental interest is *unrelated to the suppression of free expression*; and if the incidental restriction on alleged First Amendment freedoms is no greater than is essential to the furtherance of that interest. [Emphasis added]

The First Amendment provides that "Congress shall make no law ... abridging the freedom of speech, or of the press. ..." This guarantee is intended to "preserve an untrammeled press as a vital source of public information." ... Because the First Amendment's "core purpose" is to assure "freedom of communication on matters relating to the functioning of government," it "goes beyond protection of the press and the self-expression of individuals to prohibit government from limiting the stock of information from which members of the public may draw." ... [The Supreme Court] declined to exempt reporters from the ordinary duty to appear before a grand jury to testify about matters that they had personally witnessed, but nonetheless recognized that "without some protection for seeking out the news, freedom of the press could be eviscerated." ...

Recognizing that "the process of newsgathering is a protected right under the First Amendment, albeit a qualified one,'" the Second Circuit in *von Bulow* by *Auersperg v. von Bulow* ... held that whether a person "is a journalist, and thus protected by the privilege, must be determined by the person's intent at the inception of the information-gathering process." The First Amendment's protections apply where it was "the intent {of the individual} to *use material—sought, gathered, or received—* to disseminate information to the public and that such intent existed at the inception of the newsgathering process." [Emphasis added.]

The Second Circuit Court had the opportunity, when writing this decision, to limit what a journalist may seek, and equally limit the means by which it may be sought. The court declined to do so, in effect telling all journalists working within the confines of the federal Second Circuit they could actively seek[3] "material," an all encompassing word that establishes no pre-determined limits on what may be "sought." Journalistically, this Second Circuit description of the legal scope of the search for facts is limited, in the Flight 800 case, only to that which would constitute obstruction of justice.

Taking "material" that may constitute a unique or limited source of evidence for the government investigation would constitute obstruction of justice. The Justice Department admits that obstruction of justice did not occur when Terry Stacey removed two miniscule samples for testing purposes. Their singular value was the information contained within the residue—possible evidence of government malfeasance.

The entire government case against my wife and me came down to the right of a journalist to communicate a desire to acquire evidence, for scientific testing, that may reveal extraordinary illegal activity within the TWA Flight 800 investigation.

It was the government position that a journalist cannot communicate in such a manner with his source. The government maintains that the only legal route to obtain such evidence is to ask those within the government suspected of acting in a criminal conspiracy to turn over the evidence of their collective guilt. Although the prosecution would try to dress it up, that would be the thrust of their argument before the Court at Uniondale, Long Island.

Our legal team argued that my actions were protected under the First Amendment's Freedom of the Press:

... the Court noted that "an individual may assert the journalist's privilege if he is involved in activities traditionally associated with the gathering and dissemination of news. ..."

Under these standards there can be no doubt that the acts the defendants are charged with in the present indictment all relate to the constitutionally-protected process of news-gathering. As a freelance journalist and author of two previous non-fiction books, as well as numerous articles, James Sanders initiated an investigation into the cause of the crash of TWA Flight 800 with the sole purpose of gathering information for dissemination to the public. Indeed, under the government's own characterization of the facts, Mr. Sanders was gathering information for the purpose of making it known to the public, either by relaying it to other reporters or by including it in his own published book. ... Furthermore, the conduct attributed to Elizabeth Sanders—contacting Terrell Stacey and purportedly asking him to obtain residue samples—related solely to assisting her husband, or acting as his agent, in pursuit of information to be communicated to the public. ... [S]uch conduct, even when performed by someone who is not a member of the "institutionalized press," falls under the protection of the First Amendment.

In the related context of a civil rights action alleging malicious prosecution as retaliation for exercise of First Amendment rights, the Second Circuit has recognized that it is often difficult to elicit direct proof of the defendant's intent. ... Accordingly, the ... Court agreed with the view expressed by the Seventh Circuit:

> Recognizing that the ultimate fact of retaliation for the exercise of a constitutionally protected right rarely can be supported with direct evidence of intent that can be pleaded in a complaint, ... courts have found sufficient complaints that allege a *chronology of events from which retaliation may be inferred.* ... Conversely, alleging merely the ultimate fact of retaliation is insufficient. [Emphasis added.]

... In the present case, the chronology of events provides substantial circumstantial evidence from which a retaliatory intent may be inferred. Specifically, the chronology of events suggests that the investigation, threat of indictment, and ultimate prosecution of Mr. and Mrs. Sanders constituted retaliation for Mr. Sanders' exercise of his First Amendment right to promulgate a theory about the cause of the Flight 800 disaster that challenged the 'official' government version, as well as an effort to dissuade him from further efforts to investigate and communicate facts in support of that theory.

That chronology includes the following series of events:

• On March 10, 1997, the Riverside *Press-Enterprise* published a front-page article reporting Mr. Sanders' acquisition of a sample of red residue from TWA Flight 800, and his conclusions, based on laboratory analysis of the sample showing chemicals consistent with solid missile fuel [residue], as well as analysis of the pattern of debris retrieved from the crash site, that a missile had caused the crash.

• In testimony before a House of Representatives subcommittee given the day after publication of the *Press-Enterprise* article, a senior NTSB official, Bernard Loeb, attempted to discredit Mr. Sanders' conclusions, and to counter them with the assertion that the red residue was from an "adhesive."[4]

• Within hours after publication of the *Press-Enterprise* article, the FBI initiated aggressive efforts to question Mr. Sanders' wife, Elizabeth Sanders, who had been mentioned in passing and identified as a TWA employee in a related article that appeared on page A-12 of the March 10 *Press-Enterprise*. Despite being advised that Mrs. Sanders did not wish to speak to or meet with the FBI, Special Agent James Kinsley went to her residence in Williamsburg, Virginia, and to the Norfolk Airport in an apparent attempt to intercept her as she returned there from St. Louis.

• Notwithstanding the prominent discussion of Mr. Sanders' journalistic credentials in the *Press-Enterprise* article ("... author and investigative reporter James Sanders"), and its clear indication that he was conducting an independent investigation into the Flight 800 crash for the purpose of disseminating information to the public, grand jury subpoenas were issued on seeking Mr. Sanders' testimony, as well as toll records from the Sanders' telephone service provider. By approving these subpoenas, the Justice Department violated its own rules requiring prior authorization by the Attorney General of subpoenas seeking information from or relating to members of the news media; requiring that such subpoenas issue only after alternative investigative steps have been attempted and failed; requiring that, absent "exigent circumstances," they should be limited to verification of published information; and requiring negotiation with the media recipient to ensure that the demand for information is appropriately limited.[5]

• In April 1997, the government initiated a meeting with Mr. Sanders and his attorney, during which prosecutors and other law enforcement officers expressly threatened that Mr. Sanders would be indicted, and his wife would become a target, if he did not immediately agree to cooperate with the government by revealing his confidential source within the FBI/NTSB crash investigation. Citing Mr. Sanders' First Amendment rights, his attorney advised the government that Mr. Sanders would not cooperate, and that he intended to continue his investigation into possible government wrongdoing.

• During the same meeting, the government threatened to make Elizabeth Sanders a target of its investigation if she did not agree to cooperate in the government's investigation of her husband's newsgathering activities. (Since the sole source of information allegedly linking Mrs. Sanders to the acquisition of the residue samples is Terrell Stacey, who had not yet been interviewed by the government, this threat was made despite a total absence of evidence that Mrs. Sanders had engaged in any form of wrongdoing). Through counsel, Mrs. Sanders advised the government that she declined to cooperate in its investigation of her husband's journalistic pursuits.

• In late April 1997, Kensington Publishing Corporation published James Sanders' book, *The Downing of TWA Flight 800*, which detailed the information he had gathered pointing to the conclusion that the plane had collided with a United States

Navy missile that penetrated the plane's passenger compartment, and that the government had concealed this information from the American public.

• In the book's "acknowledgements" section, Mr. Sanders had written "Thank's to Liz's support system, Lee Taylor, Lucille Collins and TWA Norfolk agents." Shortly after publication of the book, FBI agents in New York demanded that Mrs. Collins, who was Mrs. Sanders' immediate supervisor at TWA, and Mrs. Taylor, a close friend and colleague, be brought to New York for questioning. Both individuals were subjected to FBI questioning, and reported that many of the questions were of a highly personal nature concerning the Sanders' marriage and private lives.

• Although the government had acknowledged that its earlier subpoena for Mr. Sanders' telephone records violated Justice Department regulations, it issued a second subpoena for Mr. Sanders' telephone records in August 1997, again without notifying him or complying fully with the provisions of [the regulations Congress forced the Justice Department to adopt in 1980].

• Continuing his probe into the FBI/NTSB investigation of the crash of Flight 800, Mr. Sanders filed a number of Freedom of Information Act ("FOIA") requests in August through October 1997.

• On November 18, 1997, Mr. Sanders told a *New York Post* reporter, Al Guart, that he had used FOIA to investigate possible wrongdoing by government officials, including James Kallstrom, James Kinsley, Valerie Caproni, and Benton Campbell. Mr. Guart said he knew Mrs. Caproni and was going to seek her comments regarding Mr. Sanders' investigative efforts.

• The next morning, November 19, 1997, Mr. Guart's 'exclusive' story appeared on page two of the *New York Post:* "Evidence-Swipers May Face Fed Charges." Mrs. Caproni was quoted in the article, again claiming that the Justice Department was not required to follow its own rules regarding media subpoenas because it found no basis for concluding that Mr.

Sanders was acting as a reporter. The article also stated that, according to "law-enforcement sources," the Sanders "will probably be charged in the next two weeks." . . .

• On December 5, 1997, Agent Kinsley's affidavit in support of a warrant to arrest the Sanders was released to the press, prior to any notification to the Sanders or their attorney. On the same date, Joseph Valiquette, an FBI agent who works directly for Assistant Director James F. Kallstrom, issued a press release alleging in part: "According to the criminal complaint, despite the laboratory test results [concerning the residue samples], JAMES SANDERS misrepresented those results in media reports for which he was a source."[6]

• Following the Sanders' surrender at the FBI's Long Island office, Agent Kinsley arranged to have them paraded in handcuffs past throngs of reporters and photographers in the parking lot of the FBI office, and attempted to do so again at the entrance to the Courthouse where they were to be arraigned, notwithstanding the availability of more discreet means of leaving and entering the respective buildings.

• The following day, during his sworn plea allocution, Terrell Stacey stated "... when I was given an opportunity or when I—when Mr. Sanders offered to me or the fact I learned that he could help in the investigation through contacts and people he had in labs, then I on my own volition took the two small pieces and gave them to him to have them analyzed."

• Notwithstanding this statement, the Sanders were indicted approximately four weeks later on the theory that they violated, and conspired to violate 49 U.S.C., Section 1155, by importuning Mr. Stacey to provide those small pieces of material to Mr. Sanders.

The chronology of events described above undoubtedly 'tends' to establish that the government's investigation and indictment of the Sanders represented retaliation for an exercise of First Amendment rights, and an attempt to chill that exercise. The investigation arose only after a newspaper article appeared in which Mr. Sanders identified evidence that a missile was the cause of the Flight 800 disaster, and implicitly accused the FBI and NTSB—which were engaged in a closely-watched official investigation of the crash, of concealing that evidence from the American public—of a criminal act. The immediate governmental response was an effort to discredit Mr. Sanders' theory, combined with aggressive efforts by federal agents to question and embarrass not only Mr. Sanders and his wife (even though there was no evidence that she was implicated in any criminal activity) through a series of contacts with her colleagues and supervisors at TWA. In seeking information from and about Mr. Sanders and his sources, the government disregarded its own rules regarding media subpoenas, and justified doing so based on a flimsy claim that it was not aware that his investigation was of a journalistic nature.[7] Indeed, the government went so far as to use the threat of an indictment against both Mr. Sanders and his wife in an effort to intimidate him into betraying a confidential source—an act that would at once derail his investigation and undermine his journalistic credibility.

When the Sanders refused to succumb to this pressure, and James Sanders continued to exercise his First Amendment rights both by publishing his book and by continuing his probe of the government's conduct, the government embarked on still more intrusive questioning of Mrs. Sanders' friends and colleagues, and further improper subpoenas of the Sanders' phone records. Finally—shortly after Mr. Sanders' inquiries concerning the Assistant United States Attorneys supervising the FBI investigation were disclosed—the government utilized the occasion of the Sanders' arrest and arraignment as an opportunity to issue a press release that gratuitously accused Mr. Sanders of misrepresenting the lab results underlying the missile theory, and to subject Mr. and Mrs. Sanders to unwarranted and unnecessary humiliation as they were transported to court in handcuffs.

When the government's overbearing adversarial measures against the Sanders following the publication of articles and a book criticizing and challenging the government's conduct are viewed in the context of the *de minimus* nature of the obscure victimless crime with which they are charged, as well as the additional evidence of a governmental motive to suppress Mr. Sanders' conclusions and accusations, the conclusion that the present prosecution constitutes an effort to retaliate for an exercise of First Amendment rights, and to chill that exercise, is compelling. Clearly, therefore, the burden of establishing evidence "tending" to establish such purposes has been met.

There is substantial evidence that the government has an interest in avoiding a public belief or perception that the crash of TWA Flight 800 was caused by a collision with a missile, and that it has gone to considerable lengths to discourage that perception. This evidence circumstantially tends to establish the nature of the animus underlying the government's retaliation against Mr. Sanders' for the exercise of First Amendment rights.

Soon after the July 17, 1996, crash, numerous witnesses reported that they had seen an object or streak of light proceeding over the Atlantic Ocean just before the plane exploded. These witnesses included two New York Air National Guard pilots who were in a helicopter a few miles northeast of Flight 800's flight path. Additionally, hours after the crash, Federal Aviation Administration ("FAA") air traffic control personnel reported to government officials, including the White House, that their radar data indicated that an unidentified object—possibly a missile—had approached and struck Flight 800 at a high speed. A December 26, 1996, letter from the NTSB's Bernard Loeb to David Thomas of the FAA reveals an effort to neutralize and quash this information.

After stating that the NTSB had determined that the original assessment of the radar data was incorrect, Mr. Loeb wrote that he "would appreciate it if you could verify that all specialists and/or managers involved in the preliminary radar analysis fully agree that there is no evidence within FAA ATC [air traffic control] of a track that would suggest a high-speed target merged with TWA 800." Mr. Thomas responded:

Although we understand and share your desire to allay public concern over this issue, we cannot comply with your request.

While qualifying his remarks by noting the technical limitations of the FAA radar system, and of the FAA's ability to interpret the data, he advised Mr. Loeb that the FAA specialists could not discount the possibility, albeit "remote," that the presence of a missile was indicated.

Subsequently, however, after two of the FAA's radar tapes, from the evening of July 17, 1996, were leaked in March 1997, the FBI's lead investigator, James Kallstrom, acknowledged that there was an anomalous, unidentified "blip" detected by radar, but he asserted that it was caused by a Navy plane that was more than 7,000 feet away from Flight 800 at the time of the explosion. ... On November 18, 1997, Mr. Kallstrom changed this story, asserting that the object detected by radar "is and was and always will be a commercial flight, not a missile." ... The one factor that remains constant in the varying assurances provided by the crash investigators is the government's evident "desire to allay public concern" by refuting any evidence suggestive of the presence of a missile.

Gutman's discovery motion narrative continued:

The government's willingness to present conflicting explanations in order to assure the public that there is no evidence of a missile, demonstrates the government's obvious motivation to suppress or discredit Mr. Sanders' research and conclusions regarding the involvement of a missile in the crash of Flight 800. That motivation supplies the animus underlying the decision to investigate Mr. Sanders and his wife, to utilize intimidation and threats in an effort to compromise and discredit his investigation, and, when those efforts failed, to follow through on their threats by pursuing the present prosecution.

In view of the obscurity of the statute under which the government is proceeding in the present case ... there is virtually no basis for a meaningful 'statistical' analysis of prosecutions brought for such offenses. Our research has not disclosed any reported decisions arising from criminal prosecutions under this statute, and a representative of the Department of Justice's Bureau of Justice Statistics has advised counsel that no such prosecutions could be found in their database. ...

On the other hand, while the NTSB's "Public Inquiries" office has advised counsel that no records are kept of reports that items are missing from the sites of airplane accident investigations ... legislative history ... indicates that its predecessor statute was enacted in response to testimony by NTSB officials that 'numerous instances have occurred where souvenir hunters thoughtlessly and, on many occasions, maliciously carried off parts of aircraft wreckage which are vital to the accident investigation.

... An apparent violation of the statute occurred within the first ten days of the Flight 800 investigation, when the FBI's James Kallstrom reportedly removed an American flag found among the debris from the crash and presented it as a souvenir to a relative of one of the victims. ... It does not appear, however, that Mr. Kallstrom has been subjected to criminal prosecution (or a sanction of any kind) as a result of this act.

It should be noted that the Justice Department covered-up the fact that two FBI Flight 800 investigators were caught red-handed pilfering debris from the Calverton hangar. It seems the NTSB became aware that more and more debris came up missing after it had passed through the FBI screening process and was given to the NTSB for processing. After complaining to the FBI but receiving no satisfaction, the NTSB set up surveillance and bagged two FBI officers, caught in the act of removing debris from the crash site.

This is exculpatory evidence the Justice Department has a legal obligation to turn over to the defense. Instead, they hid this compelling evidence of selective prosecution. These facts were uncovered during the course of a May 10, 1999, Senate hearing, *after* my wife and I had been convicted of conspiring to investigate the government by having residue tested.

In addition to the complete ... absence of prosecutions under this statute the selective nature of the government's determination to prosecute Mr. and Mrs. Sanders is demonstrated
by the fact that the alleged crime in the present case caused no
discernible harm or deprivation to any identifiable victim. The
property that was removed consisted of nothing more than a
miniscule sample of seat-backing material with no intrinsic
value whatsoever. Indeed, a criminal prosecution for the theft
or destruction of property on such an infinitesimally small scale
is simply unheard of.

Since Mr. Stacey left behind more than ample residue-bearing material to be tested by government investigators, the "removal" at issue here did not deprive the government of "parts
of aircraft wreckage which are vital to the accident investigation." Yet, the government has proceeded in the present case
not only against Mr. Stacey, the individual who allegedly removed the material, but against Mr. Sanders, on the attenuated
basis of his alleged importuning of the removal, and—under a
still more strained theory of liability—against Mrs. Sanders,
who (according to the government's allegation) acted as nothing more than an intermediary with regard to this *de minimus*
offense.

Given the extreme lack of culpability involved in this incident, it is virtually inconceivable that the removal of the material at issue here would have formed the basis for an intensive
criminal[8] investigation and prosecution if the material had not
figured in a book and other publications espousing a theory
that the government sought to discredit and suppress. Under
the circumstances present here, it surely cannot be said that
this prosecution serves "an important or substantial governmental interest" that is "unrelated to the suppression of free
expression" and that "the incidental restriction on alleged First
Amendment freedoms is no greater than is essential to the furtherance of that interest." On the contrary, the present case
smacks of an effort to penalize the defendants for the perceived

harmfulness (to governmental interests) of the contents of their communications, rather than for any harm arising from their conduct per se. Plainly, therefore, the defendants have met their burden of establishing "some evidence" that the government has proceeded from improper motives. Accordingly, they are entitled to full discovery of information and materials in the government's possession pertinent to their assertion that they have been subjected to vindictive and selective prosecution.

For the reasons discussed above, we respectfully request that the Court grant the defense motion for pre-trial discovery relating to the defenses of vindictive and selective prosecution.[9]

It was my opinion that Justice Department and FBI conduct had comfortably come under the legal doctrine of "outrageous conduct." Those I was investigating used the awesome power with which they had been entrusted to defame and injure the journalist who put them at risk. Every step of the way, the Justice Department had violated our civil rights, codified in 18 U.S.C., Sections 241-242, specifically enacted early this century to protect American citizens from being abused by local, county, state and federal officials, including Justice Department lawyers. More than 50 years of case law has accumulated stressing the protective nature of these two civil rights sections. The Supreme Court has long held these two sections to be a protective cover for journalists.

So it was my opinion, strongly voiced to the defense team, that outrageous government conduct should also be considered as a defense, giving them the ability to, pre-trial, appeal any adverse ruling of Judge Joanna Seybert—who seemed to regard the Sanders Gang as the modern incarnation of Bonnie and Clyde. After extensive research into where the Supreme Court was mentally headed on outrageous conduct rulings, it was the unanimous legal opinion that the Court had effectively removed the right not to be tried from the American legal landscape.

To attempt to revive it risked further alienating the federal court and an even more antagonistic reception at the bar of "justice." So we reluctantly agreed to follow legal counsel's advice. It was the correct decision.

32

THE INFIDEL RESPONDS

I hold the firm conviction that those I was forced to deal with in the Justice Department, FBI and NTSB were, by definition, the "Infidel." In this case, constitutional Infidel; i.e., someone committed to subverting the Constitution.

Ben Campbell, the prosecutor assigned to use the federal judiciary to complete the neutralization of the Sanders Gang, fit the role nicely. As someone who has trouble looking you in the eye when not buttressed by the courtroom legal setting, Campbell had been part of the Department of Justice team that violated virtually all its own rules and regulations in pursuit of my wife and of me, then proceeded to violate a substantial number of federal felony sections in the effort to destroy before being destroyed.

Campbell's use of the awesome power of the government for illegal purposes was thinly disguised in his response to our pre-trial discovery motion:

> On March 10, 1997, the *Press-Enterprise* newspaper of Riverside, California published a series of articles concerning the crash of TWA Flight 800. In those articles, the defendant James Sanders was quoted and interviewed about his theory that a United States Navy missile accidentally shot down TWA 800.[1]

The second sentence, in its entirety, is factually false. I was "quoted and interviewed" exclusively about my theory that the FBI and NTSB were deliberately mishandling the investigation to hide the real cause of the 747's demise—that a missile brought the plane down. Nowhere in any of these articles is the U.S. Navy mentioned, much less discussed in detail as alleged. Campbell resorts to this subterfuge in order to avoid placing before the judge confirmation of the intense battle I found myself in with the Justice Department.

Benton Campbell lied to the judge when he wrote: "... Sanders, who was identified in the articles alternatively as an accident investigator, a former police officer, and a freelance author, told the *Press-Enterprise* reporters that he was in possession of pieces of the wreckage from TWA 800."[2]

I was identified on page one, above the fold, as an "investigative reporter." The article then, in great detail, laid out my investigation of the FBI. Buried inside other articles was the additional information about my background. The reason for this statement within the Justice Department's brief was their need to paint a picture for the judge of an honest government investigation of an individual who was nothing more than an amateur sleuth throwing wild accusations at the government.

"After the publication of the *Press-Enterprise* articles," Campbell continued, "the FBI initiated an investigation into the removal of pieces of the wreckage of TWA 800 from the hangar at Calverton, New York. That investigation ultimately lead agents to the TWA pilot Terrell Stacey, who was a member of the NTSB investigative team at the Calverton Hangar. Stacey was involved in the TWA 800 investigation through the NTSB's 'party' system. ... FBI agents interviewed Stacey in June 1997. During that interview, Stacey identified James and Elizabeth Sanders as the individuals who asked him to steal pieces of the wreckage of TWA 800. Stacey stated that he reluctantly complied with their requests in January 1997 and mailed some pieces of fabric from seats inside the plane to James Sanders at his residence in Williamsburg, Virginia.

"In addition to interviewing persons connected with the

case, FBI agents also obtained a subpoena for the telephone records of the defendant James Sanders in March 1997. That subpoena was initially served on Bell Atlantic, which provided the records a short time later. After learning of the subpoena, the defendant James Sanders asserted, through his attorney, that he was a member of the media and that the subpoena was unauthorized. … [T]he government ultimately learned from a public announcement from Zebra publishing that the defendant was writing a book about the cause of the crash of TWA 800. Upon discovering this information, the government determined that James Sanders qualified as a member of the media and sought nunc pro tunc [similar to receiving forgiveness for sinning] authorization from the Department of Justice to subpoena his telephone records. Approval was granted on August 1, 1997."

The Justice Department had now placed its scheme to complete my "neutralization" before the Court. They knew I was an "investigative reporter" the instant they learned my name. The *Press-Enterprise* article, page one, paragraph three, says "investigative reporter James Sanders. …" One would have to go far beyond the legal concept of "willful blindness" to avoid the immediate knowledge that I was a working journalist, within seconds of beginning to read the article. So the Justice Department formulated a new legal avoidance theory: selective dyslexia. Until the eve of the trial, "Justice" could not see "investigative reporter" to the immediate left of my name.

Upon learning of the illegal seizure of our phone records, Jeff Schlanger, our attorney at the time, fired off a letter to the Department demanding the phone records "be recalled immediately," and that any responsive records that have already been produced "be sealed and held by an appropriate Court."[3]

Department of Justice lawyers Valerie Caproni and Ben Campbell responded:

... You ground your unusual request on your [belief] that Mr. Sanders is a member of the media and that the subpoena for his telephone records was served in violation of Department of Justice guidelines as set forth in 28 C.F.R., section 50.10, and *Branzburg v. Hayes*. ...

We can find no support for the assertion that Mr. Sanders is a member of the media. We would note that in the articles that were published in the *Press-Enterprise* James Sanders is identified as a "Virginia-based writer and a retired Southern California policeman." All indications from the article are that Mr. Sanders was simply a source of information—not a colleague. Furthermore, Mr. Sanders has a byline on none of the articles in which his allegation that missile fuel [sic] was found within the TWA crash debris was discussed. At a minimum, it would be highly unusual for a member of the media to forego any credit for a story such as this. The fact that he received no journalistic credit for his allegations persuaded us that his claim to be a member of the media is nothing more that [sic] an attempt to shield himself from a legitimate grand jury inquiry. Nonetheless, in a further effort to ascertain whether Mr. Sanders is a "member of the media" as that term is commonly understood,[4] we and the FBI ran database checks on his name. Those checks revealed no article, in any newspaper and magazine covered by WESTLAW or LEXIS/NEXIS,[5] in which Mr. Sanders had a byline. In short, we can find no evidence to support Mr. Sanders' contention that he is a member of the media. ...

Why would the Justice Department feel compelled to lie to the Court when they knew the Court was being provided with an original March 10, 1997, *Press-Enterprise* newspaper article proving beyond any doubt that the government was knowingly presenting the Court false information?

Because they had no choice at this point in their scheme. And, apparently, because they knew they could do it without reprisal from the judicial system. They were counting on the judiciary being part of the prosecution team. They were betting on it.

In 1980 Congress threatened to enact legislation defining illegal FBI and Justice Department actions, when taken against a journalist. This threatened legislation was strenuously opposed, with the Department pleading that such a law would be too much of a burden on "the people." So Congress mandated that a new section be added to the Code of Federal Regulations [CFR] that those who were empowered to enforce and prosecute the laws of the United States would abide by when dealing with journalists:

> 50.10. Policy with regard to the issuance of subpoenas to members of the news media, subpoenas for telephone records of members of the news media, and the interrogation, indictment, or arrest of, members of the news media.
>
> Because freedom of the press can be no broader than the freedom of reporters to investigate and report the news, the prosecutorial power of the government should not be used in such a way that it impairs a reporter's responsibility to cover as broadly as possible controversial public issues. This policy statement is thus intended to provide protection for the news media from forms of compulsory process, whether civil or criminal, which might impair the news gathering function. In balancing the concern that the Department of Justice has for the work of the news media and the Department's obligation to the fair administration of justice, the following guideline *shall* be adhered to by all members of the Department in *all* cases[6] [Emphasis added]:
>
> (a) In determining whether to request issuance of a subpoena to a member of the news media, or for the telephone toll records of any member of the news media, the approach in every case must be to strike the proper balance between the public's interest in effective law enforcement and the fair administration of justice.

(b)All reasonable attempts should be made to obtain information from alternative sources before considering issuing a subpoena to a member of the news media, and similarly all reasonable alternative investigative steps should be taken before considering issuing a subpoena for telephone toll records of any member of the news media.

(c) Negotiations with the media *shall* be pursued in *all* cases in which a subpoena to a member of the news media is contemplated. These negotiations should attempt to accommodate the interests of the trial or grand jury with the interests of the media. Where the nature of the investigation permits, the government should make clear what its needs are in a particular case as well as its willingness to respond to particular problems of the media.

(d) Negotiations with the affected member of the news media *shall* be pursued in *all* cases in which a subpoena for the telephone toll records of any member of the news media is contemplated where the responsible Assistant Attorney General determines that such negotiations would not pose a substantial threat to the integrity of the investigation in connection with which the records are sought. Such determination shall be reviewed by the Attorney General when considering a subpoena authorized under paragraph (e) of this section.

(e) No subpoena may be issued to any member of the news media or for the telephone toll records of any member of the news media without the express authorization of the Attorney General. ...

(f) In requesting the Attorney General's authorization for a subpoena to a member of the news media, the following principles will apply:

(1)In criminal cases, there should be reasonable grounds to believe, based on information *obtained from nonmedia sources*, that a crime has occurred.

(2)When there have been negotiations with a member of the news media whose telephone records are to be subpoenaed, the member shall be given *reasonable and timely notice* of the determination of the Attorney General to authorize the subpoena and that the government intends to issue it.

"Reasonable and timely notice" is mandatory in order to allow the journalist time to go to court, obtain a temporary injunction and schedule a hearing in which the Justice Department and journalist will square-off before a federal judge.

Case law in the Second Circuit makes it all but impossible for the Justice Department to win such a court fight—which is why they violated every CFR regulation cited above and secretly issued a third-party subpoena to the phone company in order to improperly obtain the identity of my source within the investigation. Then, in August 1997, after being caught improperly seizing our phone records, Attorney General Janet Reno authorized the second seizure of our phone records through the use of another third-party subpoena, in order to avoid the unpleasantness of having to justify their actions to a federal judge.

The government did not follow the rules because it could not without placing at risk senior people within the government. The Attorney General does not casually become personally entwined in such a scheme without direction from those above her that have been placed at risk. The alternative was to have Ben Campbell present factually false information in the Justice Department opposition to discovery.

The Justice Department opposition to discovery continued:

The defendants James and Elizabeth Sanders seek an order granting discovery on claims of selective and vindictive prosecution. The authorities from the Supreme Court on down have uniformly held that, in order to obtain such discovery, a defendant must make a substantial and credible preliminary showing based on some evidence of selective or vindictive prosecution. The Sanders have utterly failed to meet these requirements. For the reasons discussed below, the defendants' request should be denied. ...

... The Court crafted a demanding preliminary requirement that those seeking discovery on these claims must make at least a "credible showing of different treatment of similarly situated persons" to "establish a colorable basis for a finding of discriminatory effect and consequently become eligible for discovery." ...

The Second Circuit has echoed these requirements, stating that "in order to show what has been described by the Third Circuit as a colorable basis entitling the defense to subpena [sic] documentary evidence required to establish a selective prosecution defense, we would first require some evidence tending to show the existence of the essential elements of the defense and that the documents in the government's possession would indeed be probative of these elements." ...

Judicial deference for prosecutorial decisions stems in part from the relative competence of the prosecutors and the courts to assess the strengths of cases and the deterrence value of prosecution and, in part, on the judiciary's concern "not to unnecessarily impair the performance of a core executive function." ... As the Court stated, "examining the basis of a prosecution delays the criminal proceeding, threatens to chill law enforcement by subjecting the prosecutor's motives and decisionmaking to outside inquiry, and may undermine prosecutorial effectiveness by revealing the government's enforcement policy." ...

The Sanders have completely failed to meet these rigorous standards. Turning first to their request for discovery in support of their claim of selective prosecution, it quickly becomes apparent that their requests are not supported by a credible showing of some evidence but, rather, are the product of conjecture, "mere assumptions" and "generalized proffers based on information and belief." ... Neither of the defendants specifically identifies what documents or items they are requesting, additional evidence of the unsupported nature of their claims and their desire to engage in a wholesale "fishing expedition" into the government's evidence.[7]

Putting aside the poor sentence structure of running two incomplete thoughts together and the misspelling, Campbell's statement required the judge, at this point, to choose a route as she prepared her decision. In order to back the Justice Department position, the judge would have to sign on to the new legal theory used to obtain an indictment and argue against discovery that would place the government at risk: selective dyslexia.

It is not conjecture that the Justice Department violated its own internal rules in order to avoid going to court and losing the right to gain access to our phone records. Nor is it conjecture that they violated CFR 50.10 to improperly obtain a subpoena to compel my appearance before a grand jury. It is not conjecture that Justice Department violation of CFR 50.10 resulted in the violation of my civil rights, 18 U.S.C., Section 241 (a felony in itself), which prohibits the Justice Department from harassing, intimidating, injuring or otherwise obstructing a journalist's pursuit of evidence of government misconduct. It is not conjecture that the FBI violated the constitutional rights of my wife and I when they paraded us before throngs of media, with our hands bound behind our backs. Nor is it conjecture that the FBI maliciously vilified and injured us on December 5, 1997, in its press release announcing the issuing of arrest warrants.

These facts are reduced to conjecture only through the use of selective dyslexia, the inability to see "investigative reporter" to the left of my name in the March 10, 1997, *Press-Enterprise* article. The massive fog of selective dyslexia must also blot out the 30-plus column inches devoted to describing in detail my pursuit of evidence of illegal government conduct within the Flight 800 investigation. These facts had to be removed before the Justice Department could legally make its discovery presentation to the Court.

Campbell's narrative droned on:

… In order to advance a claim of selective prosecution, a defendant must "establish that (1) while others similarly situated have not been proceeded against, he has been singled out for prosecution, and (2) the government's selection of him for prosecution was based on an impermissible consideration such as race, religion or the exercise of constitutional rights." …

The Sanders have failed to meet their burden on both components of the selective prosecution defense. As an initial matter, the defendants have not made any credible showing that other persons situated similarly to them were not prosecuted for the unauthorized removal of parts from the wreckage of a downed civilian aircraft.[8]

The only "persons similarly situated" would be journalists receiving debris in order to have it tested, as part of an investigative effort uncovering criminal conduct within an airplane crash investigation. Further, "persons similarly situated" would have had to obtain this potential forensic evidence in a manner that did not constitute obstruction of justice; i.e., a government claim that the debris was a unique, irreplaceable part of the investigative puzzle. No such "persons similarly situated" have ever, in the history of the United States, been prosecuted.

Campbell's tactic was to advance the prosecution claim that this was only a case about theft. No other legal consideration existed:

In support of their claim, the defendants advance only the argument that, since 49 U.S.C. 1155(b) was enacted in response to "numerous instances" where souvenir hunters and others removed parts of aircraft wreckage, "it is reasonable to assume" that there must be many examples of such activity since the passage of the statute. The defendants cite no instance, however, where individuals were not prosecuted for taking pieces of aircraft wreckage.[9]

It's an irrational argument. No journalist has ever been indicted under this section. No similarly situated individual exists.

Campbell then began to enter into new forbidden territory, hiding exculpatory material from the defense:

> The Sanders' assertions that they were selectively prosecuted because FBI Assistant Director James Kallstrom was not charged for presenting an American flag to the son of a victim who was killed in the crash of TWA 800 are meritless and unavailing. 49 U.S.C. 1155(b) prohibits *unauthorized* removal of parts of the wreckage. ...[10] [Emphasis added.]

The Justice Department knew when this was written that there was much more to this story that had to be hidden from me if the government wished to keep us under indictment. Multiple Navy divers conspired to remove this flag from the ocean floor without first putting it through the established processing procedure. The flag was not taken to the Calverton hangar, photographed and entered into the NTSB debris-field computer. Nor was it tested for possible explosive residue. The divers secreted the flag out of the investigative area and eventually gave it to Jim Kallstrom, who did not admonish them for this indiscretion, no matter how well intentioned. Instead, Kallstrom aided and abetted this conspiracy to withhold evidence from the NTSB.

Kallstrom, it should be noted, was not legally in charge of the crash investigation. The NTSB, by law, controls all airplane crash investigations. In 1973 the FBI and NTSB established written procedures, a memorandum of understanding (MOU), establishing when the NTSB would cease to be the "lead" agency when the FBI found enough evidence to declare that a crime had occurred. That never occurred during the course of the Flight 800 investigation.

Therefore, Kallstrom was subordinate to the NTSB, requiring their approval before keeping a piece of Flight 800 debris for his personal use. Patricia Milton's book, *In the Blink of an Eye*, published in July 1999, reveals this criminal activity on the part of Kallstrom. He and the Navy divers were "persons similarly situated" to the Sanders in the sense that there was a piece of wreckage they wished to remove from the crash scene without prior NTSB approval, and for their own personal use.

Title 49 U.S.C., which gives the NTSB priority investigative status, also provides a civil remedy for such conduct by persons officially attached to the investigation. The civil remedy can be as light as a verbal warning or as heavy as a $1,000 fine. This was the proper, legal remedy for Kallstrom, the Navy divers *and* Terry Stacey.

But the government could not use the procedure mandated by law because we could not be charged with conspiracy if Terry Stacey's act of removing the residue was a civil rather than criminal act. When the government moved criminally against Stacey, my wife, and me, it made Kallstrom and the Navy divers actions criminal as well. But those criminal acts were not prosecuted, although well known to the Justice Department.

One of Ben Campbell's priorities in the development of the prosecution's opposition to discovery was to hide this information from us. It was Brady Material; i.e., exculpatory evidence, and should have been immediately made available to us. Its revelation, however, would give the judge no choice; the case would have to be dismissed. So a decision was made by the same people who had committed so many felony violations in pursuit of the Sanders Gang—the exculpatory evidence would not be revealed. Campbell continued:

Even assuming, however, that the Sanders are correct that a chronology of events can provide a basis for inferring improper animus, the defendants' chronology does not meet that requirement. As an initial matter, the Sanders point to the publication in the Riverside, California *Press-Enterprise* discussing James Sanders' theory that a U.S. Navy missile accidentally shot down TWA. The Sanders assert that it was the embarrassment of this article and James Sanders' conclusions about the cause of the crash which lead to this indictment.[11]

Again, there is absolutely no mention of the U.S. Navy being involved in an accidental shootdown in this series of articles, only that it was a missile that brought down Flight 800. Criminal acts were being committed by federal officials which, when exposed by me, placed them at risk. Government embarrassment was not the issue. Government criminality was.

Campbell strained to create a substantial reason for the Justice Department's actions against us, one the judge could glom onto:

What the Sanders' quickly gloss over, however, is the fact that the article clearly indicated that James Sanders was in possession of pieces of the wreckage of TWA 800. The secure storage facility inside the hangar at the Grumman Aircraft Facility on [sic] Calverton, Long Island was the only source for those items. The *Press-Enterprise* article raised serious doubts about the security of that location. In the article, Sanders did not tell the interviewing reporter how many pieces of the plane he had, how he obtained the items, what he had done with them, or who his "source" was inside the NTSB/FBI investigation.[12]

This entire strange paragraph is factually false. Straining to continue to mislead the judge, Campbell attempted to reduce my participation in the development of the articles to the level of an interviewee, rather than a journalist. The *Press-Enterprise* was aware of my source within the Calverton hangar and interviewed Stacey on two occasions.

The newspaper knew precisely how many pieces of residue I received and how they were obtained. Terry Stacey personally gave the newspaper this corroborating information. In fact, both pieces of residue were pictured in the article.

And, the *Press-Enterprise*, in the course of the cooperative investigation with me, retained a First Amendment attorney for the express purpose of researching legal issues pertaining to the residue. The attorney reported back that I may very well be placed in a position of going before a grand jury and revealing my source or face contempt and jail time. I was covered by the Freedom of the Press clause, the First Amendment attorney said, with one proviso: the attorney could not give a legal opinion on the probability the government would abuse its power and attack the messenger.

Also, it is irrelevant whether "serious doubts about the security of" the Calverton hangar were revealed. A journalist has an obligation to overcome obstructions created to hide criminal acts of government officials.

> The information Sanders provided to the *Press-Enterprise* reporters indicated that potential violations of federal law, including 49 U.S.C. 1155(b), theft of government property, and obstruction of justice, had occurred and that an investigation was warranted."[13]

Campbell concluded. The Justice Department admitted to Jeff Schlanger, our attorney as of March 13, 1997—and a former prosecutor with excellent contacts within the Justice Department—that they did not know of the Title 49 section when the investigation was initiated March 10, 1997.

"Theft of government property," contrary to Ben Campbell's egregious attempt to misrepresent the law, is not part of Title 49. Theft of government property would come under Title 18, Section 641. Journalists, via long-established precedence, are shielded from enforcement of this law and conspiracy violation when obtaining "government property" during the course of a journalistic investigation.

The more important point, however, is that the "potential violations of federal law" uncovered by the *Press-Enterprise* articles, were felony violations of law committed by government agents within the investigation. That is what prompted the government's hysterical response to forensic evidence outside their control.

> The Sanders also spend a great deal of time discussing James Sanders' status as a member of the media and his allegations that the government violated its own internal policies in subpoenaing his telephone toll records as evidence of improper government animus. Contrary to James Sanders' claims, the March 10, 1997 article did not clearly identify him as a member of the media. ...

This fallacious statement, so necessary to the survival of the government scheme, repeatedly surfaced in Ben Campbell's writing. Using the maxim that if you repeat a lie often enough, it will be believed, Campbell continued to stomp over the rule of law:

> The Sanders' repeated and vehement claims that the government violated its own policies in its zeal to prosecute them ring hollow, particularly given the ten-month period which elapsed between the March 10, 1997 article and the defendants' indictment in January 1998.[14]

This is an irrational sentence. The length of time between Justice Department violation of CFR 50.10 and our indictment does not magically expunge government illegality from the record except, perhaps, in the mind of Ben Campbell.

Campbell soldiers on, attempting to create a rational argument where none exists:

Moreover, even if the Sanders assumptions were correct that the government violated internal policies in the course of this prosecution, that fact is insufficient to meet the standard justifying an order of discovery on a selective or vindictive prosecution claim.

Conspicuously absent from the Sanders' arguments about the government's motivation in this case is any discussion of the numerous other persons who have expressed opinions and views consistent with James Sanders' position that an errant United States Navy missile shot down TWA 800. None of these persons have been prosecuted for their views and opinions about the cause of the disaster.[15]

Campbell's practice of repetitious misinformation in an attempt to create a diaphanous façade of government reasonableness, continued on:

...[T]he Sanders have not provided any evidence that this prosecution is motivated by a "genuine animus," the requirement of the first prong of a vindictive prosecution claim. Their myopic view that the indictment is based upon a desire to retaliate for James Sanders' views about the cause of the crash of TWA 800 are unpersuasive for the reasons noted earlier, the nature of the investigation, the lack of "vindictive" prosecutions against others expressing similar views, and the clear presence of sufficient probable cause to indicate a violation of 49 U.S.C. Section 1155(b) and other federal statutes. ...

The Sanders argue that the fact that [sic] they were engaged in news gathering activities invokes the First Amendment and entitles them to the discovery they seek. The defendants fail to recognize, however, that the First Amendment does not extend any protection to those who engage in illegal activity.[16]

And more Campbell:

Even if the defendants' claims are accepted that they were

engaged in activities connected with the First Amendment—a conclusion that the government is not prepared to concede, particularly with regard to Elizabeth Sanders—that does not translate into immunity from prosecution for their criminal acts.[17]

So it is Campbell's view that it's a crime to investigate the government.

The weight of authority makes it clear that "where we are concerned with the exercise of prosecutorial discretion and 'speech" and "nonspeech" elements are combined in the same course of conduct, a sufficiently important governmental interest in regulating the nonspeech element can justify *incidental limitation* on First Amendment freedoms.[18] [Emphasis added.]

[The statute] is clearly motivated ... by the desire to *prevent interference* with investigations into the cause of the crash of civilian airliners. ... There is little question that 49 U.S.C. Section 1155(b) involves important governmental interests including ... *avoiding interference* with an investigation into the cause of an airplane crash. These interests more than justify the incidental and minimal limitation on First Amendment freedoms imposed by the statute.[19] [Emphasis added]

... The defendants must provide a credible showing of some evidence to support their claims before they are entitled to additional discovery materials. This they have not and can not do.[20]

Thus, the government's representative concluded. Only a bureaucrat with the mindset that it's the right of the State to control information could possibly allege that this case represented an "incidental limitation on First Amendment freedoms." In direct conflict with Constitutional law, the government, in effect, was claiming it has the right to tell you what to think, and will not tolerate "interference" from the press because the government mandates that they cannot do it.

33

CLINTON ADMINISTRATION "POLICE-STATE TACTICS"

As major media becomes ever more politicized, Internet news services such as *WorldNet Daily* and *NewsMax* have assumed the responsibility of informing We The People.

The *NewsMax* headline said, "Clinton Mind Control at the CIA—Congressman Burton Stunned by Intimidation Tactics." It was a short story, revealing a thug-like mentality permeating the bureaucracy in the closing months of the 20th century:

Today's top *NewsMax* headline story, "FBI Whistleblower Sues White House, FBI," is not an isolated one.

There have been dozens of examples of the Clinton administration using [police-state] tactics against government whistleblowers.

FBI agent Sculimbrene's account is indeed horrifying. Though the most senior FBI agent at the White House, he was subjected to drug tests, demands for psychiatric examinations and threats to his job—all because he wouldn't go along with the party line.

One of the things that irritated the Clintons was Sculimbrene's decision to testify as a character witness on behalf of former White House Travel Office chief Billy Dale. At the time, the Clintons were trying to put Dale in jail on trumped-up charges.

And then there were more: Remember the two secret service agents who testified to Congress that the administration lied when they claimed nearly 1,000 FBI files were taken by the White House because of a "bureaucratic snafu"? The agents were quickly put under investigation within their agency.

Apparently, the Clintons' inquisition against opponents is permeating many federal agencies, including the nation's security agencies.

This past summer, Rep. Dan Burton, chairman of the House government Reform and Oversight Committee, held hearings on "Retaliation at the Department of Defense and Energy: Do Advocates of Tighter Security for U.S. Technology Face Intimidation?"

NewsMax.com has obtained a copy of some of the testimony given before Burton's committee on June 24, 1999.

Republican Rep. Curt Weldon told the committee there were "a couple of cases" of intimidation at the CIA, including one agent who "will not show [at the committee hearing] because his career is still in jeopardy."

Weldon said the agent "revealed to his superiors that an intelligence leak was occurring in Somalia that compromised U.S. security."

Because "he was doing his job" by warning about the transfer of classified material, Weldon said the career CIA agent "was asked to submit to a drug test, a medical exam for brain tumors, and a psychiatric evaluation."

Burton was clearly shocked by Weldon's report: "I have heard of that kind of activity in Russia, where they used to charge people with crimes against the state and commit them to psychiatric institutions. I have never heard of a professional intelligence analyst in this country being asked to undergo a psychiatric examination."

Congressman Burton should get outside the Beltway more often. He would be equally shocked to learn that such tactics are not reserved for dissident CIA officers.

34

DEFENSE, FINAL DISCOVERY

After digesting the Justice Department's, arrogant, jingoistic bluster in opposition to discovery, the defense team prepared a response, confident the government had stepped far beyond the envelope of truth and reasoned debate:

In our opening memorandum we pointed to substantial evidence that supports the conclusion that the government's actions against James and Elizabeth Sanders—culminating in an unprecedented prosecution of them for their alleged roles as accessories to a removal of valueless scraps of fabric from an aviation accident investigation site—were motivated by animus arising from Mr. Sanders' exercise of his constitutionally-protected right to publish information regarding the cause of the TWA Flight 800 tragedy, and to disseminate his conclusion that governmental investigators (including the FBI officials involved in the present prosecution) had concealed that information from the public. As we demonstrated, immediately after Mr. Sanders' views were published in an article that prominently identified Mr. Sanders as an investigative reporter and author, Justice Department officials, disregarding their own First Amendment-based policies, launched an aggressive campaign to uncover Mr. Sanders' confidential source within the official FBI-NTSB investigation. When Mr. and Mrs. Sanders refused to yield to the government's demands for information, the prosecutors followed through on their threats to indict them.

These actions, coupled with evidence that the government has a motive to discredit Mr. Sanders conclusions, and has in fact used this prosecution as a vehicle for accomplishing that purpose, tends to establish that the present matter would not be before this Court in the absence of an improper motive to suppress or penalize constitutionally-protected speech. That conclusion is further supported by the fact (now acknowledged in the government's response) that FBI Assistant Director James Kallstrom removed property from the wreckage, but has not been prosecuted or sanctioned in any way. As we will show, the government's response, including its identification of a single prior prosecution under 49 U.S.C., Section 1155, fails to defeat our threshold showing of "some evidence" tending to establish the essential elements of a claim of vindictive or selective prosecution. Accordingly, the defense is entitled to discovery related to these defenses. ...

Prior to the last conference before the Court, counsel for the defense conferred with Assistant United States Attorney Benton Campbell in an effort to resolve disputes with the government regarding our original discovery requests and thereby avoid the necessity for judicial intervention. During that conference, the government opposed all requests for documents and information relating to the government's motive for prosecuting Mr. and Mrs. Sanders, and all parties agreed that it would be necessary to litigate the present motion, and thereby clarify the general parameters of discovery, before continuing our efforts to reach agreement with the government as to particular requests.[1]

While the government "is not prepared to concede" that Mr. and Mrs. Sanders were engaged in actions protected by the First Amendment ... it offers no arguments in opposition to that contention, and it does not purport to suggest that Mr. Sanders acted with any purpose other than to gather information to be disseminated to the public, or that Mrs. Sanders acted with any purpose other than to assist her husband in that pursuit. Nonetheless, the government insists that Mr. and Mrs. Sanders "are being prosecuted for the crime that they committed, not the opinions James Sanders has advocated." That assertion is belied, however, by the Justice Department's own December 5, 1997, press release regarding the initiation of criminal charges against Mr. and Mrs. Sanders. The press release summarizes the criminal complaint's gratuitous and misleading assertions that the laboratory testing of the residue samples submitted by Mr. Sanders "provided no conclusive evidence of the presence of solid rocket fuel" and that "JAMES SANDERS misrepresented those results in media reports for which he was a source." Immediately after this effort to discredit Mr. Sanders and his published conclusions, the government's press release offers the following statement by James V llstrom, Assistant Director in charge of the New York FBI office:

This criminal investigation is far from over. *These defendants are charged with not only committing a serious crime, they have also increased the pain already inflicted on the victim's families.* This investigation will continue in an effort to identify any other individuals who may have played a role in this scheme. [Emphasis added]

Short of a signed confession, there could hardly be clearer proof that the present prosecution is indeed directed against "the opinions James Sanders has advocated." Mr. Kallstrom's reference to the "pain … inflicted on the victim's families" plainly does not relate to the removal of material from the airplane wreckage. (Was the arrest of the truck driver who removed parts from the downed Valujet plane accompanied by a press release accusing him of causing such pain?) On the contrary, it obviously relates to Mr. Sanders' propagation of the view that a missile caused the crash, and to the corollary suggestion that, notwithstanding Mr. Kallstrom's repeated assurances to the contrary … the victims could not take comfort in the belief that the massive government investigation that he headed thoroughly and conclusively laid the missile theory to rest. This statement of a high-ranking official of the agency that referred this case for criminal charges, implicitly endorsed and issued by the Department of Justice, constitutes direct evidence of the speech-based animus underlying the present prosecution.

During the December 5, 1997, broadcast of the NBC Nightly News, which included on-air statements by Kallstrom, correspondent Robert Hager reported that, "Tonight, the FBI says its investigation isn't finished, says still more may have been involved in what it calls *"a plot to rewrite the history of TWA 800."* [Emphasis added] This remark further reveals that the investigation and prosecution of the Sanders was motivated by the government's reaction to the content of Mr. Sanders' publicly-expressed views.[2]

Further evidence obtained by the defense ... demonstrates the depth of the government's motivation to discredit Mr. Sanders' published conclusions regarding the content of the red residue that appears in a portion of the airplane's cabin. In remarks to a Congressional subcommittee immediately after publication of the *Press-Enterprise* article reporting Mr. Sanders' conclusion that the red residue trail was caused by missile fuel, NTSB head Bernard Loeb "categorically" denied the existence of such a trail (which the government has since acknowledged), and asserted that "we believe that the red residue material is an adhesive." The claim that the residue comes from glue has been reiterated in numerous public statements and documents, including Mr. Kallstrom's November 18, 1997, press conference and Agent Kinsley's December 5, 1997, affidavit in support of the Sanders' arrest.

These claims were premised on a report of the NTSB Fire and Explosion Team, headed by Dr. Merritt Birky, that purported to summarize testing of "reddish brown" material from selected seat-back panels in rows 17, 19 and 27, by infrared spectroscopy at a NASA lab. That report asserted that this analysis "showed the material to be consistent with a polychloroprene 3M Scotch-Grip 1357 High Performance contact adhesive."[3] In fact, however, the NTSB lab had reported to the NTSB that "At no time during the analyses of these samples however, was there conclusive evidence to suggest that the Scotch-Grip 1357 High Performance (HP) contact adhesive was polychloroprene-based adhesive specifically used in any of these applications."[4] Furthermore, Charles Bassett, the NASA scientist who tested the residue samples forwarded to him by Dr. Birky, has not only stated that his tests do not support the conclusion that the residue was caused by the 3M adhesive, but has indicated that the 3M adhesive could not be the source of the red residue because that adhesive, when cured, is green or olive drab and, when subjected to heat, turns various shades of green and brown, but not red. ...

Thus, the government's repeated efforts to discredit Mr. Sanders' conclusions about the source of the red residue by insisting that the source of that residue has definitively been determined to be an adhesive, are based on a misrepresentation of the results of laboratory analyses. The government's willingness to make such misrepresentations in order to discredit Mr. Sanders' conclusions, and thereby assure the public that there is an innocuous explanation for the reddish residue trail, adds further, compelling support to the conclusions that the present prosecution is motivated by the government's animus relating to the content of Mr. Sanders' public communications. In this regard, it should be noted that the government has not even attempted to dispute the assertion in our opening papers that the government has consistently sought to dispel the notion that a missile was involved in the Flight 800 crash, and that it has resorted to conflicting explanations in pursuit of that effort.

In response to our argument that such animus can be inferred from the government's violation of its own rules regarding subpoenas to journalists, the government maintains, astonishingly, that "the March 10, 1997, article did not clearly identify [Mr. Sanders] as a member of the media." In making this extraordinary claim, the government obstinately* continues to ignore the fact that the article's *first* reference to Mr. Sanders, in the *second* paragraph of the front page far-left column is as "author and investigative reporter James Sanders," and that three paragraphs later the article describes Mr. Sanders' two previous non-fiction books of investigative journalism. The government also erroneously contends that Mr. Sanders' counsel offered no evidence of 'Mr. Sanders' "media status" in response to an inquiry from the government. On the contrary, while noting that the government's questioning of Mr. Sanders' "media status" failed to recognize that First Amendment protection hinges not on an individual's institutional affiliations, but on his intent to disseminate information,[5] counsel expressly advised the government that Mr. Sanders had acted as a reporter and writer in connection with the March 10th *Press-Enterprise* articles (and that the *Press-Enterprise* would confirm this fact), and also advised the government of a number of other publications in which articles by Mr. Sanders had appeared. In view of the substantial information in the government's possession making clear that Mr. Sanders was acting as a news-gatherer in connection with the information referred to in the *Press-Enterprise* article, the government's bold assertion that it had no basis for recognizing the First Amendment implications of its interactions with Mr. Sanders until his publisher announced that he was writing a book about Flight 800 is preposterous.

[*NOTE: "obstinately" is a polite legal word for "criminal act" committed by a federal prosecutor. If anyone other than an agent of the federal government deliberately lied to a judge in writing, they would be indicted for violation of 18 U.S.C., section 1001, which prohibits such conduct—and for a very obvious reason. But in federal court, it is not possible to accurately describe federal criminal conduct in simple, direct words. The judge, in far too many cases, stands perilously close to being a team player for the Justice Department rather than a neutral party.]

Contrary to the government's memorandum,[6] [case law] does not suggest that the government's violation of Justice Department guidelines can never provide relevant support to a claim of vindictiveness; [the case cited by the prosecution] simply held that, in that particular case, the defendant's allegations of such violations did not suffice to establish that the government's charging decision was vindictive. Here, however, the government's failure to follow its own regulations, its absurd disavowal of awareness that Mr. Sanders was engaged in a journalistic pursuit, and its constricted interpretation of the scope of First Amendment protections incurred in the context of an aggressive effort to expose Mr. Sanders' source and to discredit the information that he had disseminated. In that context, the government's violation of its own policy is a component of a circumstantial showing of vindictiveness.

In an effort to avoid the force of that circumstantial evidence, the government goes so far as to take issue with our position that the government's animus can be demonstrated by a "chronology of events" suggestive of retaliatory intent. ... If circumstantial evidence can establish a defendant's criminal intent sufficiently to deprive him of his liberty, it can surely establish the government's vindictiveness sufficiently to warrant additional discovery on this issue.

Here, however, we have not only presented circumstantial evidence, but, as discussed above, have pointed to direct evidence: an admission of a party to this litigation declaring, in effect, that the present prosecution is intended to punish the defendants for the "pain" caused by their speech. Viewed in conjunction, the direct and circumstantial evidence presented in support of this application constitutes far more than "some evidence" that the government has indicted Mr. and Mrs. Sanders for the purpose of retaliating against, or chilling, their exercise of rights guaranteed by the First Amendment.

In its effort to justify the prosecution of Mr. and Mrs. Sanders and to support its claim that, even absent the government's animus arising from [the Sanders] exercise of First Amendment rights, they would now be facing the same criminal charges, the government's response strains to portray Mr. and Mrs. Sanders' conduct in a sinister light. Thus, the government refers to the Sanders' "persistent instructions" to TWA Captain Terrell Stacey,[7] and asserts that he "reluctantly complied" with their requests. These characterizations, unsupported by any affidavit or other evidentiary showing, stand in stark contrast to Stacey's own statement, under oath, regarding the circumstances leading to his removal of the fabric swatches:

"I was assigned to the investigation immediately after the accident and started working on it. Well, first off I had brought that airplane back in from Paris the day before and had flown that airplane three times in the previous week. And I was assigned to [the] investigation.

We had been there for many months. I was away from the family under a lot of pressure and emotional stress to try to find out the cause of the accident. And when I was given an opportunity or when I—when Mr. Sanders offered to me or the fact that I learned that he could help in the investigation through contacts and people he had in labs, then I on my own volition took the two small pieces and gave them to him to have them analyzed."[8]

Thus, contrary to the government's unsupported insinuation, Stacey's sworn statement makes clear that his decision to remove the fabric samples was not a response to "persistent instructions" by Mr. and Mrs. Sanders, but reflected his own frustration at the failure of the official investigation to determine the cause of the accident. He provided the fabric to Mr. Sanders "on [his] own volition" because Mr. Sanders had the willingness and the ability to pursue a line of investigation that Stacey believed was important, and that the FBI-NTSB investigators were not pursuing. Stacey's statement does not indicate that Elizabeth Sanders played any role whatsoever in his decision to remove the fabric.

Furthermore, while the government's memorandum repeatedly refers to the material removed by Stacey as "pieces of the wreckage," "parts from the wreckage," or simply "the wreckage," the government ultimately recognizes that the material at issue in fact consisted of nothing more than two pieces of seat-backing fabric. The government does not dispute our assertion that these miniscule swatches of material had no intrinsic value, or that Stacey left behind a sufficient quantity of residue-bearing material to permit a full range of testing by the official investigators. The government also does not suggest that the Sanders' purpose in obtaining the samples was anything other than to further Mr. Sanders' journalistic investigation into the cause of the Flight 800 crash.

Viewed fairly and without the government's unsupported characterizations, the Sanders' conduct does not warrant prosecution under 49 U.S.C., Section 1155 any more than that of James Kallstrom, whom the government acknowledges removed a flag from the wreckage to give to the child of a victim. While the government implies that, unlike the removal of material by Stacey, Kallstrom's removal was "authorized," it does not cite any statute or regulation that authorizes an investigator—even a high-ranking FBI official—to distribute "property on the aircraft at the time of the accident" at his own discretion to the relatives of victims; indeed, since aircraft disasters almost invariably have numerous victims, most of whom are likely to have grieving relatives, such "authority" would lead to substantial, indiscriminate pilfering of such property. The government does not suggest that Kallstrom took any formal steps to notify any official body of his intent to remove the flag, or that he sought or received approval for his actions in any way.

The government asserts that Kallstrom's "public presentation of a small flag found in the wreckage to a grieving son at his mother's funeral differs in kind and degree" and that "[a]ny comparison [to the Sanders' actions] is misleading and short-sighted." If the government means to suggest that Kallstrom's conduct does not warrant criminal prosecution because it served a high-minded and worthy purpose, the Sanders' conduct is equally blameless. In seeking to uncover and disseminate the truth about the causes of the Flight 800 disaster, the Sanders were acting in the tradition of the First Amendment, which recognizes the importance of an "untrammeled press as a vital source of public information."[9] Their pursuit of the truth about this tragedy offered comfort not just to a single relative of a victim, but to all of the victims' relatives, as well as to the public at large, which, in a democratic society, has a fundamental interest in obtaining information about important public matters from sources other than government officials.

The government's suggestion that Kallstrom's "public" presentation of the flag distinguishes his conduct from the Sanders' is both puzzling and baseless. James Sanders not only revealed his obtaining of the Flight 800 material in a newspaper article, but wrote and published a book that recounted in detail his receipt and testing of that material. If Kallstrom's openness regarding his actions signifies a lack of culpability, so does Mr. Sanders'. Thus, contrary to the government's argument, Kallstrom's removal of property from Flight 800 establishes that a "similarly situated" person was not prosecuted.

The involvement of participants [such as Terry Stacey] in the NTSB "party program" surely does not provide a meaningful distinction between the present defendants and Kallstrom. If the government has a particular interest in curtailing wrongdoing by civilian participants in an accident investigation, it should have a still greater interest in curtailing wrongdoing by government law enforcement officers involved in such investigations. ...

... The government has pointed to no instances whatsoever in which individuals have been prosecuted under 49 U.S.C., Section 1155 on a theory of accessorial liability. To be truly "similarly situated" to Mr. Sanders, a defendant would have to be a journalist who did no more than express an interest in obtaining an inconsequential quantity of material from a crash site so that it could be analyzed by an independent laboratory, with the purpose of uncovering and publishing the truth about a matter of widespread significance. To be "similarly situated" to Mrs. Sanders, a defendant would have to have done no more than relay a journalist's desire for such material to a participant in the official investigation. ...

The defense has presented substantial evidence that strongly supports the conclusion that, in the absence of an improper motive related directly to the Sanders' exercise of rights guaranteed by the First Amendment, they would not have been prosecuted. Therefore this court should direct the government to provide discovery relating to the defenses of vindictive or selective prosecution.

Our legal team had presented a compelling case in the diplomatic legal writing style required—writing that did not overtly charge the government with criminal acts because that causes too many within the federal judiciary to circle the wagons and overtly join the government team.

The Justice Department, FBI and NTSB had mounted a media offensive that made me out to be a pile of human waste, a writer who preyed on human suffering only to make money. The government schemers said there was absolutely no evidence of a missile. They shrilly proclaimed the reddish-orange residue to be glue. They loudly declared that I had "misrepresented" West Coast Analytical Services [WCAS] elemental test results.

Now, both sides, in a legal setting, had presented the Court opposing sides of the argument. Our team had presented evidence, in the form of an affidavit from NASA Chemist Charles Bassett, that the FBI and NTSB had lied about the residue being glue. The Justice Department had not been able to counter with any document from the FBI lab, or any other source, countering this stunning evidence of FBI and NTSB culpability.

Our team had presented evidence that the Justice Department violated its internal regulations, mandated by Congress in 1980. Our lawyers had also presented compelling evidence that Ben Campbell, the Justice Department prosecutor assigned the case, had, in the written opposition to our motion for discovery, lied to the Court in order to avoid admitting that the Justice Department had indeed violated its own Code of Federal Regulations by selectively ignoring the *Press-Enterprise* article clearly identifying me as an "investigative reporter." At one time in American history, lying to the Court was a felony.

Now that Judge Joanna Seybert had the written arguments

in front of her, she had a decision to make. The government could not survive even limited discovery. The government scheme was in imminent peril and needed judicial protection in order not to be publicly exposed.

Justice, in a nation that adheres to the rule-of-law, mandates that a level field of battle be maintained. At this stage of the proceedings, the degree of discovery was the means by which the judge could ensure fairness.

35

THE JUDGE'S OPINION

Federal Judge Joanna Seybert had not yet begun to write her opinion by the date oral arguments were scheduled. She walked into the courtroom, sat in the high-back leather chair, turned to Benton Campbell and said words to the effect, "excellent brief." No such compliment was given to our attorneys. She then admitted she had not yet had time to do more than briefly scan the written briefs.

Nonetheless, she was prepared to issue a ruling. Our legal team was treated curtly, but pressed on in the face of a judge who did not wish to entertain a serious debate of the compelling issues before her. The prosecution sensed—or knew—not to be drawn into a debate by the defense. The judge then ruled against any discovery, saying she would mail her written decision within a few weeks.

She then attempted to roll over our right to file motions for dismissal prior to trial, suggesting in effect that the Court proceed with the hanging. She wanted the trial to begin in less than two months.

The defense objected, pointing out the right of the defendants to present motions for dismissal prior to trial. Clearly unhappy that the defendants would not just accept their fate, she reluctantly established a timeframe for submitting written arguments for dismissal of the case.

It was in this setting that our lawyers received Judge Joanna Seybert's written explanation for her oral denial of discovery:

Pending before this Court is defendants' joint motion for pre-trial discovery relating to their defenses of selective and vindictive prosecution ... The two-count indictment alleges that between October 1996 and July 1997, the defendants conspired to remove a portion of a seat cushion [sic] from the interior cabin of the now-infamous TWA Flight 800. ... The defendants allegedly sought the material because it contained samples of a reddish-brown residue, which defendant James Sanders believed would prove his theory that a Navy missile was responsible for the downing of Flight 800.

The defendants have jointly moved for discovery pertaining to their claim that the determination to bring charges against them was motivated by the Government's desire to retaliate against them for exercising their First Amendment free-speech rights, as well as to chill those rights. Thus the defendants purport to seek discovery of information and documents in the Governments' [sic] possession that are relevant to the Government's decision-making process and its motives for prosecuting the present case.

As a preliminary matter, the Court must address the defendants' contention that their conduct in obtaining the fabric from the wreckage was protected by a First Amendment "newsgathering" privilege. Under this privilege, defendants contend that the acts the defendants are charged with all relate to the constitutionally-protected process of newsgathering because James Sanders was a freelance journalist and was investigating the crash of Flight 800 for newsgathering purposes. Elizabeth Sanders, in assisting her husband, was also engaged in the newsgathering process.

While the Court recognizes that there is a "reporter's privilege" with respect to certain information subpoenaed in civil and criminal proceedings, this privilege clearly does not apply as a shield against prosecution for violation of laws of general applicability. Indeed, the Supreme Court stated that "the First Amendment does not invalidate every incidental burdening of the press that may result from the enforcement of civil or criminal statutes of general applicability." Thus, the press may not

use First Amendment protection to justify otherwise illegal
actions.[1]

The above represents a giant leap in legal logic as it per-
tains to the First Amendment Freedom of the Press. We were
not charged with entering the Calverton hangar and stealing
residue. Acting in a journalistic capacity, after four-months investigating possible law-breaking within the federal investigation of the TWA Flight 800 crash, I had obtained a volume of
documents and information creating reasonable cause to believe the FBI and NTSB at the senior levels, were in-fact acting
in an illegal manner, obstructing justice, creating a false conclusion to the cause of the accident—serious felony violations.

As part of that investigation of illegal activity, my source
within the hangar revealed that a reddish-orange residue trail
crossed three rows of the 747—the same three rows that were
the first to exit the stricken aircraft. Other journalists with in-
formants inside the hangar were able to confirm Terry Stacey's
revelation.

The FBI had removed residue samples in late August or
early September 1996 and refused to share those results, as
mandated by Title 49. I told Terry Stacey that the residue would
be tested if I received a sample.

The judicial system, for more than 200 years, has consistently said such interaction between a journalist and his source
is '"protected" by the Freedom of the Press "shield." Supreme
Court justices, in writing and in public speeches, have force-
fully described such journalistic conduct as a constitutional
obligation of those who choose journalism for a profession.
Now, for the first time in the history of the United States, the
right of a journalist to freely communicate with his source in
order to aggressively pursue criminal acts of federal officials
was being challenged by the very officials I was investigating.

The issue of obstruction of justice was not involved. The
government did not allege the samples I obtained were unique

and therefore deprived the government of potential evidence of a criminal act. In fact, the Justice Department admitted the removal of the residue did not in any manner impede their "investigation" into the crash of TWA Flight 800.

A federal law has been on the books for decades [18 U.S.C., Section 641] prohibiting anyone from receiving anything owned by the federal government without its express permission. Journalists are not exempted within the words of the statute. Case law says this federal code covers the removal of even one Xerox copy of a document. Yet no journalist has ever been indicted under this law, even though literally thousands of journalists have received copies of documents without federal permission.

Many of these documents, such as the 2,000 pages of documents illegally removed from federal control in the Pentagon Papers case, were recognized by the Supreme Court to have damaged national security. But no journalist has ever been indicted for violating 18 U.S.C., Section 641. Why? Because of the "shield" of protection provided by the constitution's First Amendment Freedom of the Press blocks prosecution for "violation of laws of general applicability."[2]

Judge Joanna Seybert was traveling down a road no federal judge in American history had traveled.

The judge next wrote:

Accordingly, the Court rejects the defendants' argument that they are immune from prosecution for the acts alleged in the indictment on the basis of a newsgathering privilege. The Supreme Court has been clear that the "First Amendment confers no such immunity from prosecution." The Second Circuit has reiterated this principle and found that where the facts involve the exercise of prosecutorial discretion and "speech" and "nonspeech" elements are combined in the same course of conduct, "a sufficiently important governmental interest in *regulating* the nonspeech element can justify *incidental limitations* on First Amendment freedoms.[3] [Emphasis added]

The judge had begun to develop a key theme: Justice Department conduct in its pursuit of my wife and of me amounted to "incidental limitations on [the Sanders'] First Amendment freedoms." It is a specious argument.

It was the Court's opinion that the Justice Department can ignore the congressionally-mandated Code of Federal Regulations calling for a strict set of rules under which the FBI and Justice Department "shall" operate when dealing with a journalist; can violate 18 U.S.C. Section 241 and 242, which offers journalists and others civil rights protection from lawless government acts; and, can treat communication between a journalist and source as a conspiracy.

Having effectively expunged Freedom of the Press from the Constitution, the judge then addressed the second part of the defense discovery motion:

> The Court now turns to defendants' motion for discovery relating to their defenses of selective and vindictive prosecution. ...
> ... The defendants raise a number of arguments attempting to distinguish the prosecution of Gadsden [who was prosecuted for taking a piece from the 1996 ValuJet crash as a souvenir]. For example, they point to the fact that he was also accused of denying having the wreckage parts when interviewed by the FBI. ... In addition, the part stolen by Gadsden was a circuit breaker relevant to the investigation of the crash. Here, however, they claim that their conduct is minimal in comparison because there was ample other [sic] seat portions available for government testing and the fabric was not "vital to the accident investigation." Defendants also suggest that Gadsden's motive for removing the wreckage as a souvenir also falls squarely within the purpose of Section 1155(b) to stop souvenir hunters from carrying off parts of aircraft wreckage. In this case, on the other hand, the parts were taken not as souvenirs,

but to further the investigation of the cause of the explosion."[4]

The last sentence is a factually false repeat of the Justice Department's mantra that was a mandatory part of the government's legal efforts to avoid addressing the factual issues of the case. The primary reason for obtaining and testing the residue was the pursuit of illegal government conduct within the Flight 800 investigation.

The Court then attempted to wrap up its core argument:

> Finally, the Sanders suggest that a distinction exists because they were not the principals who removed the property and the government has failed to uncover any instances of "accessorial liability" under the statute that have been prosecuted. They conclude that to be "similarly situated," a defendant would have to have done no more than relay a journalist's desire for such material to a participant in the official investigation to be prosecuted. The court simply disagrees with this latter assertion. The indictment charges much more than a simple relay of a message from Sanders to Stacey; rather, the indictment charges that the Sanders actively conspired to have the fabric removed from the hangar and delivered to James Sanders.[5]

The final sentence above is factually false. The portion of the indictment dealing with this issue is presented below in its entirety to remove any doubt about who is presenting fact and who is presenting factually false information:

> Count One [indictment, p. 5]. (Conspiracy to Remove Parts of TWA 800 From Calverton)

> 13. On or about and between October 1996 and July 1997, both dates being approximate and inclusive, within the Eastern District of New York and elsewhere, the defendants JAMES SANDERS and ELIZABETH SANDERS and others knowingly and intentionally conspired to remove, conceal and withhold,

without authority, parts of a civil aircraft involved in an accident and property on the aircraft at the time of the accident, in violation of Title 49, United States Code, Section 1155(b).

14. In furtherance of the conspiracy and to effect the objects thereof, the defendants JAMES SANDERS and ELIZABETH SANDERS and their co-conspirators committed and caused to be committed the following:

OVERT ACTS

A. In or about December 1996, JAMES SANDERS asked Terrell Stacey to remove some of the reddish residue from the seats that had been recovered from TWA 800 so that JAMES SANDERS could test the residue for the presence of missile fuel exhaust.

B. In or about December 1996 and January 1997, ELIZABETH SANDERS spoke to Terrell Stacey and asked him to remove a sample of the residue from the seats that had been recovered from TWA 800.

C. In or about January 1997, in Calverton, New York, Terrell Stacey attempted to scrape a portion of the reddish residue from the seats of TWA 800. Being unable to scrape off the residue, Terrell Stacey cut a portion of fabric from the seats on which the reddish residue could be seen.

D. In or about January 1997, Terrell Stacey sent the fabric he had removed from the seats of TWA 800 to JAMES SANDERS at the SANDERS' home in Virginia.

The indictment states only that James Sanders once "asked" Terry Stacey to remove a residue sample for the specific purpose of testing. Elizabeth Sanders' charge was that she "asked" twice. Nothing in the indictment even hints at any other activity.

The Court then moved on, revealing why the above statement was inserted into the record. Without it, the Court could not have made the following ruling:

... the Court finds that the prosecutions of Gadsden and the Sanders are sufficiently similar to convince the Court that the defendants have failed in their efforts to establish evidence tending to support the first prong of a selective prosecution defense.

The Court then addressed the second element in the selective prosecution "test":

The defendants contend that they have provided sufficient evidence to meet their threshold showing that the present prosecution was motivated by a desire to chill the defendants' exercise of rights protected under the First Amendment, or to retaliate against them for exercising those rights. ...

Specifically, the defendants point to the following "evidence" of a discriminatory or retaliatory animus.

[NOTE: Some of the points are factually inaccurate. The actual words, taken from our discovery brief, are inserted in brackets below each point to allow a direct comparison]:

(1) On March 10, 1997, the Riverside *Press-Enterprise* published a front-page story reporting Mr. Sanders' acquisition of a sample of red residue from TWA Flight 800 and his conclusion that the residue was solid missile fuel.

[On March 10, 1997, the Riverside *Press-Enterprise* published a front page article reporting Mr. Sanders' acquisition of a sample of red residue from TWA Flight 800, and his conclusion, *based on laboratory analysis of the sample showing chemicals consistent with solid missile fuel, as well as analysis of the pattern of debris retrieved from the crash site, that a missile had caused the crash.*]

(2)On March 11, 1997, during testimony before the House of Representatives, a senior NTSB official attempted to discredit Mr. Sanders' theory and stated on the record that "there is no such thing as a red residue trail in that airplane." In complete contradiction, FBI Special Agent James Kinsley stated in his affidavit supporting defendants' arrest warrants on December 5, 1997, that "[f]rom Row 17 to Row 28 of the seating area, there is a reddish residue on the metallic frame and backs of the passenger seats" that is "manifested strongly on seats from Rows 17 through 19."

[In testimony before a House of Representatives subcommittee given the day after publication of the *Press-Enterprise* article, a senior NTSB official, Bernard Loeb, attempted to discredit Mr. Sanders' conclusions, and to counter them with the assertion that the red residue was from an "adhesive." That testimony included Mr. Loeb's claim that "one thing I can say categorically is there is no such thing as a red residue trail in that airplane." This "categorical" denial conflicts with the sworn statement of FBI Special Agent James Kinsley in his December 5, 1997, affidavit in support of an arrest warrant that "[f]rom Row 17 to Row 28 of the seating area, there is a reddish residue on the metallic frame and backs of the passenger seats" that is "manifested most strongly on seats from Rows 17 through 19."]

(3) Within hours after the publication of the *Press-Enterprise* article, the FBI initiated aggressive efforts to question Elizabeth Sanders, although she stated that she did not wish to speak with the FBI.

[Within hours after publication of the *Press-Enterprise* article, the FBI initiated aggressive efforts to question Mr. Sanders' wife, Elizabeth Sanders, who had been mentioned in passing and identified as a TWA employee in a related article that appeared on page A-12 of the March 10 *Press-Enterprise*. Despite being advised that Mrs. Sanders did not wish to speak to or meet with the FBI, Special Agent James Kinsley went to her residence in Williamsburg, Virginia, and to the Norfolk Airport, in an apparent effort to intercept her as she returned there from St. Louis.]

Also immediately following the publication of the *Press-Enterprise,* grand jury subpoenas were issued to obtain Mr. Sanders' testimony, as well as toll records from the Sanders' telephone provider, even though it was obvious that Mr. Sanders was acting as a journalist. The Department of Justice concedes that it approved these subpoenas in violation of its own rules regarding seeking subpoenas relating to members of the news media.

[Notwithstanding the prominent discussion of Mr. Sanders' journalistic credentials in the *Press-Enterprise* article ("... author and investigative reporter James Sanders"), and its clear indication he was conducting an independent investigation into the Flight 800 crash for the purpose of disseminating information to the public, grand jury subpoenas were issued seeking Mr. Sanders' testimony, as well as toll records from the Sanders' telephone service provider. By approving these subpoenas, the Justice Department violated its own rules requiring prior authorization by the Attorney General of subpoenas seeking information from or relating to members of the news media; requiring that such subpoenas issue only after alternative investigative steps have been attempted and failed; requiring that, absent "exigent circumstances," they should be limited to verification of published information; and requiring negotiation with the media recipient to ensure that the demand for information is appropriately limited. In a letter to Mr. Sanders' attorney, Assistant United States Attorney Caproni asserted that the government had disregarded those regulations because nothing in the March 10th articles indicated that Mr. Sanders was acting as a journalist. This assertion is preposterous in view of the article's extensive discussion of Mr. Sanders' journalistic credentials . . . .]

(4)In April 1997, prosecutors threatened James Sanders with prosecution if he would not reveal his confidential source within the FBI/NTSB crash investigation. Mr. Sanders refused to cooperate on the basis of his First Amendment rights. At the same meeting, prosecutors also threatened to make Elizabeth Sanders a target if she did not agree to cooperate in the investigation of her husband, even though at that time they had absolutely no evidence of her involvement.

[In April 1997, the government initiated a meeting with Mr. Sanders and his attorney, during which prosecutors and other law enforcement officers expressly threatened that Mr. Sanders would be indicted, and his wife would become a target, if he did not immediately agree to cooperate with the government by revealing his confidential source within the FBI/NTSB crash investigation. Citing Mr. Sanders' First Amendment rights, his attorney advised the government that Mr. Sanders would not cooperate, and that he intended to continue his investigation into possible government wrongdoing. During the same meeting, the government threatened to make Elizabeth Sanders a target of its investigation if she did not agree to cooperate in the government's investigation of her husband's newsgathering activities. ... [T]his threat was made despite a total absence of evidence that Mrs. Sanders had engaged in any form of wrongdoing. Through counsel, Mrs. Sanders advised the government that she declined to cooperate in its investigation of her husband's journalistic pursuits.]

(5)In late April 1997, James Sanders published his book, *The Downing of TWA Flight 800,* which also detailed the information he had gathered and asserted that the government was covering up the fact that the flight was downed by a Navy missile. The book's acknowledgements thanked Elizabeth Sanders.

(6)Shortly after publication of this book, the FBI attempted to question Elizabeth Sanders' supervisor and another close friend and colleague.

[In *(The Downing of TWA Flight 800)* "Acknowledgements" section, Mr. Sanders had written, "Thanks to Liz's support system, Lee Taylor, Lucille Collins and TWA Norfolk agents." Shortly after publication of the book, FBI agents in New York demanded that Mrs. Collins, who was Mrs. Sanders' immediate supervisor at TWA, and Mrs. Taylor, a close friend and colleague, be brought to New York for questioning. Both individuals were subjected to FBI questioning, and reported that many of the questions were of a highly personal nature concerning the Sanders' marriage and private lives.]

(7) The government issued a second subpoena for James Sanders' telephone records in August 1997, again in violation of 28 C.F.R., 50.10.

(8) Mr. Sanders filed Freedom of Information Act ("FOIA") requests in August, September and October 1997, seeking information relating to FBI Assistant Director James Kallstrom, FBI Special Agent James Kinsley, Assistant United States Attorney Valerie Caproni and Assistant United States Attorney Benton Campbell.

(9) On November 18, 1997, Mr. Sanders reported to a *New York Post* reporter that he was using the FOIA requests to investigate the prosecutors and FBI agents involved in the investigation of him and his wife.

(10) On November 19, 1997, the *Post* reporter published an exclusive story, quoting Valerie Caproni of the United States Attorney's Office for the Eastern District of New York as stating that the Justice Department was not required to follow its regulations because there was no basis to conclude that Mr. Sanders was acting as a reporter and that charges would be filed within two weeks.

(11) On December 5, 1997, FBI Agent Kinsley's affidavit in support of the defendants' arrest warrants was released to the press without notification to the Sanders or their attorneys. On the same day, the FBI issued a press release stating that James Sanders had misrepresented the results of his lab reports of the red residue.

(12)In December 1997, at the time defendants surrendered, Agent Kinsley arranged to have the defendants paraded in front of the press in their handcuffs even though more discreet actions could have been taken.

[Following the Sanders surrender at the FBI's Long Island office, Agent Kinsley arranged to have them paraded in handcuffs past throngs of reporters and photographers in the parking lot of the FBI office, and attempted to do so again at the entrance to the courthouse where they were to be arraigned, notwithstanding the availability of more discreet means of leaving and entering the respective buildings.]

(13)On December 12, 1997, Terrell Stacey, the Sanders' contact inside the investigation, stated during his plea allocution that he took the fabric samples on his 'own volition' and gave them to James Sanders to analyze.

[The following day, during his sworn plea allocution, Terrell Stacey stated, " … when I was given the opportunity or when I—when Mr. Sanders offered me or the fact that I learned that he could help in the investigation through contacts and people he had in labs, then I on my own volition took the two small pieces and gave them to him to have them analyzed."]

(14)On January 6, 1998, the Sanders were then indicted on the grounds that they orchestrated the efforts to have Stacey remove the fabric samples.

[Notwithstanding this statement, the Sanders were indicted approximately four weeks later on the theory that they violated, and conspired to violate, 49 U.S.C. Section 1155 by importuning Mr. Stacey to provide those small pieces of material to Mr. Sanders.]

Some of the Court's changes minimized defense accusations of government wrongdoing and embellished our alleged acts. The judge continued:

On the basis of this chronology, the defendant's argue that

they have made the required threshold showing that the government's investigation and indictment of the Sanders was in retaliation for their efforts to publicize their theory that a Navy missile was the cause of the Flight 800 explosion.[6]

Once again the factually false Justice Department mantra appears, fatally distorting the facts. We repeatedly and clearly stated the retaliation was a direct result of criminal acts uncovered within the investigation.

The Court has reviewed these allegations and finds that the defendants have failed to establish a substantial and concrete basis sufficient to allow further discovery to overcome the presumption of regularity on the part of federal prosecutors," the Court continued.

... Although the court does recognize that circumstantial evidence is relevant and admissible in both the criminal and civil context, the circumstantial evidence presented in the *chronology above* does not persuade the Court that this is credible evidence that tends to show the existence of a discriminatory or retaliatory animus against the defendants.[7] [Emphasis added]

The judge's decision was that the wife of a journalist could be made the "target" of a Department of Justice investigation even in the absence of any information or evidence that she may have been involved in wrongdoing. The judge ruled the congressionally-mandated Code of Federal Regulations applicable to Justice Department lawyers and FBI agents can be ignored at their whim. And, the judge said it is permissible for the Justice Department to knowingly present false information to the Court; i.e., alleging not to know I was a journalist, and falsely stating the animus was the result of something other than my uncovering government wrongdoing.

But that was not the extent of the judge's beliefs which appear to reside outside the Constitution:

Perhaps defendants' chronology would have more weight if James Sanders in the March 10, 1997, *Press-Enterprise* article had merely propounded his theory that a missile downed Flight 800. The article, however, goes much further. It expressly states that "He used classified documents obtained from a confidential source inside the official investigation." "Someone whom Sanders declined to identify passed him a 104-page printout of the FBI-NTSB catalog of every article recovered from the undersea crash site," that "Sanders said he later obtained samples of the residue" and that "The residue test was initiated by James Sanders, who said he obtained pieces of one of the seats." Prominently placed on the front page of the newspapers is a color photograph of the "samples of seat material with residue." Based on these statements, the Court agrees with the government that the article raised serious doubts about the security of the hangar and clearly indicated a potential violation of 49 U.S.C., Section 1155(b).[8]

The judge, in effect, ruled that when the Justice Department feels insecure about "security" within any investigation, it can violate all CFRs and civil rights codes.

Judge Seybert stated her belief that journalists investigating improper conduct within a federal investigation must be limited to he-said/she-said stories—the kind of stories the government can easily deflect because they are without substance.

The judge believed it was improper for a reporter investigating federal crimes to receive documents from within a federal investigation. If her beliefs are upheld by the Second Circuit Court and Supreme Court, it will no longer be possible to conduct an in-depth investigation into federal lawlessness while facing the probability that those who are the target of the journalistic investigation will use their power to attack and indict the journalist, and harass and indict the journalist's wife. According to the Court, such harassment is proper activity for Justice Department lawyers and investigators to engage in when concerned about security within any investigation.

In a federal courtroom it is reasonable to draw inferences from facts during the course of a criminal trial. From facts presented, compelling evidence emerges, as does proof beyond a reasonable doubt.

In Judge Seybert's courtroom the prosecution was allowed to infer that when I met secretly with Terry Stacey, it was evidence of a "consciousness of guilt," not a normal journalistic practice. But mention of journalistic pursuit of criminals within the government was not allowed inside the courtroom.

The legal playing field had been dramatically altered. The effect was to give the schemers within government an enormous advantage in their effort to destroy the messenger.

36

PRE-TRIAL MANEUVERING

The case was approaching a trial date, and the young prosecutor made it evident that this was going to be the government's attack. Prosecutor David Pitofsky did not know the NTSB was scrambling to find a way to give him scientific tests backing their glue allegation without actually having to test my residue samples.

It was against this backdrop that the final exchange of pre-trial motions occurred. After observing the judge in action during the discovery phase, no one inside the defense believed the motion to dismiss was going to fare any better. It was, however, a necessary legal exercise in order to preserve the right to appeal, so on January 25, 1999, the final pre-trial round of motions began when our attorneys filed a motion to dismiss:

> Defendants James Sanders and Elizabeth Sanders submit this memorandum of law in support of their joint motion to dismiss the indictment on the ground that it imposes an over-whelming and unjustifiable burden on First Amendment freedoms, and in support of Mr. Sanders' motion to suppress the confidential notes, correspondence, memoranda and other First Amendment materials that were unlawfully seized without a warrant from his computer. Based on the arguments and facts set forth in their earlier motions to compel discovery, both defendants also formally move to dismiss the indictment on the ground of vindictive and selective prosecution.[1]

A new wrinkle had been added. Under pre-trial discovery, documents from the computer I used to research and write *The Downing of TWA Flight 800*, alleged to be in storage in Kansas City, Missouri, began showing up. Over a period of time the Justice Department admitted it had seized the computer without bothering to get a warrant—a warrant they could not get. No federal judge would entertain such a request. So the Justice Department created yet another sub-scheme, and without authority seized it. This issue would not be resolved until after the trial started.

Gutman's narrative continued:

The present prosecution seeks to impose criminal sanctions against James and Elizabeth Sanders based on conduct that arose solely in the context of a journalistic effort to obtain an inconsequential quantity of material that had no value apart from the light it might shed on a matter of widespread concern. From its inception, the threat of such a prosecution functioned as a means by which the government—bypassing constraints designed to safeguard freedom of the press—attempted to compel an investigative reporter to disclose a confidential source. In view of these unique circumstances, we contend that the governmental interest in prosecuting the alleged offense is so overwhelmingly outweighed by the harm that this prosecution inflicts on rights protected by the First Amendment that the indictment should be dismissed. ...[2]

Our courts have recognized the "paramount public interest in the maintenance of a vigorous, aggressive and independent press capable of participating in robust, unfettered debate over controversial matters, an interest which has always been a principal concern of the First Amendment."[3] The constitutional guarantee of a free press "assures the maintenance of our political system and an open society,"[4] and secures "the paramount public interest in a free flow of information to the people concerning public officials."[5] "The central meaning of the First Amendment" is the "profound national commitment to the principle that debate on public issues should be uninhibited, robust and wide-open."[6]

In view of the First Amendment's vital function of safeguarding "freedom of communication on matters relating to the functioning of government,"[7] the Supreme Court has recognized that learning about, criticizing and evaluating government requires some "right to receive" information.[8] "The First Amendment goes beyond protection of the press and the self-expression of individuals to prohibit government from limiting the stock of information from which members of the public may draw."[9] Indeed, the value of the press as a check against abuse of government power has been championed even when the government, in the Pentagon Papers case, suggested that national security concerns were implicated. In the same case, Justice Black, joined by Justice Douglas, praised journalists for fulfilling their essential democratic role to "bare the secrets of government and inform the people." Notwithstanding that the plaintiffs in that case had obtained thousands of pages of confidential government documents, Justice Black concluded that, "far from deserving condemnation for their courageous reporting, *The New York Times,* the *Washington Post,* and other newspapers should be commended for serving the purpose that the Founding Fathers saw so clearly."[10]

The carefully formulated guidelines for safeguarding a journalist's freedom to investigate and report on newsworthy events fell by the wayside. Rather than comply with those rules, the government … took the more expedient course of threatening to prosecute not only Mr. Sanders, but his wife as well, if he refused to betray the confidentiality of his source. Thus, the government parlayed a de minimis statutory violation into a tool for bypassing the procedural constraints designed to protect an investigative journalist's First Amendment freedoms. By proceeding with the present prosecution, which is a direct result of the Sanders' refusal to relinquish their constitutionally-protected rights in the face of that pressure, the government enlists the assistance of the Court to make good on its threat.

The present prosecution represents an unprecedented effort to impose criminal sanctions for a *de minimis* statutory violation that occurred in the course of a reporter's effort to gather information to be shared with the public. While, as we have argued previously, law enforcement authorities have articulated improper motives for pursuing this prosecution—for example, a desire to condemn those who would dare to "rewrite the history of TWA Flight 800." In view of both the negligible harm arising from their alleged conduct and the disturbing utilization of this prosecution as a means to circumvent First Amendment-based guidelines, any such governmental interest is vastly outweighed by the profound harm this prosecution imposes on First Amendment values. Indeed, if permitted to proceed, the prosecution of the Sanders will stand as an ominous warning to all journalists who refuse to be satisfied by the information that the government chooses to dispense about its activities, but instead strive to "bare the secrets of government and inform the people."[11] Accordingly, under the extraordinary circumstances of this case, vindication of the freedom guaranteed by the First Amendment requires that the indictment be dismissed.

The Justice Department response was "mailed in." They knew they did not have to break a sweat. The judge was not going to do anything that would result in the dismissal of the case, or offer the defendants the opportunity to tell their story to the jury. It was okay to say they disagreed with the government conclusions, but it would be forbidden to allege government wrongdoing was the focus of my investigation. Nor would it be possible for the defense to tell the jury about government violation of the CFR, case law and our civil rights.

The stirring words of Supreme Court justices through the ages, proclaiming the right of journalists to aggressively pursue government lawlessness, would not be allowed. We were limited to saying we did what we did because we disagreed with the government's conclusions.

The judge never issued a written ruling to the motions to dismiss. At the start of the trial she merely mentioned that the motions were denied, indicating that her written ruling on the discovery motion was a sufficient response.

37

THE TRIAL BEGINS

The Justice Department had seized my computer without a warrant. After the jury was selected and before opening arguments, oral arguments were presented.

This microcosm of the criminal case presented the first hint that the judge had moved away from the Justice Department camp. Her discovery, First Amendment and vindictive prosecution rulings had severely harmed the defense. But from this point forward, Judge Seybert took a balanced approach to running the trial.

The courtroom was put on notice that they would see some excellent lawyering. Bruce Maffeo was the dominant presence in the court. Jeremy Gutman's legal expertise made the two lawyers a very good team. Roland Acevedo was in court for the express purpose of arguing the defense side of the computer seizure. His ability to extemporaneously argue the micro and macro side of the law was impressive.

David Pitofsky, the prosecutor, was certainly up to the task of countering the defense team's presence. Pitofsky was a good speaker—with the potential to be a commanding presence a little further into his career. He had a gift for drawing inferences where none actually existed—and getting away with it. On the multiple occasions he reached too far, he went into his "I'm too cute to have done it on purpose" routine. The judge's motherly instincts invariably kicked in and Pitofsky would walk away with a very mild slap on the wrist.

On the computer issue, Pitofsky was perilously close to

misrepresenting the facts, and Maffeo made a brilliant counter-move that carried the day. The defense won a hard-fought victory. The Justice Department cannot seize a journalist's computer.

Additional legal maneuvering then kicked in over the government motion to excise the First Amendment from the trial:

> Pitofsky: ... There is the issue of the actual testimony of the defendants. ... This is obviously a very serious matter. As the government said up front, it [recognizes] it is seeking to preclude what the defense regards as a defense in this case. ... I think the Court would be hard-pressed to deny a defendant on trial in a criminal case from telling their story. And the government would not seek to preclude *general testimony* from the defendants, of that nature, *explaining what that conduct was*. I'm not sure that it is entirely relevant, but the government realizes it is a dangerous thing to keep that sort of testimony out. [Emphasis added]

Pitofsky was willing to allow us to give testimony explaining our personal conduct, but he would adamantly oppose any mention about the government's conduct at the Calverton hangar or in our pursuit.

The judge refrained from making a specific ruling at that time, saying: "I would direct defense counsel from refraining from making any lengthy references or statements to newsgathering privilege, and how that might excuse certain conduct, in their opening statement."

Pitofsky then began his opening statement to the jury, dramatically turning and pointing to my wife and to me as he began to explain the government theory of the case. He also wanted the jury to understand that "this case is not about the government's investigation as to what caused the crash. It arises out of the government's investigation, and you will hear testimony about the investigation. But this case ... *you will not be asked to decide anything about how that investigation was conducted.* [Emphasis added] As you heard in the indictment the defendants are not charged with obstruction of justice. They are simply charged with conspiring to remove a piece of evidence ... and with aiding and abetting that removal."

Because of the pre-trial rulings, the prosecution would be able to put NTSB and FBI personnel attached to the Flight 800 investigation on the stand. They would describe a thorough, legal investigation. But the defense was not allowed to delve into the corruption inside the investigation. The prosecution was allowed a complete offense, but we were forced to remove the majority of the defense from the playing field.

Bruce Maffeo, my attorney, went next. It was his job to weave as much of the story as possible into his opening arguments without provoking the prosecution into objecting. Maffeo knew, as he walked to the podium, that he could push the envelope because Pitofsky was somewhat intimidated by his presence.

Maffeo began quietly, building volume and emotion, then bringing the audience back down—combining emotion with the story he had to tell:

What you will hear from the evidence, ladies and gentlemen, as the weeks and months of the investigation that unfolded of Flight 800, people such as Terry Stacey ... who were working on the investigation into the cause and crash of Flight 800 became disturbed, disturbed with what they saw going on with respect to the investigation. ... Terrell Stacey and others like him within the investigation began to conclude that the investigation was covering up the true cause of the tragedy. ... You will hear from ... Terrell Stacey, his complaints of information that was not being pursued, witnesses not being interviewed, leads within the investigation not being followed through. ... [Y]ou will hear that people like Terrell Stacey and others like him inside the investigation sought out the assistance of Jim Sanders ... for one simple reason. Jim Sanders was ... known within the TWA community as a journalist, investigative journalist, not only worked with the media but published two other books, published investigations as to governmental misconduct. ... Terrell Stacey provided Mr. Sanders with information relating to the investigation and relating to the possibility that the cause of the plane's explosion was not a mechanical failure, not a malfunction on the part of the plane, but that a missile that had hit the plane ... caused it. Captain Stacey came to the conclusion that not only was there evidence, substantial evidence that a missile had caused the crash of Flight 800, but the official governmental investigation ... had covered up that evidence. ... [A]s a direct result of Mr. Sanders having published his conclusions ... that a missile had caused the crash, he found himself and his wife threatened with indictment if they did not reveal the source inside the Calverton hangar. They did not. And as a result they have been indicted and they stand on trial before you today.

Maffeo then got to the single, picayunish issue this case had degenerated to as a direct result of judicial pre-trial decisions: Did Stacey act of his "own volition" as he stated under oath when pleading guilty? Or did some influence make this senior TWA manager do something that was not of his own free will? Maffeo then told the jury:

Terrell Stacey ... will testify that not only did he provide Mr. Sanders with information, and also ultimately the seat fabric, he will testify he did so only because he was pressured to do so by James and Elizabeth Sanders. We submit, ladies and gentlemen, as you will have an opportunity to hear the evidence in this case, you will conclude that Terrell Stacey provided that information and, indeed, provided those materials to Jim Sanders not because of any pressure he was receiving from Jim Sanders, not because of any pressure he was receiving from Elizabeth Sanders, but because he, Terrell Stacey, had come to believe that a missile had caused the explosions ... and that he, Terrell Stacey, wanted that information to come to the public eye.

Maffeo then wrapped up his presentation, and Jeremy Gutman, my wife's attorney, approached the podium to open. In many ways Gutman reminded me of a well-dressed Lt. Colombo. His mind is always filled to capacity with legal facts, each vying to be at the forefront of his conscious thought. When Gutman pauses in mid-sentence, you can almost hear the thoughts screaming for recognition.

Like Lt. Colombo, Gutman would appear to walk away from whomever was being questioned, then turn and say, "just one more question."

He opened on a very personal note in regards to my wife, characterizing Elizabeth as a mother who, at the age of 40, realized her life-long dream to be a flight attendant. When Flight 800 went down, she was in charge of TWA's flight attendant new-hire program. Several of her students were on that plane when it crashed.

Gutman then described Elizabeth's call to Terry Stacey, asking if Stacey would talk to me. He then went to the heart of the issue:

> ... and [Terry Stacey] agreed to bring [Sanders] documents, and eventually they talked about his residue and [Stacey] brought [Sanders] a tiny piece of [foam rubber] ... that had a small amount of residue, which had no value, no worth of any kind, other than as information, as something that might provide a clue, maybe the key clue to what happened on that very sad night in July of 1996. The government wants to portray this act ... as a criminal conspiracy. They are not going to provide ... a shred of believable evidence ... that Liz Sanders asked anyone to commit a crime, or that she expected anyone to commit a crime. ... She never sought for anybody to do anything that she believed was unlawful. But you are going to hear what

she did do, and I believe the evidence will show it is what leads her to be here today, is that she respected Captain Stacey's desire for confidentiality. She understood that this is the way reporters and investigators and journalists find out what is going on in the government. There are a lot of things that the government doesn't voluntarily tell the citizens of this country. ...

At that point, Pitofsky objected. Gutman appeared poised to leap into government cover-up and conspiracy, which was what this case was really about. The judge sustained the objection.

So Jeremy Gutman took another route to get to the same point. Within a couple of minutes he had constructed a verbal road to where he wanted to go:

And ... is there a chance that they, that the government would have brought this case, a case involving a journalist and a wife of a journalist who are accused of a conspiracy based on receiving a little scrap of information and doing so without any intent to cause any harm, without any intent to cause any loss to anyone, and only with an intention to find out the truth about an important question, is it possible we would be here about this if the journalist hadn't written a book?

Again, Pitofsky was on his feet, yelling "objection." Again, it was sustained. Gutman then wrapped up his opening comments.

Pitofsky at this point decided he was going to get the Court to stop this attack on the government. He asked that the lawyers approach the Bench. The following sidebar occurred:

Pitofsky: It is the government view that Mr. Gutman brought up some impermissible points in his opening, specifically that there was a cover-up. I chose not to object because of courtesy. ... Mr. Gutman violated the Court's ruling, bringing up the cover-up, or a motive to tell the truth, and suggesting to the jury that the motive had anything to do with [the jury's] responsibility in this case.

The Court: Mr. Gutman, you did mention a journalist, we wouldn't be here ... if it wasn't for a journalist. I think that's when you really did step over the line.

The judge struggled with the prosecution demand and eventually developed an instruction to the jury to deal with it. The prosecution remained adamant about any attempt to introduce to the jury the government's actions in this case. The playing field had been tilted severely in their favor by the Court's pre-trial rulings, and Pitofsky wasn't going to give anything back. The Justice Department is not about "justice." Its goal is to convict those they have targeted, regardless of the facts.

Pitofsky called a senior FBI agent to the stand. His purpose for testifying was to enable Pitofsky to draw an inference that did not exist. The Flight 800 investigation had never been declared a crime scene. It was a "crash scene." The NTSB was the lead agency. The FBI legally had an inferior position. Agent Kenneth Maxwell admitted this on the stand. He also admitted that unless enough evidence accumulated to publicly declare it a crime scene, it remained an NTSB crash scene. But Pitofsky needed to be able to talk about the "inviolate" crime scene. So he began using the phrase "crime scene." Maxwell soon caught on and began to parrot Pitofsky.

Another witness was called to bolster Maxwell's testimony. I had communicated by e-mail with someone in California who had contacts within the law enforcement crime labs. One e-mail had the phrase, "under color of authority," a term Pitofsky knew meant an on-duty law enforcement officer, acting in an official capacity. But that is not why Pitofsky wanted to have access to the phrase. He had decided to tell the jury that it actually meant "without authority."

38

DAY TWO

Terry Stacey spent most of day two on the witness stand. He was the prosecution's only substantive witness. All others were for introducing e-mail, phone records, and as a tool for Pitofsky to draw his infamous inferences.

Pitofsky, on direct examination, led Stacey through his work at the Calverton hangar, his first meeting with me, and how our journalist-to-whistleblower relationship developed. Stacey was then led into the portion of his testimony where another NTSB investigator took him to the passenger cabin mockup to show Stacey the reddish-orange residue trail that could be seen across the backs of the seats in rows 17, 18 and 19:

Pitofsky: Returning to your telephone conversations during this period, what sort of conversations did you have with Jim Sanders about the existence and importance of this reddish coloring on the seatbacks?

Stacey: That from the standpoint of the investigation he was doing, that it would be, that it would be very important, or nice to have that—I remember him using the term once, that it would [be a] slam dunk, if it came out positive for explosive residue, then it would [be a] slam dunk as far as being absolute proof that some outside force affected the airplane.

Pitofsky: What, if any, discussion did you have about what you might do with regard to this red coloring?

Stacey: Well, he being an investigator, former investigator with the police department, indicated to me we would just need a very small sample of it. To just take a pen knife and scrape off a little of it on to an envelope, and it would just take a very minute sample to have analyzed.

Pitofsky: And how specific were your discussions about what would be done with the sample once you obtained it and sent it to Mr. Sanders?

Stacey: That they would be taken to a private lab to be analyzed.

I sat there listening, thinking, "so what's your point?" They were talking about normal journalist-to-source conversation. Stacey did not say I had browbeat him into getting a sample. Nor did I "ask" him for a sample. I did make it clear I would gladly accept a sample and have it tested. That isn't a conspiracy, it is how journalists gain access to the facts they need to take a story past the he-said/she-said stage, to where those exposed were truly placed at risk by the specificity of the journalist's writing.

Pitofsky then went to the heart of Stacey's story, his reluctance to obtain the residue. Had he not been reluctant, the government would have lost the rationale for the alleged conspiracy. If it was something he wanted to see outside government control, Stacey acted "of his own volition." At that point the Justice Department would have lost all claim to a conspiracy—even by the tortured logic of this case:

Pitofsky: And what was your reaction to the idea of removing the sample?

Stacey: I was concerned about it, or leery about it because I knew we had been warned many times to maintain a confidentiality of the investigation and we knew we weren't supposed to take anything out of the hangar.

Pitofsky: Do you recall what if any discussion did you have with Mr. Sanders over the phone about those types of concerns?

Stacey: Each time I talked with Jim I relayed to him what

we were doing had to be in the strictest confidentiality. And my being jeopardized, my position with the company being jeopardized as well as my position in the investigation, as well as the company's position with the investigation.

Pitofsky: Approximately how long did it take you to decide whether to get involved in this scheme to remove the evidence?

Stacey: I would say three weeks, or approximately so. I was vacillating back and forth in my mind as to whether or not to take this step.

This alleged vacillation, requiring Stacey to be coerced into doing something he allegedly did not want to do, formed the basis for the charges.

I had tape-recorded all source interviews during the course of this investigation. Unfortunately, I hadn't created a library of tape. My normal practice was to take notes from the tape recording, then reuse the tape. Only conversations in the latter portion of the cassettes were not taped over.

On December 8, 1996, in the middle of the timeframe Terry Stacey alleged he was vacillating and I was attempting to coerce him into doing something he did not want to do, we had a telephone conversation that was not later taped over. We discussed several issues from inside the investigation, but the residue issue did not surface until the last couple minutes when I began to sign off:

Sanders: In any case, I won't keep you anymore, here; I wanted to check with you. So I'll just anxiously await the residue and whatever else ...

Stacey: Whatever else I can scrounge.

Sanders: Yeah. Exactly. Yeah. I can either come up and get it or, whichever is more convenient, I can either come up and get it, or mail it. But it's a little easier for me now normally because Liz lands at her apartment this evening. She's driving up there right now.

Stacey: Oh, my.

Sanders: Then she ends up next week going right back to St. Louis for five days. Then from the twentieth through the end of the year she's flying or at least on-call to fly.

Stacey: Does she get the holiday off, or Christmas off?

Sanders: No. No. She's working both that and probably, assuming they grab her for a flight—she said the thirtieth, but I presume she meant the thirty-first. Unless her schedule is— unless that's when they end her schedule. I don't know if they do them in 30-day cycles or what.

Stacey: I think this one ends on the thirty-first.

Sanders: So if they grab her for one of those, where she's halfway through a flight on the thirty-first, she's working on the first, too. In any case, I'll have easier access to places to stay and cars and that kind of stuff. I also have a forensics expert online to analyze it very quickly so we don't have to stand in line at a crime lab somewhere, probably out on the West Coast, and wait for a month while they get around to it.

Stacey: *I'll make that my top priority*, because that group, like I say, Les and them were talking about finishing up, so that place ought to be fairly secluded in a few days. ...There won't be a lot of people. [Emphasis added]

Sanders: Oh, outstanding, good.

Stacey: OK

Sanders: OK. Well, give me a buzz whenever and we'll figure out how to do a handoff on it and go from there. I appreciate all the help.

Stacey: OK. Very good.

Sanders: OK. Talk to you later.

This tape recording presented words which reflect the true status of Terry Stacey's mental thought process at that time. There was no hesitation, no coercing. Obtaining the residue was, he volunteered, his "top priority" along with anything else he could "scrounge."

The tape accurately reflected the journalist-source relationship. We were comfortable discussing all issues related to the Flight 800 investigation.

When Liz's name came up, and the knowledge that she was driving to her apartment, perhaps 30 miles west of Calverton, no talk occurred about her participating in any manner in this journalist-to-source relationship.

Terry Stacey was not a reluctant source. He was an enthusiastic source volunteering to obtain residue thought to contain "facts" that would offer compelling evidence of government culpability. Within 24 hours the existence of this tape would be revealed to the jury.

But on this day inside the courtroom, the prosecution did not know what awaited them when our attorneys began to cross-examine Terry Stacey. So Pitofsky continued to lead Stacey through the story he had been coerced into delivering by the Justice Department in exchange for their not filing felony charges:

> Pitofsky: During that time did you speak to anyone else about the idea of obtaining a sample from the Calverton facility?
> Stacey: Yes.
> Pitofsky: Who was that?
> Stacey: Liz Sanders.
> Pitofsky: Under what circumstances—first of all, how many conversations did you have with Liz Sanders on this particular topic?
> Stacey: On this particular, only one.
> Pitofsky: You testified that after the initial conversation with Jim Sanders, it took about three weeks to make your decision. Where in the two- or three-week period while you were trying to make your decision, did the telephone call from Liz Sanders occur?
> Stacey: All I can say is it occurred during that time. I couldn't recall if it was the beginning of it, the middle or end. I honestly don't know.
> Pitofsky: What do you recall having been said by both yourself and herself in as much detail as you can recall?
> Stacey: Just the thing that I remember about it is she just

indicated to me that it would be nice to have that sample, or we really needed that sample.

Pitofsky: Did there eventually come a time when you decided whether or not you would obtain this sample?

Stacey: Yes.

Pitofsky: And did you in fact decide that you would obtain the sample?

Stacey: Yes.

Pitofsky: Why did you decide to go ahead and take the sample from the Calverton facility?

Stacey: Again, there was a heavy burden with the investigation, frustration with the investigation, the lack of sharing the information by the NTSB and, of course, the FBI. Many theories going around and NTSB people trying to prove the theories; being away from the family; constantly being involved in the investigation of the wreckage and so forth. I thought this would be a means of me obtaining some more information, more analysis to find out the cause of the accident of Flight 800.

So, by Stacey's own words, under oath, my wife and I played no role in his decision to take the residue.

When the prosecutor heard this answer, he knew his case was on the ropes. The correct answer, from the Justice Department's view, was: "Jim and Liz Sanders made me do it." But Pitofsky wisely declined a leading follow-up question designed to elicit the answer Pitofsky wanted to hear. If answered incorrectly, Pitofsky's case was gone.

Bruce Maffeo began his cross-examination of Terry Stacey. Within minutes Maffeo guided the cross-examination toward debunking Stacey's alleged reluctance to remove the residue.

Pitofsky was blindsided when Maffeo dropped the transcript of the taped interview onto the prosecutor's table. He rapidly leafed through the pages and soon read the dreaded words, "I'll make that my top priority."

The defense would have had to turn the audiotape over to the prosecution before trial if it was going to be introduced into evidence. But the prosecution would then use it to re-shape Stacey's testimony. So a decision was made not to introduce the tape into evidence.

On cross-examination, the tape could be used to impeach Stacey's testimony without turning it over to the prosecution under discovery. The moment had arrived. Maffeo gave Stacey a copy of the transcript and asked him to read it. After Stacey read the key passages, Maffeo began:

Maffeo: Have you had an opportunity to review it, Captain Stacey?

Stacey: Yes.

Maffeo: Having had an opportunity to review it, does it re-fresh your recollection that you told Sanders in December 1996 that you would make removing the residue your top priority?

Stacey: No, sir.

Maffeo: Does it refresh your recollection at all?

Stacey: No, sir.

Maffeo: Do you recall telling Sanders in the same conversa-tion that you would have to wait until the people who were working in that area of the hangar completed their job and wait a couple of days?

Stacey: No, sir.

Maffeo: No recollection of it at all as you sit here today, sir?

Stacey: No.

Maffeo: Isn't it a fact, Captain Stacey, that you removed the red residue of your own volition and to find out the cause of the accident?

Stacey: Yes.

Maffeo was on a roll. Stacey was precariously close to abandoning the script the prosecution had carefully implanted in his brain, so Maffeo pressed hard:

Maffeo: My question to you, Captain Stacey, is this: At the time that you snapped off these two three-inch samples of seat fabric, you didn't believe at the time that you were compromising the ability of the NTSB or the FBI to conduct an investigation [with the] remaining samples left in the cabin; is that correct?

Stacey: Correct.

Maffeo: In fact, Captain Stacey, is it not true that at the time that you performed those actions, you did not believe that you had violated or that you were breaking the law?

Pitofsky: Objection.

The Court: Overruled.

Stacey: Repeat the question, please.

Maffeo: At the time you snapped these two samples off, Captain Stacey, you didn't, in fact, think you were breaking the law?

Stacey: That's correct.

Outside of a confession that the Department of Justice had coerced Terry Stacey, there was nothing else the defense could have hoped to get out of him. Within minutes, court was adjourned for the day and a very happy defense team walked out the front door.

Every day had been a "win" day for the defense. The courtroom audience reflected that fact; they were certainly on our side.

The dour major media journalists glumly admitted it looked bad for their team. *The New York Times* resorted to making up portions of Terry Stacey's testimony in order to run an article that favored the government. *Newsday* followed *The Times'* lead and published a story questioning why our lawyers were not putting on a First Amendment defense, in effect suggesting they doubted my credentials. But the local reporters, much more friendly to the defense, described the prosecution as sinking fast.

39

DAY THREE

Pitofsky had one last chance to get Stacey back onboard the prosecution team. His answers the previous day had been devastating to the prosecution.

Before the trial continued on day three, Pitofsky had a legal excuse for being with Terry Stacey even though he was still under oath. Stacey was to listen to the audiotaped conversation I had recorded on December 8, 1996. The audiotape was all Pitofsky was legally allowed to discuss with Stacey. But much more occurred between the prosecution and Terry Stacey than what they were legally entitled to discuss.

Pitofsky's questions, when court resumed, and Stacey's answers, demonstrate a clear case of witness tampering:

> Pitofsky: Good morning, Captain Stacey. I will remind you are still under oath. Do you recall, Captain Stacey, yesterday you were asked by Mr. Maffeo on cross-examination whether you removed the red residue, and I quote, "of your own volition, and to find out the cause of the accident"? Do you remember being asked that question?
>
> Stacey: Yes.
>
> Pitofsky: And you remember your answer to that question was "yes"?
>
> Stacey: Yes.

The next question would not have been asked unless Pitofsky had coached Stacey before entering the courtroom:

Pitofsky: Would you please explain to the jury what that phrase means, that you "acted of your own volition" in this matter?

If Stacey had not been tampered with, Pitofsky would not dare ask such an open-ended question—a question that would allow Stacey to head off in any direction he wished. Pitofsky, instead, would have had to use a series of questions to narrowly focus the witness. Now Pitofsky's questions would be answered in a transparently well-rehearsed, and expected, manner:

Stacey: That I was to—it was during the time that I came and appeared before Judge Pohorelsky, and I was accepting responsibility for my actions, as well as making certain that it was clear that no other TWA or investigative personnel at the hangar had assisted me in taking the material.

Pitofsky: I just want to make clear that it is your testimony this morning that what you meant when you used that phrase at your plea hearing and what you meant when you answered yesterday, had to do with whether any TWA or other hangar persons had assisted you or worked with you on this matter?

Stacey: That's correct.

Pitofsky: Did you mean you didn't receive influence from anyone in this matter?

Stacey: No.

Pitofsky: And did you receive influence from persons in this matter?

Stacey: Yes.

Pitofsky: And who did you receive influence from persons in this matter?

Stacey: From Jim and Liz Sanders.

Less than 24 hours before, Stacey had categorically denied that my wife had any influence on his actions. Now that his memory had been "refreshed," Stacey's recollections more closely followed the prosecution's take on the "truth." Miraculously, the train had regained the tracks.

But Pitofsky's machinations only temporarily salvaged the government's case. On re-redirect, Maffeo, the dynamic presence, honed in on the facts:

Maffeo: And do you recall telling this jury yesterday in substance that when the discussion first arose regarding the red residue, that you were, to use your words, concerned about it, were leery about it, because you were warned many times to maintain the confidentiality of the investigation?

Pitofsky: Objection. Outside the scope of the redirect.

Maffeo: Judge, I think it relates directly to the tape.

The Court: I will allow that latitude.

Maffeo: Do you recall telling this jury that yesterday?

Stacey: Would you say that again, please.

Maffeo: Let me pose the question differently. Do you recall being asked this question and giving this answer in this courtroom yesterday, sir, by Mr. Pitofsky: "Question: and what was your initial reaction to the idea of removing the sample? Answer: Well, I was concerned about it or leery about it because I knew we had been warned many times to maintain the confidentiality of the investigation, and we knew we weren't supposed to take anything out of [the] hangar." Do you recall giving that answer to this jury to that question yesterday, sir?

Stacey: Yes.

Maffeo: You had an opportunity to listen to the tape that was just played to the Court today, sir?

Stacey: Yes.

Maffeo: You listened to it . . . before you came to court this morning?

Stacey: Yes.

Maffeo: You recognize your voice on that tape?

Stacey: Yes.

Maffeo: It is your voice saying you will make getting the residue your top priority?

Stacey: Yes.

Maffeo: Your voice saying you will get anything else you can scrounge up, right?

Stacey: Yes.

Maffeo: And your voice telling Jim Sanders you would wait to remove the residue until other members of the investigation had moved out from that section of the Calverton hangar?

Stacey: Yes.

Maffeo: Anything in that conversation you heard, sir, relating to your concerns about the confidentiality of the investigation? Did you hear yourself give concern to those words to the conversation you listened to this morning, sir?

Stacey: No.

Maffeo: Did you hear anything of your words talking about being leery about removing the residue in that conversation, sir?

Stacey: No.

Maffeo: Captain Stacey, you were also asked questions earlier this morning by Mr. Pitofsky about the phrase, "of my own volition." There came a point that this was established yesterday that you entered a plea of guilty in this courtroom; is that correct? And there came a point, sir, during the appearance before the magistrate judge, did there not, that Magistrate Judge Pohorelsky asked you in your own words to describe what it is that you did correct?

Stacey: Correct.

Maffeo: And, specifically, do you recall being asked this question by the judge and giving this answer, on page 17: "Question by the Court: Mr. Stacey, can you describe briefly in your own words what you did in connection with the crime charged? Answer: I was assigned to the investigation immediately after the accident and started working on it. Well, first off I brought that plane back from Paris the day before and had flown the airplane three times in the previous week. And I was assigned to the investigation. We had been there for many long months. I was away from the family, under [a] lot of pressure and emotional stress to try to find out the cause of the accident. And when I was given an opportunity or when Mr. Sanders offered to me, or the fact that I learned that he could help in the investigation through contacts and people he had in labs, then I on my own volition took the two small pieces and gave them to him to have them analyzed." Do you recall giving that answer to that question posed by the Court in your plea appearance?

Stacey: Yes.

Maffeo: And anything in your statement to the Court under the oath on December 10 about Jim or Liz Sanders pressuring you to take the residue? Did you say anything like that to the Court on December 10, 1997?

Stacey: Say the first part of the question?

Maffeo: During the course of your allocution before the magistrate judge on December 10, 1997, did you tell the judge that you had been pressured by Jim or Liz Sanders to take the samples of the red residue?

Stacey: No.

Maffeo: You were asked a question by Mr. Pitofsky yesterday before this jury … Do you recall being asked this question and giving this answer …

The Court: Can you just slow down a bit?

Maffeo: I am sorry, Judge. [Captain Stacey] Do you recall being asked this question and giving this answer before the jury yesterday: "Question: Why did you decide to go ahead and take the [residue] from the Calverton facility? Answer: Again, there was a heavy burden with the investigation, frustration with the investigation, a lack of sharing the information by the NTSB, and of course, the FBI; many theories going around with NTSB people trying to go around and trying to prove the theories, being away from the family, constantly being involved in the investigation of the wreckage and so forth, I thought this would be [a] means of me obtaining some more information, more analysis, to find out the cause of the accident of Flight 800." Do you recall giving that answer to this jury yesterday, Captain Stacey?

Stacey: Yes.

Bruce Maffeo then wrapped up the re-cross-examination

and Jeremy Gutman took over. Being Liz Sanders' attorney, the
focus changed somewhat:

Gutman: Captain Stacey, you testified yesterday under oath
to this jury about one telephone conversation with Liz Sanders
that touched on the subject of residue; is that correct?

Stacey: Correct.

Gutman: And you couldn't remember when that took place?

Stacey: That's correct.

Gutman: And you really couldn't—let me read your testimony to you. You testified, "just the thing that I remember
about it is she just … indicated to me that it would really be
nice to have that sample or we … really needed that sample,"
correct?

Stacey: Correct.

Gutman: Your testimony, yesterday?

Stacey: Yes.

Gutman: You don't remember the exact words you said in
that?

Stacey: No.

Gutman: And is that the conversation that you believe influenced you to remove the residue?

Pitofsky: Objection. Outside the scope of redirect.

The Court: Sustained.

Gutman: Your honor, that was …

The Court: Do you want to approach on this?

Gutman: If it's necessary.

[The following takes place at the sidebar:]

The Court: Where in the redirect did the government get
into conversations concerning Liz Sanders?

Gutman: He [Stacey] said, "I was influenced by Liz Sanders." I am asking him if this is what he meant when he said
that.

The Court: That I will allow.

[The following takes place in open court:]

Gutman: Were you referring to that partially remembered bit of conversation when you said on your redirect testimony just a little while earlier this morning that you were influenced by Liz Sanders?

Stacey: No. Specifically, no.

Jeremy Gutman then wrapped up his re-cross-examination of Terry Stacey. The prosecution's case against Liz was in shambles. Stacey continued to testify that her alleged phone call to him had not influenced his decision to take the residue.

Pitofsky's case against me was also tottering on ruin. After months of maneuvering and having the First Amendment removed from the courtroom, Pitofsky saw his case going down for the third time. What happened next provides compelling evidence that Pitofsky hatched a scheme at that moment, a roll-of-the-dice, to resuscitate his moribund case:

Pitofsky: Captain Stacey, I want to focus on the events of your plea of guilty in this case. There was some question as to what occurred there. Sir, what did you understand to be the issue before the Court during that hearing? Let me ask you this way: Whose guilt or innocence did you believe to be in issue on that day?

Stacey: Mine.

Pitofsky: And did you believe that the guilt or innocence of Liz and/or Jim Sanders was in issue on that day?

Stacey: No.

Pitofsky: And did you believe what was [at] issue that day was your guilt or innocence and your willingness to accept your responsibility for your participation in this conduct?

Stacey: Yes.

Pitofsky: And were you charged with a conspiracy in this case? Did you plead guilty to a conspiracy count in this case?

Stacey: No.

Pitofsky: The count you pled guilty to was focused entirely on you; is that correct?

Stacey: Yes.

Pitofsky: And you were also asked questions about what you said about Liz Sanders and her influence or lack of influence during your plea allocution. Do you remember during your plea allocution you were asked questions about Liz Sanders, or you gave information about Liz Sanders, that you mentioned Liz Sanders during your allocution?

Stacey: No, not that I recall.

Pitofsky: I will read you the question and answer and you tell me if it is accurate to your recollection. Do you recall the *Judge* asked you, during this period did you speak to anyone else about obtaining [t]his red residue? And you answered, "yes, Liz Sanders called me." And the *Court* then asked you, "how did that conversation go?" And you answered, "she just indicated we really needed to get that sample in order to find out what happened." Does that refresh your recollection as to whether you mentioned Liz Sanders during your plea allocution? [Emphasis added]

Gutman: Can we have a page reference, please?

Pitofsky: I am sorry. Page 34, lines 17 through 23.

Stacey: You lost me, and I was thinking of plea allocution, so let's start over, please.

Pitofsky: Let me represent to you what I just read.

Maffeo: Objection.

Gutman: Objection, objection, objection. Can we approach?

The Court: Yes, you certainly may. Please bring up the document.

[The following takes place at the sidebar:]

Gutman: Your honor, this is grand jury testimony. I move for a mistrial. This is an inadmissible statement.

Pitofsky: Then I made a mistake.

Pitofsky's claim to having made a mistake was as weak as the government's case. Pitofsky is an experienced attorney. This experience has exposed him to tens of thousands of pages of transcripts, from trials, depositions and grand jury testimony. The formats are distinctly different. Transcripts taken outside the courtroom setting have the witness name at the top of each page. This type of transcript has the transcriber's company name and phone number at the bottom of each page.

Transcripts generated inside the courtroom do not have either of these. It is an instantly recognizable distinction that would preclude any experienced attorney from making the alleged "mistake" Pitofsky had just made. Pitofsky, however, had an additional stop sign glaring him in the face—whenever a judge is making a statement or asking a question, the transcript says "The Court." If an attorney is asking the question, the transcript says "Q."

Pitofsky was reading from a transcript page that had "Q" before each question. He was clearly looking at a transcript page in which an attorney was asking Stacey questions, not "The Court." Additionally, unless Pitofsky wishes to claim that, like Moses parting the waters of the Red Sea, the pages before him magically opened and he saw Liz's name before him, he had to search through a number of pages to find the quote. Each page was like a neon sign saying, "This is not an allocution plea."

A law school 1-L would not have made such a "mistake." Pitofsky's move was indeed a desperation move to contaminate the jury. His hope was that the defense attorneys' strenuous objections would cause the jury to believe they were using legal tactics to withhold highly damning evidence.

Our attorneys moved for a mistrial because of the likelihood the jury had been contaminated by that false impression. The judge denied the motion, and Captain Stacey stood down.

Pitofsky then called Lee Taylor to the stand. Ms. Taylor

had been Liz Sanders' best friend at TWA. Because Taylor was mentioned in *The Downing of TWA Flight 800*'s acknowledgement section, the FBI wanted her for interrogation. Taylor refused and was subpoenaed to appear before a grand jury in Brooklyn, New York.

She retained an attorney and eventually reached an agreement with the Justice Department for immunity from prosecution if she cooperated by testifying against her friend and her friend's husband. When our lawyers gained access to the FBI field notes of Lee Taylor's interviews and her grand jury testimony, they discovered that she had elected to go far beyond any legal requirement.

At Pitofsky's prompting, Lee Taylor told the jury we referred to my Flight 800 manuscript as "the big one." She suggested the term meant we anticipated a financial windfall from the book.

Lee Taylor knew the story behind "the big one." Every book I had written had been predicted by the publisher to be "the big one." By the third book, it had become a rather sarcastic statement.

Under cross-examination, Bruce Maffeo forced Taylor to admit it was a joke, not an inference of anticipated financial gain. She was also forced to admit that she purchased a coffee mug inscribed "The Big One" and gave it to Liz for Christmas.

It was a highly personal, devastating moment for Liz to sit there and watch her best friend so callously disregard the truth at her expense. Taylor's testimony allowed Pitofsky to construct two new non-existent inferences: We had demonstrated a "consciousness of guilt" by not making ourselves available for FBI interrogation without the FBI having to first go through our lawyer; and the motive for pursuing the Flight 800 story was financial gain.

The prosecution then rested. Our defense lawyers believed the prosecution had failed to prove their case "beyond a reasonable doubt." They believed that, absent the jury being tainted by Pitofsky's antics, the government had presented nothing. Terry Stacey, the government's prime witness, had been completely rebutted by the tape-recorded conversation I had made on December 8, 1996. So the defense announced it was only going to call one final witness on our behalf, Jeff Schlanger, our attorney in 1997.

As a lawyer, and therefore an officer of the Court, Schlanger's sworn testimony carried significant weight, particularly if not rebutted by the prosecution.

Schlanger testified that the Department of Justice promised to "target" Liz Sanders as of April 19, 1997, almost two months before they interrogated Terry Stacey. Therefore, "Justice" had absolutely no evidence, real or imagined, with which to justify making her a target.

Pitofsky apparently could not find anyone within the government who had been at that April 19, 1997, meeting willing to perjure themselves in order to rebut Jeff Schlanger's testimony.

The defense then rested, and Jeremy Gutman filed a motion asking the judge to dismiss the charges against Liz Sanders. The unrebutted testimony of Jeff Schlanger created a *prima facie* case of Justice Department vindictiveness as the reason Liz Sanders was indicted.

The judge denied the motion, in effect ruling that such government conduct is acceptable to the federal judicial system.

40

CLOSING ARGUMENTS

No one had testified under oath that the Flight 800 investigation was declared a crime scene. In fact, the opposite had occurred. FBI agent Kenneth Maxwell had admitted that the NTSB was in charge of the investigation until such time that the FBI developed sufficient evidence to declare Flight 800 a crime scene. He also testified that never happened.

But Pitofsky needed to create a false impression for the jury to consider, so he had personally inserted "crime scene" into the record as he questioned Agent Maxwell. Now, in the opening minutes of his summation, Pitofsky again dragged "crime scene" into the picture he was painting for the jury.

Although more artfully argued, Pitofsky then told the jury that aiding and abetting was established because Terry Stacey would never have removed the residue unless a journalist was waiting to receive it. Excising the First Amendment from the trial permitted such egregious foolishness to become a serious part of the government argument.

That foolishness was compounded when Pitofsky was permitted to argue that "none of this would have occurred in the first place" if Liz Sanders had not called Terry Stacey and asked him to talk to her husband. Prior to the excision of the First Amendment's Freedom of Speech from the trial, this was considered "protected" activity by an American citizen.

Pitofsky then absolved Liz Sanders from any alleged criminal conduct. Telling the jury about the tape recording they had heard earlier in the week, he said: "Now, you heard that during this period of time in December [December 8, 1996] while Captain Stacey—I guess, after he had decided he was going to remove the residue, but before he had actually done it—there was an audio-taped conversation involving the two of them [James Sanders and Terry Stacey]." No communication between Stacey and Liz Sanders occurred between the end of October and December 15, 1996. The prosecution and defense all agreed on this point. Both sides also agreed that during the December 1996, Christmas party where the two exchanged "chit-chat," no conversation related to residue occurred.

Pitofsky said Terry Stacey had "decided he was going to remove the residue" as of December 8, yet Liz's only phone call to Stacey was 32 days later. From the prosecutor's own mouth came the truth: Liz Sanders had not coerced Terry Stacey.

Pitofsky merely slipped up and let the truth slide out before recognizing his mistake. He continued, unfazed, next describing normal journalistic procedure as evidence of a consciousness of guilt:

> First of all, you have evidence of the sort of the cloak and dagger way that Mr. Stacey and Captain [sic] Sanders were meeting in, Mr. Stacey says in his own book—Sanders, in his own book saying they were meeting in ways to allow Captain Stacey to go back and forth without anybody noticing their movement.

Pitofsky continued, telling the jury this was not the manner of activity that journalists and confidential sources usually engage in during the course of a journalistic investigation of the government.

Pitofsky then brought up something for which no inference, real or imagined, had been introduced into the record. "Color of authority," as Pitofsky and all law enforcement officers know, deals with a police officer, on the job, acting under the "color of authority" granted him to enforce the law. I had used the phrase to a law enforcement-related contact I had sent an e-mail to, seeking advice on which crime labs on the West Coast I could use to analyze my residue samples. But Pitofsky needed the jury to believe there was something sinister in the phrase I used:

> If the issue you have to decide—is Mr. Sanders aware he was operating without authority, he almost says the words. Can you find room between the concept of acting without authority, or acting without color of authority? Maybe. But it is as close, I submit to you, as you can possibly come to a flat-out statement by the defendant that he was acting without authority.[1]

This is the one document the jury would later ask to review during their 45-minute deliberation.

Pitofsky hammered away again at the sanctity of the crime scene, and attempted in his own skewed way to equate a defendant's right to protect himself from accusation and unlawful prosecution, as an admission and demonstration of a consciousness of guilt.

His closing arguments came down to three basic points: (1) the Calverton hangar was a crime scene; (2) Stacey did not decide to take the residue until coerced by the defendants; and (3) Stacey's testimony was truthful.

Bruce Maffeo then began his closing arguments. I sat there during the opening minutes of Maffeo's remarks, watching the jury and audience. It was apparent that Maffeo's forceful presentation was having a significant impact—on the audience. The jury was difficult to read.

The meat of the defense had been removed pre-trial; i.e., the criminals were the ones chasing us. Within the confines of what the Court allowed, Maffeo pointed to facts:

> If you had a sense that what you were doing was wrong, if you had some belief that you committed a crime, would you

have gone ahead and participated in an article that lays the entire story out, your involvement in a front-page article in a newspaper?

I mean, Jim Sanders wasn't walking around using any pseudonyms as a result of this. He uses his name, uses his e-mail, provides name, address and telephone number to [West Coast Analytical Service].

There is not a hint of evidence that Jim Sanders did anything to conceal his identity. And there is plenty of evidence that what Jim Sanders strove to do, the penalty for which he is paying today, was to conceal the identity of his source, nothing more, nothing less.

One of the most shocking things to me, and maybe I have been living with this case too long, but the government has put into evidence in these large poster boards quotations from portions of Jim Sanders' book, and argued, well, this is direct evidence of his guilt.

What it is, ladies and gentlemen, is more compelling evidence that neither Jim or Liz Sanders thought they had committed a crime. Otherwise why do you in addition to all the other steps, publish a book laying out every step of the investigation?

[T]here is no argument or sense by anyone, certainly Terrell Stacey, by taking this evidence he in any way compromised the government's ability to test. There was plenty of material left there when he left the Calverton hangar. And, indeed, the FBI had apparently claimed to have taken portions of that residue earlier and tested, although the results were not shared with anyone within the NTSB.

The significance of this scraping, ladies and gentlemen, however small and infinitesimal it is, the true significance of [the] scraping came through Terrell Stacey's testimony. And I think what that testimony shows is that the residue in this case was important to Terrell Stacey, very important.

It was important to him because it was his belief and his hope that if this material were tested by an independent laboratory it would shed some light on what had caused the crash of Flight 800.

Those pressures, ladies and gentlemen, inside of Terrell Stacey, had nothing to do with Jim or Liz Sanders. Those pressures on Terrell Stacey were created by the government, by the FBI, by the NTSB.

Terrell Stacey had spoken to the two air national guard pilots who were closest to the plane when it exploded, so close they had to veer away. ...

He had met them face to face and was told by them that they had seen a missile hit the plane before it exploded.

You also heard Terrell Stacey say that those very witnesses had been told inside the investigation to stop using the word "missile."

We heard about Mr. Stacey's vacillation, his concerns. His leeriness about taking that red residue, I submit to you, is a sop that he has thrown to the government and TWA, simply to keep his job.

But Terrell Stacey now finds himself, some short years before retirement, caught between the weight of the federal government on one hand, and the weight of his employment with TWA [on the other].

So, what he does, he does what anybody under those circumstances does. He gives the government a little piece of what he thinks they want. "So, there were procedures, I was leery and concerned."

I don't mean to be unpleasant with Captain Stacey, because it really is unfair to the man. But, ladies and gentlemen, you know it is a sop to the government, because you know, ladies and gentlemen, it is nowhere else in evidence in this case.

You know it when you heard the tape that was played for him, with his own voice, December 1996, the very period that the government would have you believe that Terrell Stacey was anguishing and torn about taking this extra step about removing a scraping of red residue.

I think what we will walk out of this with, ladies and gentlemen, is a better sense of what drove Terrell Stacey and what drove Jim Sanders, which is not to have conspired to commit a crime. Terrell said it in open court that he didn't think what he was doing was breaking the law.

I think we will have a better understanding of what it is that drove these people. What happened … after two-and-one-half years of this tragedy, and when you ask yourself those questions, then the narrow question before the trial before you is: Did Jim Sanders conspire with anyone to break the law? Did Jim Sanders knowingly and intentionally break the law? I submit to you that the only answer to that, ladies and gentlemen, that is supported by the evidence and supported by the law, and supported by your conscience, is that he did not.

With that last statement, Maffeo ended his closing arguments.

Jeremy Gutman then began to present the case for Liz Sanders. He is a scholar, an intellectual. You can envision Maffeo occasionally at a rowdy Manhattan Island pub, having a great time. Jeremy Gutman would fit perfectly in a room with soft piano music and good wine. Gutman began a very logical, focused presentation:

Mr. Pitofsky told you that Captain Stacey will tell you that he was initially reluctant to accept [the Sanders] request and remove this residue; that he did not give Jim Sanders an answer for several weeks, but then he received another phone call from Liz Sanders and she encouraged him to participate in this project to remove the sample and give it to Jim Sanders, and at that point he agreed that he would do it.

Now, ladies and gentlemen, it is a very compelling, well-plotted scenario. It has a very well planned beginning, middle and end.

First, it is Jim Sanders who puts the whole thing in motion. Then there is this three- or more-week period where Captain Stacey is tortured, conflicted in trying to make up his mind, but he can't decide what to do until finally the crucial moment arrives when Liz Sanders, my client, comes to him and like Lady Macbeth, tells him to do the foul deed.

This is the scenario that the government [says] they are going to prove to you. It reads a little bit like a play. It is neat and symmetrical. We have Stacey on one end, Jim and Liz on the other, but it is fictional, ladies and gentlemen.

Stacey did, it is true … testify about his reluctance. He did testify that for several weeks he couldn't make up his mind. But we know without any doubt that that is not true. We had a tape from December 8 … The fabric was supposed to have been taken in early January, and [on] December 8 we heard Captain Stacey saying, getting that residue is my top priority, and I will scrounge around for anything else I might be able to find.

Now, it doesn't matter—the fact is he denied that tape until it was played for him. And then he admitted, yes, that's me, that was me talking. It doesn't matter from your perspective whether he is lying or hopelessly confused. Either way it doesn't matter; a tape recording is not subject to pressures because it has an agreement with the government. And a tape recording can't revise its story to suit its current interest.

The tape doesn't lie. The tape tells you on December 8 he already had gotten over whatever reluctance he may or may not have had about [getting] the residue. We don't know if he ever had any reluctance. But certainly by December 8 he made it his top priority.

This does two things to make your job easier. It tells you the facts I just talked about, and maybe more importantly, like it or not, you can't rely on Captain Stacey's testimony, you just can't. …

We heard all sorts of things, influenced—what does that mean? He was influenced by his personal history with the airplane, having flown it the day before. He was influenced by the fact that he was away from his family What does that mean to say he was influenced? And what words or actions does the government want you to find beyond a reasonable doubt that Liz Sanders engaged in, that influenced him.

If Captain Stacey himself can't answer that question, and he couldn't ... the question was never asked of him, and he never did tell us what exactly did she do that influenced [him].

Well, if he can't guess ... how can the government ask you to guess?

Earlier in his closing argument, Mr. Pitofsky told you that but for Liz Sanders, Stacey would never have taken the residue. Well, Mr. Pitofsky, as you know, is not a witness. He can't testify. And you didn't hear from any witness. The only person who said, but for Liz Sanders, Terry Stacey wouldn't have taken that residue—was Mr. Pitofsky. Captain Stacey, the alleged co-conspirator, didn't give you that evidence and didn't give you any basis to find Liz Sanders guilty.

But there is an even bigger flaw to their argument, because it is based on another premise, and that is that an innocent person would have no reason to fear harassment by the FBI, or baseless prosecution by the United States government.

Terry Stacey may be willing to have the government rewrite the story of what he has done, and turn him into someone that fits within the government's scenario of a criminal conspiracy.

Liz Sanders is not willing to let them rewrite her story that way.

Jeremy Gutman detailed the phone-call evidence, which, when combined with all other documents introduced as evidence, prove beyond a reasonable doubt that Liz did not talk to Terry Stacey until after the residue had been removed.

After Gutman closed, Pitofsky had one last chance to give his side of the story to the jury. He focused on issues that should not have been allowed inside the courtroom. The defense was prohibited from introducing evidence of government wrongdoing, yet Pitofsky was allowed to use the counter-argument: to what end was the government's motive of falsely implicating the Sanders? Pitofsky had hit a new low with that. He had spent months legally maneuvering to preclude the defense from answering that very question during the course of the trial.

The prosecution and defense then rested, and the judge read the jury 50 pages of instructions.

The jury deliberated for a few minutes then took a lunch break. A rather raucous party atmosphere could be heard through the jury-room door that entered directly into the courtroom.

After deliberating for 45 minutes, the jury filed back in. They found my wife and me guilty on all counts.

41

SENTENCING

*In Germany they came first for the Communists,
and I didn't speak up because I wasn't a Communist.
Then they came for the Jews,
and I didn't speak up because I wasn't a Jew.
Then they came for the trade unionists,
and I didn't speak up because I wasn't a trade unionist.
Then they came for the Catholics,
and I didn't speak up because I was a Protestant.
Then they came for me,
and by that time no one was left to speak up.*

Reverend Martin Neimollar

The judge was 90 minutes late. The crowd in the court-room divided up into groups to discuss the upcoming proceedings—Justice Department law school interns on one side of the room, and an eclectic group of people supporting us on the other side. One such supporter had flown in from Arizona; another flew in from Florida. Others from as far away as North Carolina and Massachusetts drove to Uniondale, Long Island, to demonstrate their support.

David Pitofsky, the federal prosecutor, was in rare form, pumped for the proceedings to come. He had an audience of interns to watch his masterful performance as he battled the evil Sanders' Gang. He knew the probation report submitted to the judge had recommended Liz not be imprisoned or fined, but be placed on probation for one year.

Liz was not the enemy of the State. I was. The Federal Probation Department was recommending I not be imprisoned, but given a $5,000 fine and three-year probation. Pitofsky's assignment was to vilify me once again and demand that I serve a prison term.

Pitofsky had two lines of attack he could use to achieve his goal. He had filed papers with the judge alleging I had obstructed justice in May 1997 when I had a conversation with Liz's best friend at TWA, Lee Taylor.

Lee had heard via the TWA Legal Department that the FBI wanted to talk to her. She had called me in a panic. I told her she did not have to talk to any federal official unless served with a grand jury subpoena. At that point she was legally obligated to answer the grand jury's questions.

In a later conversation I pointed out that Hillary Clinton's friends, then prominently featured on C-Span during the Whitewater debacle, were unable to recall anything tougher than their first names. I suggested to Lee that this performance, a televised public spectacle for weeks on end, without any Justice Department targeting for obstruction of justice, represented the baseline upon which a Department operating under the rule of law must look for guidance when considering any obstruction of justice charge. In other words, under the Janet Reno Justice Department, a foggy memory was not a crime.

The FBI had been enraged when Lee Taylor told them of my advice to her. It was a clear case of contempt-of-cop, advising anyone they did not have to live in fear of FBI bullying.

All of this occurred about two months before Lee Taylor received a subpoena to appear before the grand jury. It was a political discussion from which facts were discerned and discussed, called Freedom of Speech.

But not to Pitofsky. He and Jim Kinsley had massaged the FBI field notes as they passed information to the Federal Probation Department and the judge. The judge understandably formulated the belief that I had told Lee Taylor she could develop a foggy memory—after she had received the subpoena.

So Judge Joanna Seybert unwittingly fell in with Pitofsky's scheme shortly after she entered the courtroom at 3:00 p.m. on July 16, 1999, one day shy of the third anniversary of the downing of TWA Flight 800.

Bruce Maffeo rose to object to the misinformation under which the judge was preparing to sentence me. Pitofsky, in answer to the judge's question, stated that he believed I had spoken to Lee Taylor after she received the subpoena. Maffeo produced the FBI field notes, which disproved this attempt to present factually false information to the court.

Pitofsky was somewhat taken aback at being caught in such an underhanded venture. In federal court, this is normally not an impediment to further underhanded behavior by the prosecution.

He soon rallied and began his second line of attack. Jim Hall, chairman of the NTSB, had written a letter to the judge demanding, by inference, severe punishment because I had misrepresented the facts for financial gain, causing pain and suffering to hundreds of families of the victims lost in the TWA Flight 800 tragedy.

My actions, Jim Hall said, brought the government's honorable investigative conduct into question. So, Hall concluded, it was not a victimless crime as the defense suggested. I must be severely punished:

> . . . this is not a so-called victimless crime. [The] NTSB has recently been given a statutory responsibility to keep members of families affected by airline tragedies informed. These duties have put us in close contact with the families of the victims of TWA Flight 800, and we are well aware of the confusion and distress caused by the perpetuation of groundless speculation about criminal destruction of the aircraft, and the even more insidious claims of a federal government cover-up. These defendants have traumatized the families with the release of misinformation, the only plausible cause for which is commercial gain.

This was the cross upon which Pitofsky intended to nail my hide, demanding I be hauled away in chains and incarcerated. Pitofsky took Jim Hall's malicious statements and further embellished:

Mr. Sanders has repeatedly asserted that his actions were motivated by a desire to discover and "bring to the American public the truth" about the cause of the Flight 800 crash. However, the evidence shows that his motives were more complicated, more personal and more selfish. For example, it is undisputed that Mr. Sanders sought and obtained a book contract worth $125,000 based on his "investigation" into the crash. As Lee Taylor testified at trial, Mr. Sanders discussed in private his hope that the Flight 800 disaster story would be the "big one"—that is, the story that would generate for him (not for the American public) substantial financial and professional benefits. Additionally, attached hereto is a letter to Your Honor in aid of sentencing from Jim Hall, the Chairman of the National Transportation Safety Board ("NTSB"), which brings to Your Honor's attention some of the adverse consequences of the defendants' actions. Among other things, Mr. Hall writes about the trauma visited upon the bereaved families of those who perished in the crash, whose grief was only exacerbated and prolonged by Mr. Sanders' dissemination of misinformation.

Mr. Sanders has also repeatedly endeavored to cast his actions in the heroic light of investigative journalism; however, the fact that he published his opinions in a newspaper article and book militate against his plea for leniency. It goes without saying that the press plays an absolutely vital role in American democracy; and that it does so, as it must, unfettered by State control. The duty of monitoring the press falls with journalists themselves, along with their editors and publishers, all of whom occupy positions of awesome responsibility and trust. Where, as here, such individuals abdicate their duty, and deploy the power of the press irresponsibly and for personal advantage rather than for the public good, they threaten the very principles that they claim to champion.

Once again the judge seemed to be agreeing with the argument presented by a government agent. She read a portion of Hall's letter into the record. Her comments revealed that she was inclined to believe this malicious line of attack.

Then Maffeo stood up and began the counter-attack. His extraordinary courtroom presence and ability to tell a story in a manner that brings out the facts and literally drives emotion into the words, had an impact. Many in the audience were in tears as he pointed out that there are two sides to this story. The NTSB doesn't have a monopoly on truth, Maffeo argued. Terry Stacey sat before the judge a few short weeks before and painfully told the judge and jury that one of the factors that compelled him to take the residue and give it to me for testing was the fact that two military pilots who had seen a missile approach and strike Flight 800, had been ordered not to say they had seen a missile, Maffeo pointed out. He also pointed to the many discrepancies; anomalies misinformation and disinformation that drove journalists like me to question the integrity of the FBI/NTSB investigation.

This was a case that should have been fought in the court of public opinion, not in the federal courts. Yet, once again, here was the chairman of the NTSB maliciously attacking me when the government had never produced a shred of proof to substantiate this reprehensible attack, Maffeo said.

It was a powerful performance that devastated the prosecution. The judge turned to Pitofsky, and asked him if he had any recommendations before she passed sentence. The formerly cocky prosecutor could barely get out of his seat or formulate a coherent thought. He took a deep breath, shrugged his shoulders, then told the judge "the people" had no sentencing recommendations whatsoever to make.

The judge then addressed us, saying we would not be imprisoned, nor be required to pay a fine. She gave me three years probation and Liz one year. The judge then commented to Maffeo that she assumed the defense would be filing an appeal. Maffeo assured her that the notice of intent would be filed Monday morning. Probation was lifted during the appeal process.

Pitofsky had heretofore always remained in the courtroom for post-proceeding verbal jousting with Maffeo. Not this time. He grabbed his briefcase and made for the door, with Kinsley in hot pursuit.

The interns solemnly filed out as our support group celebrated.

42

PROPAGANDA OR JOURNALISM?

You cannot have a corrupt government without a corrupt press, unless of course, you have no free press at all.

James Berquist
FAA whistleblower

The day after sentencing was the third anniversary of the Flight 800 crash. Patricia Milton, an Associated Press reporter, used the third anniversary to launch her book, *In the Blink of an Eye, The FBI Investigation of Flight 800*. It is an unabashedly pro-FBI view of the investigation as seen through Jim Kallstrom's eyes and the eyes of his senior staff. If they said it, it was pure gold—no need to fact-check, just write it down.

Patricia Milton quotes these FBI officials inner-most thoughts to inform the reader of their compassion, caring, wisdom and high-minded dedication to humanity. Her single-minded devotion to Jim Kallstrom builds with each page until, on page 284, it reaches a climax as she gushes:

> And then, as Higgins watched through the panes of the West Wing's double French doors, Kallstrom cinched the belt of his Marine Corps green trench coat and strode off with the weight of a very, very tricky investigation balanced effortlessly, or so it seemed to Higgins, on his big broad shoulders.

Such commentary should have alerted those hard-bitten major media personalities who so love to ask the tough questions, probing for the weakness in the author's story. But it wasn't even hinted at when Patricia Milton began her media tour.

Chris Matthews, CNBC's "Hardball" anchor, questioned Patricia Milton, throwing up nothing but softballs. As a "counter" to Milton, Matthews' other guest that night was Jim Kallstrom!

Milton was telling the story the major media had committed themselves to defending, at the cost of all appearance of journalistic integrity. If the government said it, major media broadcast it as fact without any attempt to balance the story with the wealth of evidence casting doubt on each government missive. Milton's book defended major media's politically-correct view of the Flight 800 tragedy, therefore it was proper for major media to serve up softballs to the defender of the status quo.

Was Milton profiting from the misery of the victims' families by releasing her book on the third anniversary? Of course. Did the major media question her motives? Of course not.

Did the major media pour over her book, looking for weak points and outright false statements? No. Even the most egregious of disinformation was ignored by major media. For instance:

• "The FAA was also rushing a copy of the [radar] tape with the mysterious blips over to the White House. … It could very well" be a missile, "the FAA advised the FBI, but it could also be a computer glitch, or a 'ghost blip,'" Milton alleges on page 22, leading the reader to believe the confused or indecisive FAA was passively sending radar tape to the White House and FBI. This is factually false. The FAA technicians saw what they believed to be a missile converge on Flight 800. They first contacted the White House, not to say they were confused, but to say they believed a missile was seen on the radar merging with Flight 800. A November 15, 1996, NTSB report, cited elsewhere, provides the facts. Milton provides fiction. The FAA technicians were pressured by the NTSB to recant, but refused. FAA senior management did attempt to appease the NTSB by stating the possibility of a missile being seen on the radar was "remote." This was not the technicians' statement. It was a political statement during a heated exchange where the FAA was being pressured to be a team player. Nor does Milton mention that two New York Air National Guard pilots had seen a missile strike Flight 800. They were so close to the event they had to maneuver their aircraft out of the way of falling debris.

• "In fact, Kallstrom was grateful for all the help he could get, not only from the Coast Guard and local police but from the National Transportation Safety Board (NTSB), which by federal protocol would be the FBI's partner. ..."[1] This is a factually false statement put out by the FBI to cover the actions of the Justice Department and FBI during the course of the Flight 800 investigation. Federal code, i.e., a law passed by Congress and signed into law by the President, mandates that the NTSB is the "priority" investigative team. The FBI and other federal investigative agencies can participate, but the NTSB controls the investigation—all evidence and scientific testing done by the FBI must be promptly shared with the NTSB investigation. But the FBI from the beginning began to muscle the NTSB into accepting an inferior role. When elements within the NTSB resisted, the Department stepped in and told the NTSB it could not interview witnesses to a missile.

• "The men [Kallstrom and the NTSB's Bob Francis] also agreed that, as a practical matter, the FBI would conduct all eyewitness interviews. ..."[2] NTSB documents proclaim this factually false. The Department of Justice forced the NTSB Witness Team to cease and desist in the opening days of the investigation. According to the NTSB documents, the Justice

Department and FBI did not want any eyewitness accounts that might conflict with the FBI version of what the eyewitnesses said.

• Patricia Milton, on page 50, gives the eyewitness account of a "U.S. Navy electronic-warfare technician" on USAir Flight 217, which was descending into the New York area from 21,000 feet, headed in a north-northeast direction toward TWA Flight 800, which was climbing from 13,000 feet, heading east from JFK Airport. The witness, sitting on the right side of the plane, saw a "flarelike streak" heading in a "east-northeasterly direction." He tracked the flare-like object visually for about 10 seconds. Then, he "saw a small explosion in the area where he had last seen the" flare-like object. "A second later, the small explosion became a large one. All this appeared to occur about three- to four-thousand feet below the USAir plane."[3] The witness then watched TWA Flight 800 fall toward the water. A passenger sitting one row behind this witness also saw events unfold before his eyes: "Nugent said he could see the cabin lights inside the plane a moment before it erupted into a fireball." Rather compelling eyewitness accounts. So, what golden kernels did Kallstrom and his minions spread before Patricia Milton? For months these two eyewitness stories "haunted the [FBI] agents as almost irrefutable evidence that some kind of missile had hit Flight 800." But alas, "the most important details were absent. At no point ... had he seen TWA Flight 800, so at no point had he seen the projectile hit the plane—or anything else." So there *could* have been a missile that missed Flight 800 just before the "mechanical" overpressure blew the plane out of the sky, according to Milton's logic.

• "... [N]or did anyone claim to see anything that might indicate a possible missile launching site," Milton alleges on page 80. That is factually false. Multiple witnesses, including

Paul Angelides, saw a missile in the initial stages of flight and graphically described the sound of a missile launch and acceleration as it streaked off to meet Flight 800. Then Patricia Milton alleges something that was almost impossible for her not to know was false when she wrote it: "… only a few had seen the streak ascending. Most, in fact, had thought it might be descending or moving horizontally. …" NTSB eyewitness statistics prove that 94% of the witnesses who expressed an opinion said the streak was ascending. But "ascending" does not conform to the CIA depiction of fuel streaks descending. Milton ends this sad paragraph with: "… and none seemed to have seen an object strike the aircraft. Bauer, the Air National Guard pilot who saw Flight 800 explode, thought he might have, but he couldn't be sure."[4] Milton seems to have comfortably settled into the theory that a missile *may* have approached the plane. Unless, however, it was actually seen striking the plane, it must be assumed the missile flew *past* Flight 800 just before the mechanical event destroyed the 747.

- "The radar maps showed no hostile fighter planes or warships in the area that could have fired a more sophisticated missile."[5] Misleading as well as factually false. There were, of course, no "hostile" fighter planes. None would have the range, unless we consider Canada a hostile neighbor. Many ships and planes were in the area. NTSB analysts have publicly admitted that three surface ships were in the area, one traveling in a southerly direction at 30 knots, three miles from TWA Flight 800 when it went down. The 30-knot radar target continued south. What the NTSB and FBI have been withholding from the public is that an entire flotilla of warships was to the south-southeast of Flight 800 in Warning Zone W-105. The 30-knot surface vessel headed straight for the flotilla. Navy radar reveals even more ships and an above-top-secret military platform at 98,000 feet. Let us not forget the Navy admitted in writing that large Naval units were in the area, but protected additional facts from disclosure by invoking national security.

• "By the end of July [1996], investigators would be able to deduce from the radar that the nose had come off after the initial explosion, while the plane continued to ascend without it. ..."[6] Factually false. Radar cannot determine if a plane is ascending or descending unless the transponder is functioning. Radar does tell a compelling story debunking this CIA myth passed on to the reader by Milton as fact. The stricken 747's speed initially increased, making it virtually impossible for the nose to have immediately come off or for the 747 to ascend. Instead, the evidence points to the plane going into a dive before the nose was blown off in the secondary explosion.

• "... [T]he radar tapes offered no clue as to why Flight 800 had fallen out of the sky and revealed nothing that might indicate a missile approaching or hitting the jetliner. ..."[7] Factually false. In the precise location where Paul Angelides and a second group of witnesses heard the missile launch, saw it shortly after launch, and watched as it accelerated into the darkening sky, a primary radar hit can be seen. About 20 seconds later these witnesses saw an explosion off in the distance. This conforms precisely to the primary radar hit where the missile was seen shortly after launch and where, because of its slow initial speed, it may have been "seen" by FAA radar. And, Navy radar appeared to have been tampered with in order to remove evidence of a missile approaching Flight 800 2.8 seconds before its demise.

• Patricia Milton, by inference, claims on page 135, that no 30-knot radar target can be seen speeding from the scene of the crime. Factually false. It is admitted to in NTSB documents and shown on radar printouts.

- "… [T]he FBI shared interviews—of eyewitnesses … only after blacking out the names of the interviewees."[8] Factually false, during the summer 1996 timeframe in which Milton is referencing. The NTSB was prohibited access to all eyewitness accounts until the end of November 1996. Then they were prohibited from re-contacting these witnesses for further information. The NTSB role was reduced to compiling statistics about information contained within each statement—which is how we know that 94% of those who saw a flare-like object, and expressed an opinion, thought it was ascending.

- On page 153, Milton says the Navy P-3 Orion flying near Flight 800 "had instruments to alert them if their plane was being locked on[to] by a missile launcher." This is presented as "significant evidence against the missile theory." Why? Because "A terrorist in a boat planning to lock-on to Flight 800 would likely have tested his launcher's lock-on capability with other planes passing by moments before Flight 800." Milton does not enlighten the reader as to why a terrorist would wait until the final seconds before testing the launcher. Nor does she reveal how the terrorist would see a plane at 20,000 feet, through the haze in the gathering darkness. When reviewing the radar tapes, the mystery is further compounded. The P-3 came over the top of Flight 800 seconds before a missile hit it. Factoring in aim, launch, acceleration and impact, it would be impossible to first lock-on to the P-3. Flight 800 would have been in the way. But the FBI had to provide an answer for her to print in the book. So the real question is: who is the expert within the FBI that gave her such a statement?

- On page 154, Milton alleges that Admiral William Flanagan had "supplied Kallstrom with charts and records to show the coordinates of every" military asset that could have been involved in friendly fire. "At five, sometimes six command levels, FBI agents conducted interviews and obtained signed documentation certifying that each asset was what, and where, Flanagan said it was." Factually false. Kallstrom and the Navy have always maintained that the closest surface military vessel was the U.S.S. *Normandy*, almost 200 miles to the south, when, in fact, an entire armada was a few miles from Flight 800.

• "On the day of the crash, the [FBI] agents learned the airspace defined by W-105, -106, and –107 was open to commercial air traffic. ... No military exercise ... was scheduled to take place in those areas."[9] In fact, W-105 was restricted the entire day. A second AEGIS CEC exercise kept W-105 off-limits to commercial air traffic between 0900 and 1300 hours, July 17, 1996.

• "In any event, Flight 800 had never come close to any of the Whiskey areas."[10] Factually false. Flight 800 was about 10 miles from the northwest corner of W-105 when struck by a missile.

• "An explosive would have left powder, discoloration, and material embedded in the bodies. But there was none."[11] Factually false. The coroner has stated that most of the bodies had shrapnel embedded in them. An FBI agent was at each autopsy to immediately take possession of the shrapnel and remove it from the premises, where it has disappeared into the dark fog of obfuscation that permeates the Flight 800 investigation.

• "The brief sound—more like a click than a loud crack— was indeed like the one heard on the cockpit voice recorder of Pan Am 103. ..."[12] Factually false. All parties involved in this portion of the NTSB investigation acknowledge that this final sound is unlike any ever before recorded on a doomed cockpit voice recorder. The NTSB issued a lengthy "factual report" stating this. What the NTSB neglected to mention is that the Pan Am 103 sound traveled through the plane's structure at about 340 feet per second (fps). The final Flight 800 sound traveled at more than 2,000 fps, approximating the speed at which a missile would have been traveling when it struck the 747.

- "… [T]he radar maps the NTSB had studied from stations as far-ranging as Nashua, New Hampshire, and Norfolk, Virginia, added nothing to the picture."[13] Factually false—needs no further comment.

- On page 189, Patricia Milton alleges the FBI missile team decided to "study the kinds of missiles known to exist" in an attempt to determine how each might relate to the Flight 800 crash. "In essence, there were three kinds: the ICBM, the SM-2, and the MANPAD, or shoulder-launched missile. …" The SM-2 "was designed to be fired from the silo of a warship like the *Normandy*," Milton confidently assures the reader. This statement ignores the missile between the large SM-2 and MANPAD used by NATO and the U.S. military, including a new [in 1996], relatively small, underwater-launched Navy anti-aircraft missile designed to give the Seawolf-class of submarine protection when operating in a littoral warfare situation.

- "As all commercial, military, and satellite radar had confirmed, no warship of the necessary size … had been situated and remotely within the SM-2's ninety-mile maximum range. …"[14] Factually false. More than 30 military vessels were in the immediate area and seen scurrying away immediately after the plane was shot down.

- On page 190, Milton's gullibility is fully exposed. She

alleges that "… the FBI determined that no U. S. armed forces" including Navy Seals, Special Forces, Delta Force and Marine Recon, were conducting clandestine exercises with Stingers or any other MANPADs. Milton says the FBI contacted "all" these units, and "all denied having conducted any exercises on Long Island or off its coast. …" But Kallstrom did not stop there, she said. The FBI "interviewed all command levels" of the Special Forces, Navy Seals, Delta Force and Marine Recon, "scrutinized training logs, deployment, and other background information. …" Then the FBI lined up each unit, on multiple occasions, and interviewed each and every elite-force member in the United States military "until they were satisfied that no MANPAD could possibly have been fired by U.S. forces, and that no cover-up of such a launching could have occurred." Factually false, and downright absurd.

• "Why was there no visible explosive damage to the metal or other pieces where the" PETN/RDX explosive "traces were found?"[15] Factually false. The PETN and RDX found on the right side of the passenger cabin, at row 25 or 26, is in the area over the hole in the RSOB discussed elsewhere in this book. Directly above this hole, the seats in rows 21 through 26 are severely fragmented, distorted and burned, with fist-sized holes through the seats. The FBI and NTSB were so fearful of my obtaining photos of this damage when I went to the Calverton hangar on December 22, 1998, they had these seats removed prior to my arrival. But I was able to obtain photos of these seats. They reveal extensive blast and heat damage to the seatbacks in the same area where explosive residue was found.

• On pages 230-231, Milton relates the FBI version of why the PETN/RDX evidence fell apart. The FBI learned that a St. Louis K-9 police team had used a TWA 747 to give the dog practice locating explosives inside an airplane. The test, conducted about one month before Flight 800 went down, was on the 747 parked at the gate *next* to the plane that would eventually become Flight 800. But the FBI needed an explanation, so they declared the wrong plane to be the one where the K-9 practice was conducted. The officer's notes do not identify which 747 was used. But records and crew statements do reveal which 747 was *not* used for the training exercise. The flight crew of the plane that would eventually be Flight 800 kept records of that day in St. Louis. These records confirm they were on the plane preparing for the flight, loading passengers and food, and conducting the extensive pre-flight at the exact time the airport police officer says he was training his dog in a totally empty 747. But the FBI did not interview the crew. Why? Because the politically-correct answer in their grasp would evaporate before the truth revealed in crew interviews. The 747 at the adjacent gate was totally empty during this timeframe and was, beyond a reasonable doubt, the plane where the canine exercise was conducted.

• Linda Kabot took a photo the evening of July 17, 1996, that shows a cylindrical object in the sky with an exhaust plume apparently being turned downward by the projectile's thrust-vector control steering mechanism. It could be a drone, which uses such a steering mechanism and sometimes has such a configuration. But no plane on earth uses this kind of steering mechanism. Patricia Milton, on page 234, offers the FBI reasoning for not believing the cylindrical object, without wings [or wings so small they were invisible in the gathering darkness], is an airplane: "it had only two of the three necessary signatures of a missile ... a white dot that would signify a burning propellant, and a dark streak that would be the missile itself. It was missing the exhaust trail that would follow the missile." Factually false. Depending on the missile and stage of flight, an exhaust trail may or may not be seen. A drone does not normally leave an exhaust trail in flight.

• On page 234, Milton continues her attempt to explain away the eyewitness accounts. Repeated throughout the book is the FBI contention that because the witnesses used descriptive words such as "flare-like object" rather than "missile," it must mean they had not seen a missile. Taking this line of reasoning to its logical absurdity, the only rational explanation is that some big, really fast fireflies zoomed skyward that night just as spontaneous combustion destroyed the 747. Or, the witnesses had seen a missile that missed the 747.

* On the next page, Milton attempts to discredit the two New York Air National Guard pilots who had both seen a missile approach and destroy Flight 800. The third person in the aircraft, "had seen neither a missile-like flare nor the explosion itself," Milton disingenuously tells the reader—apparently forgetting that in the opening pages of her book she had reported this third person was not in a position to observe what was visible to the two pilots. But Patricia Milton soldiers on, revealing that both pilots were arrogant and may not have liked each other. By this process of elimination, Milton then declared the third person in the aircraft "seemed the most credible."[16] So, arrogant pilots are bad witnesses, and even less credible if they do not like each other.

• "No chemical traces were found on any of the tank parts retrieved as yet. ..."[17] Factually false. The NTSB has withheld the NASA-KSC chemical analysis report exposing the fact that nitrate was found on part CW-504, located at the left side of the front spar. Another nitrate sample was also found in an adjoining CWT ceiling part. I was able to obtain a copy of this report and interviewed the NASA chemist who discovered the nitrate, Charles Bassett. Bassett says he called the NTSB's Flight

800 senior scientist, Merritt Birky, to advise him that additional testing was needed to determine whether the nitrate was from an explosive. Birky ordered Charles Bassett to cease further testing.

• "A reconstructed wing might show the passage of a spark-lit fire after all."[18] But there was a problem. The NTSB did reconstruct the left wing and it showed a hydraulic event that could not be explained by any mechanical hypothesis, so it was disassembled. The NTSB made no attempt to reconstruct the right wing because, as a BATF report exposed, there was an exterior-to-interior path ending at the hole in the RSOB, from which significant right-to-left damage crosses the CWT.

• On page 304, Patricia Milton talks about Pierre Salinger releasing a report March 6, 1996, and a few days later "Salinger convened a news conference in Paris to call for a congressional investigation into the missile ... theory. ... But there was a more commercial reason for the news conference, Milton alleges: "... the real object of the conference appeared to be the promotion of a newly published paperback book by James Sanders. ..." Factually false. At the moment the news conference took place, I was in Kansas City, working on the manuscript. The final draft went to the publisher at the end of March, and the first copies appeared on bookshelves the third week of April, one month *after* the Salinger press conference. Pierre Salinger and I had never met or communicated with each other. We would not meet until August 1997, in Washington, D.C.

• One page later, Milton repeats a Jim Kallstrom disinformation line that has been repeatedly debunked by the FAA, NTSB and U.S. Navy—that the streak seen toward Flight 800 on the radar tapes the FBI confiscated from Richard Russell, was actually a ghost image of a plane many miles away. Faulty fact-checking? Apparently. The "company" line? Absolutely.

• On the same page, Milton claims the ever-vigilant FBI rode into Williamsburg, Virginia, in March 1996 and "[Sanders] was questioned closely about a piece of seat fabric from Flight 800 that somehow had come into his possession." Factually false. The FBI never questioned me, nor did I ever receive "seat fabric." I received foam rubber with reddish-orange residue attached.

• Continuing on the same page, Milton says: "Sanders had no experience studying plane crashes or debris from missile attacks." What she fails to mention is that no one *inside* the government investigation had any knowledge of what missile-damaged debris from a 747 would look like. This statement can be found in the FBI's own words as well as in the missile report sent to Kallstrom by the missile experts at China Lake. They did not know how a civilian airliner's fuselage would react to a missile hit. Nor was it correct that I had "no experience studying plane crashes." In fact, Flight 800 was the *third* aircraft incident investigation in which I had been involved.

• [Sanders] "did, however, have a wife who was a TWA employee, and who appeared to have heard much intriguing speculation from 'insiders' at the airline."[19] Factually false, and part of a series of statements inserted into Milton's book to defame and injure my reputation and credibility. Milton knew, when she wrote those words, that I had sources inside the Calverton hangar with access to documents the government did not ever want released, such as the location of all debris when and where originally found—contradicting the mechanical hypothesis and the NTSB chairman's November 15, 1996, memo, where it is revealed for the first time that the FAA technicians monitoring Flight 800 saw a missile merge with Flight 800.

• Milton's prejudice spilled over onto page 306, where she alleges that an FBI agent saw the reddish-orange residue in August 1996, took samples back to the FBI lab in Washington, D.C., "where he worked all night testing it. His conclusion was that the reddish-orange chemical was upholstery glue." Factually false. The FBI was required to turn over such documents during the discovery portion of the criminal case. No such document was ever unearthed from the FBI files. But, Milton continues, that was not enough proof for Kallstrom. The FBI "double-checked [its] findings with the seat manufacturer, who confirmed that the substance was glue." Factually false. At least four journalists, including myself, interviewed a Webber Seat representative. In each interview, Webber Seat's story remained consistent: their seats contained an insignificant amount of adhesive and they did not know what adhesive had been used on the Webber Seats installed in Flight 800. Milton next says: "Kallstrom did not stop there. He had agents obtain the patent and formula for the glue and compare its elements to the chemicals found on the seats. They matched. The residue was glue." Factually false. My tape-recorded interview with Merritt Birky contains his admission that 3M did not know what its formula for 3M 1357 HP Adhesive was when the seats were last refurbished. They had upgraded the adhesive and failed to keep a record of the old elements. Furthermore, the government chemist who the FBI and NTSB said had independently confirmed their findings, said that was not true. The chemist provided me with a notarized affidavit politely saying the government was not telling the truth. And finally, Florida State University obtained a sample of the 3M 1357 HP Adhesive and conducted scientific testing to determine whether it was consistent with the elements found in the residue I had received from Terry

Stacey and had tested at WCAS.

• On page 334, Milton presents the CIA version of what the witnesses really saw, acknowledging that "of the 240 eyewitnesses, 58 reported hearing a loud explosion first and then looking toward the horizon. Each of these witnesses had observed a streak descending." Factually correct. Sound travels much slower than light. In reacting to the sound of an explosion, one would expect to, at best, see the final stages of that explosion. But then, Milton's house of cards falls apart: "Though the other eyewitnesses failed to report hearing an explosion, most of them also saw a streak descending." In fact, NTSB documents confirm that 94% saw a streak *ascending*. She continued: "Either the sound was blocked by objects in front of them . . . or they simply failed to hear a sound that did, in fact, reach them." We must now add hard of hearing to all Long Island residents—at least those who hang around the beach during the summer. Milton's analysis wraps up with: "Either way, they, too, were seeing the last seconds of Flight 800's fall."

• "From radar as well as the satellite sensors, the CIA determined that after the explosion the plane climbed from 13,800 feet to about 17,000 feet. ..."[20] Factually false. Radar and satellite sensors cannot determine if a plane is climbing or descending unless the transponder is working. It wasn't. No one has been able to produce a computer analysis confirming this CIA hypothesis, not even when the most optimistic numbers are factored into the equation.

• In Milton's characterization of the military missile expert on USAir Flight 217 who saw a "flare-like projectile" streak past and a short time later saw Flight 800 explode, she explains away such a highly credible witness in the following manner. First, he "didn't hear the explosion because" he was "sitting in a pressurized cabin, but" he "did see fire spreading from" Flight 800, "which was in fact the 'projectile.'"[21] So, this missile expert had not really seen a missile streaking past his plane and toward Flight 800. He had seen flaming fuel from Flight 800 streaking in the opposite direction, past his plane. The same "reasoning" is used on the following page to explain away two more highly credible military witnesses, Major Fritz Meyer and Captain Chris Baur, who were adamant that they saw a streak impact Flight 800, *followed* by the explosion of the 747. Milton's assurances that all these witnesses had the events reversed, is unsupported by *any* facts.

   • On page 344, Milton addresses the 30-knot vessel seen by the FAA radar about 2.9 miles from Flight 800 when it blew up. The FBI has alleged the boat was "about 25 feet long." Factually false. FAA radar blips do not reveal the length of a vessel or airplane. This disinformation was released by the FBI to give major media an excuse not to pursue a vessel 100 feet long—much more likely to maintain such a high speed and be seen by an FAA radar. Kallstom's reason for not attempting to determine what ship it was and interview its crew: "The FBI has not continued to seek this vessel because there is no evidence to indicate the plane was brought down by a missile." There is a lot of evidence that a missile was launched and approached Flight 800. Apparently, Milton's reasoning is that as long as the missile missed, it is irrelevant.

   • On page 346, Kallstrom declares that "not one of the conspiracy theorists has even seen the wreckage, yet they say they know this plane was brought down by a missile." By virtue of being indicted, I personally got to inspect the "wreckage," taking more than 200 photos in the process. These photos tell a story of evidence being altered by the government to remove evidence of a missile strike. The Department of Justice has threatened to imprison me if I release this evidence.

The question arises: How could such a book be published, and why is it not attacked by major media and exposed as government disinformation? The answer must focus on the power centers that corrupt major media, frequently turning an important constitutional institution into a lapdog of the most powerful people on earth.

Power corrupts unless held in check by the media. When the media becomes a willing servant to those who possess power, there is absolutely nothing stopping the powerful within government from destroying those who place them at risk.

Unfortunately, Milton is not unique among major media reporters—she is the norm. CBS News anchor Dan Rather's statement on the back of the book's dust cover demonstrates what depths the major media has descended to in obsequious pursuit of acceptance by the powerful:

> Meticulously researched ... *In the Blink of an Eye* is ... driven by an investigator [Jim Kallstrom] who's every bit the match for any hero out of Agatha Christie ... yet the story is fact. ..."

Back in 1997, Dan Rather's CBS News had volunteered to be the neutral arbiter of the glue-versus-missile residue fight that sprang before the public on March 10, 1997. CBS told me they wanted my second piece of reddish-orange residue to test, with the intention of announcing the results to the world. When Jim Kallstrom found out, he told CBS News he would take the place apart, piece by piece, if they did not immediately return the residue without first testing it.

Did Dan Rather manfully lead the resistance, manning the CBS ramparts, recording every moment of the unlawful FBI attack on journalism? No. Dan Rather's CBS News meekly turned the residue over to the government. And now, the man who promised to take CBS news apart, piece by piece, is being hailed as a hero by Dan Rather. Does this make Dan Rather a conspirator? Of course not. It makes him a typical representative of major media.

Nor did Patricia Milton actively engage in a cover-up. Her gullibility made her an easy mark for psychological operations that have been used by the federal government at least since World War II to massage and shape the news.[22]

Three days after the *Press-Enterprise* article, ABC's Good Morning America (GMA) tried to find someone to represent the government side of the residue issue, for an on-the-record, prime-time morning debate featuring me on one side of the issue and a government representative on the other. GMA failed in its search to find someone to debate me and cancelled the March 13, 1997, episode, saying they could not put me on the air without an opponent, since it would present an unbalanced story for the viewing public.

The morning of March 13, I tuned in to GMA to see what had replaced this face-to-face debate. There sat Jim Kallstrom, being fed softball questions. Is Good Morning America part of a conspiracy? No. Just typical major media.

Dateline NBC contacted me two days after the *Press-Enterprise* article ran, saying they wanted to tell my side of the story. Dateline NBC correctly pointed out that the government had exclusive access to the media at that point, and no one within major media was providing balanced coverage of the residue story. Heavy emphasis was placed on Dateline NBC's desire to level the playing field and tell my side of the story.

Shortly thereafter, I prepared to sit down with Chis Hansen to tape an interview. A young Dateline producer, Eric Worth, took me aside and quietly warned me to expect tough questions from Hansen—but not to worry. Dateline was committed to telling my side of the story.

As it turned out, Hansen's primary objective during the

multi-hour-taped interview was an apparent attempt to get me to say there was no hole through which a missile could have traveled, even though my sources inside the hangar had said there were any number of areas a missile could have traveled through.

When Hansen could not get the statement he wanted out of me, he and Dateline NBC's producers resorted to some questionable behavior. Hansen's statement, "But there's no hole," was part of the program that ran the evening of March 13, 1997. A voiceover was used to give the appearance that I agreed with Hansen's allegation.

Then Dateline NBC introduced a government memo they had received the day after the interview. This was the first time the document had left government control. I had never seen it, and Dateline NBC knew it. The document was flashed on-screen, with words highlighted. Hansen's voiceover suggested I was in possession of the document, and had failed to reveal the only two words inclusive that were favorable to the government: "remote possibility."

Does this sad performance make Dateline NBC a conspirator? No. It makes them the norm in major media "journalism."

The New York Times and other major media placed a total embargo on the First Amendment issues involved in my case. They sent a reporter, John McQuiston, to the trial, who either sat alone or with Patricia Milton. McQuiston never attempted to approach me, on or off the record. The stories he filed were replete with false information, devoid of balance, and designed to provide his readers the Justice Department's spin. On April 14, 1999, McQuiston wrote: "He [Stacey] told the jury that Mrs. Sanders had pleaded with him to help provide evidence for her husband's investigation into the crash." Nowhere in the trial transcript can a Terry Stacey statement be found that even hints at such conduct on the part of Liz Sanders'. But it created a public impression favorable to the government in the minds of more than a million readers.

McQuiston wasn't just having an off day. On April 8, at the start of the trial, he had written:

> Captain Stacey told the jury ... that he had stolen the seating material from a government hangar in Calverton, on Long Island, *at the repeated insistence of the Sanderses.*[23] [Emphasis added]

Terry Stacey had testified to the exact opposite, yet *The Times* was firmly committed to telling the story the way the government wanted it told. Facts were not relevant.

Newsday, on the same day as *The Times* article, joined the revisionist fray when Robert Kessler filed a report making the following allegation:

> Although James Sanders had given many interviews saying he was a journalist protected by a reporter's privilege in looking into the crash, the defense did not bring up First Amendment issues during the trial, apparently feeling there is no clear basis for a reportorial privilege in federal law.[24]

For 16 months our legal team had fought to keep the First Amendment from being excised from the courtroom—without success. This was not privileged information, it was available to the press and public.

Liz's attorney, Jeremy Gutman, attempted to insert some modest balance into the pages of *The New York Times*, with an Op-Ed piece published on April 16, 1999, two days after these factually-false articles appeared:

> The *Times* has recently reported that a Cincinnati *Enquirer* reporter's disclosure of his confidential source as a part of a deal struck with prosecutors "is echoing through the legal and

journalistic communities as a major assault on the revered principle of protecting sources" (April 11: "For a Reporter and Source, Echoes of a Broken Promise"). The article quoted a number of media representatives and scholars who viewed the reporter's capitulation as a breach of journalistic ethics and a threat to an essential component of investigative reporting: the ability to obtain information about corporate and public corruption from whistleblowers who will come forward only if they are assured confidentiality.

On April 13, 1999, investigative reporter James Sanders, author of *The Downing of TWA Flight 800*, and his wife, former TWA employee Elizabeth Sanders, paid the price for resisting similar pressure from federal prosecutors. They were convicted on charges that never would have been brought if they had agreed to reveal the identity of the TWA pilot who, frustrated by the misdirection and apparent corruption of the official Flight 800 investigation to which he was assigned, secretly provided Mr. Sanders a small sample of the plane's residue-bearing fabric so it could be tested.

After publication of a March 1997 newspaper article in which Sanders disclosed his possession of the residue and accused the FBI of covering-up evidence that a missile had caused Flight 800's demise, prosecutors demanded that he reveal his source. They could have sought this information by means of a grand jury subpoena, but that would have required them to comply with First Amendment-based guidelines that limit intrusions on freedom of the press, and would have permitted Sanders to challenge their demand in a court of law.

Instead, prosecutors offered Sanders a stark choice: either give up the source, or both you and your wife will face indictment. When the Sanders refused to compromise their ethical and journalistic principles, the United States Attorney made good on the threat. [Prosecutors] located the source, secured his testimony against the Sanders by means of a plea bargain, and instituted an unprecedented prosecution for the unauthorized removal of a miniscule quantity of "property" that had no value other than its potential for answering questions about the Flight 800 disaster.

In view of the obvious parallels, it is puzzling that the mainstream journalistic community, which is alarmed at the "chilling effect" that the Cincinnati *Enquirer* incident has had on reporters' vital relationships with confidential sources, has failed to recognize that the prosecution of the Sanders poses a similar threat. The critical issue in the Sanders case is not, as some reporters have suggested, whether the First Amendment gives reporters a license to break the law. The Sanders have never suggested that it does. Rather, the question that will be addressed when the Sanders' convictions are appealed is whether courts are powerless to check the government's use of its awesome prosecutorial power as a means of compromising the confidential relationship between a reporter and a source.

The resolution of that question should be a matter of concern not just to those who share Mr. Sanders' views regarding the cause of the Flight 800 disaster, but to all who understand and value the connection between a free press and an informed public.

To run such an Op-Ed piece would mandate coverage of the extraordinary constitutional issues at stake, delving into Justice Department abuse of power. *The New York Times* would be on the slippery slope to balanced reporting on this issue. They spiked the article.

Does this mean *The New York Times* is involved in a conspiracy? No. This is how major media practices journalism as we approach the new millenium.

43

PRIOR RESTRAINT

With the post-sentencing combat swirling in the background, my investigation into the actions taken by the FBI, NTSB and Justice Department at the Calverton hangar brought together a picture of debris removal, debris alteration, alteration of radar, false statements about the residue being glue, and a military presence in the area when Flight 800 went down.

I had gained possession of "before" and "after" hangar photos providing compelling evidence the center wing tank had been altered in order to make it possible for the NTSB and FBI to say there was no evidence of a missile strike.

This was compelling evidence with which to go on the offense. But there was a problem. My attorney had been forced to sign an agreement with the Justice Department in order to get inside the "crime" scene at Calverton:

> It is hereby stipulated and agreed between the parties that any and all photographs, videotapes, or other recordings made during the visit of the defendants James and Elizabeth Sanders and their attorneys to the NTSB facility at Calverton, Long Island ("The Hangar"), will be strictly for the preparation of the defendants defense in the above-captioned criminal matter and will not be reproduced, disclosed, used, published or distributed in any fashion outside of this litigation.

I had a right under Rule 16 to inspect and photograph the recovered wreckage without signing a stipulation. But the Justice Department had stalled for months in a transparent attempt to avoid complying with the rule.

The trial was set to begin early in 1999. Up to that point the judge had consistently ruled against any motion brought before the court by the our attorneys. If the judge said Rule 16 did not really mean what it said, or severely reduced the area that could be photographed, my investigation of NTSB, FBI and Justice Department conduct would be severely hampered. So I agreed, through my attorney, to an inspection under the stipulation in order to get at what I was certain was evidence the mockup had been altered.

The agreement stated the photos would only be used in the criminal case. But the photos did, in fact, produce powerful evidence that the government was engaged in a scheme to rewrite the history of Flight 800. The motive for harassing and prosecuting my wife and I was strongly reinforced, with these photos providing graphic evidence the center wing tank area had been altered.

I now had a manuscript under development that brought the misconduct within the Flight 800 investigation together with the altered evidence inside the hangar and the radar evidence, as well as the tale of government harassment and vindictive prosecution. For the first time, it would give the American public the other side of the story.

The photos taken during the December 22, 1998, inspection of the hangar were vital to presenting the public with a balanced picture of the Flight 800 investigation. As the FBI, NTSB and Justice Department knew at their respective senior levels, such revelations would once again place them at risk. They had just spent more than two years and hundreds of thousands of taxpayer dollars trying to neutralize me once and for all. But like the proverbial phoenix rising from the ashes, I wasn't done yet.

My attorney, Bruce Maffeo, wrote a letter to David B. Pitofsky, the Justice Department prosecutor, in an attempt to get him to voluntarily agree that the American public should be fully informed:

> I write at the request of my client, James Sanders, to request your consent for him to be released from the pre-trial stipulation entered in this case, which restricted Mr. Sanders' use of photographs that he took during the course of his visit in December of last year to view the wreckage recovered from the crash of TWA Flight 800, which was maintained at a hangar located in Calverton, New York. That stipulation, a copy of which is enclosed, restricted Mr. Sanders' use of the photographs to the preparation of the defense of the criminal case and prohibited them from being "reproduced, disclosed, used, published or distributed in any fashion outside of [that] litigation."
>
> The basis for Mr. Sanders' request is the recent publication of *In the Blink of an Eye* (Random House, 1999), which is written by Pat Milton, a reporter for Associated Press, with the publicly acknowledged cooperation of the Federal Bureau of Investigation ("FBI"). Among other matters, the book featured several photographs taken of the wreckage contained inside the Calverton facility that were taken with the FBI's express permission. The book also quotes extensively from James Kallstrom, the former Assistant Director of the New York office of the FBI, regarding his agency's investigation into the cause of the crash of Flight 800 and specifically attacks the conclusions regarding the plane's crash reached by Mr. Sanders in his book, *The Downing of TWA Flight 800* (Zebra Books, 1997).
>
> As no doubt you appreciate, the ongoing debate into the cause of the crash of TWA Flight 800 remains an issue of significant public concern. Moreover, there is no legitimate basis for Mr. Sanders to continue to be prevented from publishing photographs that in his view call into question the FBI's public account of the crash and its handling of the investigation, particularly in light of the FBI's decision to release selective photographs in support of its position to other journalists. Under these circumstances, we view the continued restrictions placed

on Mr. Sanders' use of the photographs that he took as implicating serious First Amendment concerns, a view that we note is apparently shared by Mr. Kallstrom, who is quoted in Ms. Milton's book as prizing "the right of [American] citizens to voice opinions and challenge their government." *In the Blink of an Eye, supra,* at 345.

Accordingly, I request that you consent to release Mr. Sanders from the terms of the stipulation entered in this case. Please advise me of your position as soon as possible.

When Pitofsky received the letter it was immediately pushed onto the front burner at Janet Reno's Justice Department. They would need to formulate a response that would deny me the use of photos—placing Reno, et al, at risk—while avoiding the image they'd taken on as thugs trampling on the First Amendment. The wisdom of Solomon would be required to get them out of the corner they had painted themselves into.

As it turned out, wisdom continued to be in short supply within the Department. They declined a written response, but made it clear that they would move to imprison me if the photos were published.

I then engaged the NTSB in a dialogue in order to solicit the government side of the story explaining how portions of the mock-up could legally be altered. I sent the following message, dated August 31, 1999, to Peter Goelz, head of NTSB's public affairs:

SUBJECT: Photos. A number of Flight 800 debris photos taken between August 1996 and March 1997 will be used in my soon-to-be-published book.

One series of photos will be similar to the photos available in NTSB Exhibit 17D, photos R-8 through R-11. These photos reveal the beginning of an apparent ongoing metamorphosis of CW-601.

Note the apparent puncture holes visible in your R-8. When compared to the photos taken by me [on] December 22, 1998, it appears that the metamorphosis observed in 1996 and 1997 continues. The holes are now gone. One lonely, moderate tear remains. Also note that the outline of CW-601 has undergone further alteration.

Can you provide a reasonable explanation?[1]

Peter Goelz messaged back: "Yes I can, but I will not. Your first book was an insulting fabrication—can't wait for number two."[2]

Peter Goelz, in writing, said he knew about the alteration of the center wing tank. I followed up with a second message to Goelz:

Peter, first, I would like to thank you for your confession. Having knowledge of obstruction of justice, i.e., altering debris, is a felony.

Second, I have NASA Chemist Charles Bassett's notarized affidavit saying the NTSB "glue" allegation is factually false. I followed up with a lengthy interview of Mr. Bassett and he assured me any allegation that 3M glue represents my sample, would be an insulting fabrication.

Florida State University has tested 3M 1357 HP Adhesive and determined that it cannot be my residue.

And let us not forget that Merritt Birky also confessed—he says the NTSB was afraid to test my residue and instead decided to go with the "glue repels missiles" hypothesis; i.e., if the NTSB can find glue inside the passenger cabin, missile residue cannot also be found.

You were personally responsible for spewing the "glue" disinformation to the press and public, so I can see why you would be petulant and whiny. Please enlighten me on any other area of The Downing of TWA Flight 800 you perceive as an "insulting fabrication."

Goelz apparently loved the rest of the book because he never wrote back.

44

NEUTRALIZE THE MESSAGE, DESTROY THE MESSENGER

There is strength in the union even of very sorry men
Homer

Tom Stalcup is a young man in his final year at Florida State University. In May 2000, he officially becomes "Doctor" Stalcup when he walks across the stage and accepts a diploma, with a physics major.

As might be expected, Stalcup has a very curious mind. When Flight 800 went down and major media soon began to publish official government leaks as fact instead of hunting down witnesses to a missile rising into the sky, he decided to begin his own investigation.

Eventually, this effort developed sources within the government. One of these sources handed him a disk containing the FAA radar database from the evening of July 17, 1996. He soon realized the government had withheld stunning information from the American public.

Stalcup picked up the phone and called *Insight* Magazine's Kelly O'Meara. Within days she had obtained the radar database from the NTSB and began to develop a story for the magazine. The story initially was given three pages—a major story for a Washington, D.C.-based magazine.

Without question, politics would become involved when the government learned the story was being developed. But Kelly O'Meara's almost 20 years of political and journalistic experience had not prepared her for what was about to happen.

O'Meara had Navy documents revealing extensive areas of the ocean south and east of Long Island reserved for significant military activity in the days surrounding the crash of TWA Flight 800—including live-fire, missile-fire, and submarine exercises. As she reviewed the radar database, surface ship and aircraft movement resembling a major military operation appeared on the screen. There was even a plane flying directly over a 30-plus-ship flotilla, constantly moving in a racetrack pattern, exactly like an AWACS-type plane involved in a Cooperative Engagement Capability (CEC) exercise. She watched as this armada steamed toward, and into, military warning zone W-105, which was activated that day for military operations.

The radar blips were "consistent with" such a Navy operation. One thing was certain, the FBI, NTSB, CIA, Department of Defense and White House all had access to this database. What is equally clear is that a decision was made to withhold this radar data from the public.

This Clinton administration decision makes it reasonable to journalistically infer that the decision was made because the revelation would cause political pain the government did not wish to endure. Although it would have been reasonable to make these inferences in the *Insight* Magazine article under development, O'Meara and her boss, Paul Rodriguez, eliminated inferences. The story was designed to inform the public of vital data not revealed by the government during the course of the TWA Flight 800 investigation.

Would the story develop "legs," forcing the Clinton administration to deal with it or face a media feeding frenzy? Or, would the government find a means to neutralize the story?

One obvious means of neutralization would be to reveal precisely what was going on that night. In an administration known for its attack-dog mentality and lack of willingness to admit mistakes, this did not seem to be a likely route.

As the article came together, the time finally came to pick up the phone, tell various government agencies the radar database had slipped out of government control, and ask for a response. The FBI refused to consider commenting, saying they didn't have the desire or will to assign someone the task of digging into the files to formulate a response.

The NTSB had a different reaction. They refused to answer questions on the phone, insisting that Kelly O'Meara meet with them face to face at NTSB headquarters.

The following day at 3:00 p.m., she arrived at the NTSB office. Instead of inviting her in for an incisive go-over of the radar data, explaining just what was going on out there south of Long Island that night, Bernie Loeb and Peter Goelz began to attack, alternately alleging nothing could be seen out of the ordinary on the radar, then claiming that even if activity could be discerned, it didn't mean anything.

This was the first step in "neutralize the message, destroy the messenger." Step two began within minutes of O'Meara turning off her tape recorder and walking out of the room.

Peter Goelz, managing director of the NTSB, "was taken aback when he was interviewed by a reporter for <u>Insight Magazine</u>," the *Washington Post* article by Howard Kurtz, began. "He [Goelz] says Kelly O'Meara was extraordinarily antagonistic," Goelz continued.

This mean-spirited response was not dissimilar to what I received when I wrote Goelz earlier. Now, Howard Kurtz had volunteered to help the NTSB beat back another budding scandal. Kurtz wrote:

> Goelz quickly realized he knew O'Meara from previous incarnations. She had pursued the missile theory while working as chief of staff for Representative Mike Forbes, then a New York Republican who had questioned whether there was a terrorist attack on the plane. And, she had worked on an Oliver

Stone docudrama about TWA 800 that the filmmaker was preparing for ABC before the project was cancelled. "She really believes that the United States Navy shot this thing down, and that there was a fleet of warships," Goelz said.[1]

Kelly O'Meara had not pursued the "terrorist attack" hypothesis, nor had she brought up anything about a missile during her tape-recorded interview of Goelz and Loeb. They brought the subject up. She had not alleged that a "fleet of warships" were depicted in the radar. O'Meara was there to get a reasonable explanation for what could be seen on the radar database the government had heretofore not revealed to the public.

It was Goelz' job to provide an answer to this reasonable journalistic question. Instead, he picked up the phone, called the *Washington Post*, and attacked a reporter who was just trying to do her job. That should have given Howard Kurtz a heads-up that this was a story the *Post* should pursue. Instead, he gave the government a helping hand.

Insight Magazine then altered its approach to launching the radar-database story. Two stories were written, instead. Because of their importance, they are presented below to fully inform the reader of the issues involved. The first *Insight* article, by Kelly Patricia O'Meara, was entitled, "New Radar Data, New Questions"[2] :

New radar data relating to the July 17, 1996, explosion of TWA Flight 800 that went down off the coast of Long Island, New York, inexplicably have just become available. The well-publicized previous data focused narrowly on a 20-nautical-mile circle centered on the crash site and was the basis of the FBI's conclusion that there was little air or naval traffic in the selected area at the time of the crash. But that restricted data pattern, it turns out, is only a subset of a larger radar field.

The new data just obtained by *Insight* from sources at the

National Transportation Safety Board, or NTSB, show that between the perimeters of a 22-nautical-mile circle and a 35-nautical-mile circle, a concentration of a large number of radar blips appears to be moving into a well-known military warning area closed to civilian and commercial traffic.

The anomaly presented by the additional data is as yet unexplained. The Clinton administration previously has stated that no concentration of military vessels was in the area that night. Indeed, the Department of the Navy specified that the closest naval vessel was the USS *Normandy*, 185 nautical miles to the south.

The two radar charts accompanying this story [see Exhibit A, back of the book] are a representation of the official data supplied by the NTSB, one of the federal agencies tasked with investigating the crash of TWA 800. ...

Chart A [see Exhibit A, back of the book] focuses on the area within a circle of 20 nautical miles centered on the crash site. NTSB identified only a Navy P-3 Orion anti-submarine airplane, U.S. Airways Flight 217, TWA Flight 900, and four unidentified tracks moving at 30 knots, 15 knots, 12 knots and 20 knots, as the only vehicles and/or objects noted within a 10-nautical-mile radius of the crash site. The NTSB has concluded that the unidentified tracks in Chart A all were consistent with the speed of surface vessels.

The newly obtained data in Chart B include the same information available in Exhibit 13A, but present additional data showing that the level of surface vessels and aircraft activity increases significantly outside the 20-nautical-mile boundary set by the NTSB review.

Chart B shows the identical tracks of the aircraft and unidentified surface vessels revealed in Chart A. But Chart B also shows in excess of two-dozen surface vessels and aircraft detected by radar just beyond the 20-nautical-mile mark. Of interest to experts who have reviewed the data plot is that most of the surface vessels in Chart B appear to be heading in a parallel movement toward Whiskey 105, or W-105—a military warning area highly publicized to mariners and aviators, designed to keep commercial aircraft and surface vessels out of harm's way during military exercises. On the evening of the explosion, W-105 was activated for military exercises along with several other warning areas along the Atlantic Coast.

Furthermore, Chart B reveals two aircraft just outside the NTSB's 20-nautical-mile boundary, one traveling at 475 knots in an east-southeast direction heading toward W-105, and a second aircraft that, in a span of approximately 30 minutes, appears to fly into and out of W-105 on two separate occasions. When the earlier data were released, both FBI and NTSB investigators said that they were unable to identify all surface vessels and aircraft within the area of the crash.

Radar technical experts who reviewed the data on Chart B for *Insight* identify the tracks of approximately 30 surface vessels and at least two aircraft that were outside the narrow perimeter of the previously announced results and have not been made public until now. When questioned about the newly released radar data, Bernard Loeb, director of the Office of Aviation Safety at the NTSB, said, "There are lots and lots of things out there, lots and lots of surface vessels and airplanes. It's New York City." However, when specifically asked whether the NTSB was aware of any apparently synchronized parallel movement of vessels, Loeb replied, "We don't see some large number of vessels running in a parallel track in the same direction."

The FBI, which took the lead on the criminal investigation of the downing of the Boeing 747 aircraft, was unaware at first that the new radar data from NTSB had come to light. When the differences in scope between the earlier data and the new data were presented to Joe Valliquette, an FBI special agent in the New York City office, he responded, "This is ancient history. There is no one who is willing to make one of our agents available here to talk about the radar data. Everything we have to say about the TWA 800 investigation was said on November 18, 1997" [the day the FBI put its criminal investigation on an inactive pending status].

Because Kelly O'Meara had been attacked by the NTSB through a *Washington Post* article, *Insight* Magazine published a second article in the same edition, entitled, "The Anatomy of a Mystery," by Paul Rodriguez:

> Intimidating the press and carping about bold reporters are old tricks. But rarely do government officials seek out rival news organizations to malign a writer before a story even is written.
>
> "Here, ruining people is considered sport." So wrote the late Vincent Foster, the deputy White House counsel whose body was found in Fort Marcy Park in Northern Virginia, dead by apparent suicide due to complicated reasons only he knew—among them, perhaps, the relentless hounding of junkyard dogs in the Washington press corps.
>
> I know a little now about how he must have felt. Until recently, reporters avoided launching public smear attacks against one of their own. And certainly in my experience as a veteran newsman, journalists would never roll over and allow government bureaucrats to use them to slime their colleagues.
>
> Yet that precisely is what recently happened to an *Insight* reporter whom I asked to unravel a new mystery involving the doomed Flight 800. Specifically, the reporter—Kelly Patricia O'Meara—was detailed to find out why recently unearthed radar tapes never seen before showed significant numbers of "hits" compared with previously released government radar tapes. And why were so many of the new blips passing beyond the crash site into a military no-fly/no-sail zone?
>
> Government investigators for the National Transportation Safety Board, or NTSB, the FBI and the military previously had said such data didn't exist or stated bluntly there was no such traffic.
>
> The blind reporting of potentially new data refuting the government would have been an irresponsible thing for this magazine—or for any bona fide newsmagazine—to do. But just as certainly it probably would have fueled cries of cover-up from the so-called black-chopper crowd. One of the favor-

ite theories still buzzing around Internet groups and skeptics is that a missile from friendly or hostile fire brought the plane down, although no evidence has been forthcoming proving that happened.

Armed with documents—interestingly, at one point supplied by an NTSB employee—O'Meara's assignment was simple: Ask the NTSB why the "new" radar data had not been previously released and determine what the data actually showed.

Notwithstanding the dog-eat-dog mores now prevailing in Washington, it still came as some surprise to me how NTSB officials managed to convince a legitimate writer at a competing news organization—the *Washington Post*—to try through innuendo to intimidate the *Insight* reporter for leveling aggressive questions about the data at testy and flippant bureaucrats.

Maybe it was O'Meara's gender or her tailored pantsuit that provoked the attack. Or perhaps it was her background as having worked for a member of Congress who initially disbelieved government reports that TWA 800 blew up due to mechanical failure. Then again, perhaps it was a former stint working for an Oliver Stone production company hired by ABC to do a since-dropped documentary on the doomed flight that may have been the reason.

But regardless of the excuse, NTSB Managing Director Peter Goelz decided not to complain to any of *Insight's* top editors—including me—about what he felt were "extraordinarily antagonistic" questions from the magazine's reporter. Instead, he went to *Washington Post* media writer Howard Kurtz. And while Matt Drudge is known to report on stories about to be printed by competitors, Kurtz reported on a "story" that had not even been written nor was going to be written as slyly suggested by Goelz in the *Post* article.

"Kelly O'Meara was questioning Goelz about secret government radar reports that she said show plenty of activity nearby on the day in 1996 that TWA Flight 800 crashed," Kurtz wrote in the August 23 issue of his newspaper. "The government says it found no evidence to support theories that the plane was downed by a missile," Kurtz continued. And later he quoted

Goelz as saying: "She really believes that the United States Navy shot this thing down and there was a fleet of warships."

Kurtz wrote these words without interviewing O'Meara. And he wrote it after being told by me that the reporter hadn't yet returned from the Goelz interview, so there was no basis to judge the accuracy of the bureaucrat's rendition of events. Moreover, I recall telling Kurtz, missiles and such were not the issue for the magazine, but the issue was what may be on never-before-seen radar data. "If anyone has questions about [the reporter's] bias, wait 'till they see a printed product," I was quoted by Kurtz as saying. Otherwise, "it's just carping about an aggressive reporter." Kurtz seemed to be assuaged sufficiently, at least to the point of waiting to find out what actually did happen at the allegedly aggressive interview—especially since neither one of us knew fully. That was about 5:00 P.M. on a Friday. Then, in Monday's August 23 *Post*, Kurtz, without hearing back from this editor, went ahead and printed a one-sided story that had been cleverly placed with him by the bureaucrats three days earlier.

An examination of the transcript of the reporter's interview, however, paints a different picture from the one Goelz portrays and Kurtz displays. It also puts into context the so-called rude reporter's tactics. It demonstrates, perhaps, how nervous, worried and reactive bureaucrats become when faced with tough questions and persistence. Challenged with straightforward questions, they evade or turn flippant.

Curiously, O'Meara never brought up in her August 23 interview the theory that the plane had been shot down. It was the NTSB officials themselves who raised it, as they did in subsequent interviews with me on August 23 and August 25. They were the ones who also brought up errant-missile theories—only, admittedly, to mock them.

Some exchanges from the O'Meara interview with the NTSB officials perhaps show best what transpired. For example, when asked where the latest data showing significantly larger numbers of previously unknown radar hits have been—at least since the NTSB issued an interim report 18 months ago, along with CD-ROMS—NTSB's Bernie Loeb said: "It's not on the CD, but it's on the floppy disk. All you had to do was to ask for it. It's been available since last April." Floppy disk? What floppy disk?

According to NTSB sources and officials who spoke privately to *Insight,* no one knew about the floppy disk—a point even Loeb suggests could have happened because "the public-inquiries office shifted locations at some point and it may have been a period of time simply because they misplaced it." When asked whether the newly obtained disk from the NTSB showing the expanded data could have been the wrong "tape," Goelz replied: "you know, it's hard to believe, but, who knows?"

As can be seen by the charts accompanying O'Meara's story ... there are significant differences from the previous publicly released NTSB reports and the newly acquired radar data.

And the differences beg questions, such as why are there two versions of what supposedly are the same set of data? What does the new information show? Do the blips represent military, civilian or commercial boats and planes on the new radar tapes? Why are so many targets moving beyond the crash site into a military no-fly/no-sail zone? And, certainly not least, why were these additional targets scrubbed or otherwise not reported in previous published NTSB reports?

In response to such commonsense questions posed by O'Meara—they were not loaded ones nor did they presuppose anything—NTSB officials speaking to a tape recorder in plain sight were evasive, mocking and circular in their answers. And, again, contrary to what Kurtz quoted Goelz as saying, it was the NTSB officials who first raised the issue of missile conspiracies in the *Post* story. In the actual interview they limited the scope of such off-the-wall chatter to Internet conspiracy theorists.

Loeb and Goelz subsequently confirmed to me that the NTSB had, in fact, left out much of the additional and "new" radar data obtained by *Insight* and that, indeed, it will lead to further questions. But that said, they also maintained that in the final analysis it doesn't matter what additional information comes out because in their judgment, nothing will change. A mechanical fault brought the plane down.

Fine. *Insight* was not questioning that or any other conclusion, but it was—and still is—questioning the handling and release of the radar data.

If conspiracy theories are fueled, it will be partly because the NTSB saw fit to play fast and loose—for whatever reason, innocent or not—with material that should have been released to the public promptly, clearly and professionally.

Too bad Kurtz didn't wait to get the full facts himself before taking a dud-filled potshot. No wonder the public has grown weary—and wary—of a media that rushes into print before it has the whole story.

The truth is that mechanical theories have been fueled by the NTSB playing fast and loose with the facts, knowing it had nothing to fear from major media.

The Howard Kurtz story is a microcosm of today's major media, which does not have the institutional integrity or courage to conduct an investigation of the Clinton administration based on fact instead of political consequence.

45

Conclusion

In a nation where the rule of law is revered, a primary objective in the Flight 800 crash investigation would be to fully inform We The People. "We" must remain confident in the government's veracity.

In such a society the government must release all data gathered during the investigation that requires explanation in order for confidence in government to be maintained. If data is leaked suggesting evil intent by the government to misinform and cover-up, the burden of proof shifts to the government.

And what a burden it is. Highly credible witnesses describe a missile. The pre-altered debris field says missile. The pre-altered Flight 800 mockup says missile. The residue says missile.

Most significant is that government actions say missile. FAA and Navy radar says "significant Naval units" were in the area. Navy radar says an above-top-secret platform was at 98,000 feet in the area—undoubtedly involved in a military exercise.

Every step of the way, government words and actions altered the facts. Words and actions constitute evidence. The evidence says missile.

EXHIBIT A[1]
OVERVIEW OF COOPERATIVE
ENGAGEMENT CAPABILITY (CEC)

The Secretary of Defense has said that Cooperative Engagement Capability (CEC) is the biggest breakthrough in warfare technology since Stealth. The CEC program is designed to link together Battle Group Anti-Air Warfare Units and Airborne Early Warning aircraft into a force-wide anti-air combat system. CEC provides real-time, high-quality composite data over highly jam-resistant links.

John W. Douglas,
Assistant Secretary of the Navy
March 29, 1996

A CEC exercise was conducted by the Navy in W-105 the afternoon of July 17, 1996. That evening a large "movement of significant Naval units" was observed by FAA and Navy radar. Also seen on the Navy radar was a military asset with transponder number 1275, at 98,000 feet, near this group of Naval units south of Long Island.

According to military and journalist sources, only two military assets are capable of operating at 98,000 feet: the SR-71, and a new, above-top-secret vehicle developed in recent years by the Lockheed Skunk Works. The SR-71 travels at very high speed, at altitudes up to 110,000 feet. The new military asset can travel above 100,000 feet, but is not dependent on forward speed to stay aloft.

This new military asset is what the Navy radar [RP44] tracked at the time Flight 800 crashed. For these reasons, CEC is included in this book.

The CEC program actually came into existence in 1988 "under the auspices of the Battle Group Anti-Air Warfare Coordination program." In 1990, tests were conducted at sea. By 1992, the program had reached a sufficient level of maturity to rapidly accelerate. Acquisition of software and hardware began in 1992, and by early 1994, "after a series of preliminary trials, five CEC-equipped ships, including the amphibious assault ship *Wasp* and the aircraft carrier *Dwight D. Eisenhower*, as well as P-3 Orion maritime aircraft, verified the ability of CEC units"[2] to independently "construct identical composite tracks and identification pictures"[3] by remotely linking their radar software. In other words, the Navy was fairly sure the theory would work.

This new system would be tied together via Cooperative Engagement Capability, laboriously described in 1994 as a system that will significantly enhance capabilities in joint theater air and self-defense missions against reduced-signature cruise and theater ballistic missiles by combining tracks from dispersed-force censors into a real-time, accurate, fire-control-quality Anti-Air Warfare (AAW) picture shared force-wide. Cooperative Engagement's high data rate and real-time exchange of fire-control sensor data will greatly expand mission effectiveness in the littoral."[4] Littoral literally means between the low- and high-water marks.

"Today, since no nation can challenge our ability to control the seas, we have concentrated our planning on winning the contest for control of the land and sea areas of the littoral," the 1994 Navy publication began.[5] Generally, "littoral" warfare covers the area from the shore to the open sea, and "inland from the shore over that area that can be supported and controlled directly from the sea."

The 1994 littoral concept envisioned fully integrated joint operations with the Army and Air Force as well as with allied forces. Now that the Cold War is over, there is a shifting concept to a much greater emphasis on fighting on land rather than over vast stretches of the ocean. Isolated Naval missions take a backseat to the need for a "seamless" integration of the fighting equipment, particularly the software that operates the sophisticated AEGIS radar system.

Operation Desert Storm, in 1991, clearly demonstrated that "the proliferation of theater ballistic missiles (TBMs) poses increasing danger to the national security of the United States and our allies."[6] So the Navy decided to focus its advanced concept thinking around the AEGIS system. In 1994, the Navy predicted that, "In the near future, AEGIS cruisers and Arleigh Burke (DDG51) destroyers will provide a somewhat limited, but nonetheless highly mobile and credible theater ballistic missile defense (TBMD) capability. When AEGIS SPY-1 radar software improvements are combined with improvements to the Standard missile, these ships can provide lower-tier defense against incoming ballistic missiles."[7]

By 1995, the Navy's CEC concept was more clearly defined, not to mention more readable: "CEC is a system of hardware and software that allows the sharing among ships of radar data on air targets. Radar data from individual ships of a battle group is transmitted to the other ships in the group via a line-of-sight data distribution system. Each ship uses similar data-processing algorithms resident in its cooperative engagement processor, resulting in each ship having essentially the same displays of track information on aircraft and missiles. An individual ship can launch an anti-air missile at a threat aircraft or an anti-ship missile within its engagement envelope, based on track data relayed to it by another ship.[8]

"To augment these capabilities and provide over-the-horizon early warning, we have embarked on a joint program with the Army to develop and field Joint Tactical Ground Stations (JTAGS). JTAGS will allow in-theater processing of space-based warning data, greatly enhancing the abilities of active theater defense." And all that high-tech equipment will work with that being developed by the other services. This level of cooperation had been talked about over the decades, but this was the first time it appeared that true cooperation would exist. Shrinking budgets and the demands of 21ˢᵗ-century warfare finally overpowered inter-service rivalry.

Then the Navy correctly identified the problem that may have lead to the Flight 800 tragedy two years later:

> Congestion in littoral war zones combined with the complexities of the sea, air, land, and space interfaces will increase the difficulty of identifying and sorting the dispositions of friendly, neutral, and hostile forces. Doing so has become increasingly critical as weapon lethality has increased and target engagement response times have decreased. Enhancements to the current Position Location Reporting System and increased fielding of the Global Positioning System have provided greater capability for the positive identification of friendly ground forces.[9]

The P-3 aircraft that may have played a role in the July 17, 1996, tragedy were also due for upgrade in order to play a role in the littoral warfare future: "In particular, we are improving the surveillance systems of the P-3 to make it more useful in the missions we now envision. Upgrades include addition of long-range optical systems, radar upgrades, and improved command and control systems."[10]

In September 1995, tests were conducted in the Gulf of Mexico. Two CEC-equipped AEGIS cruisers and an "airborne early warning (AEW) P-3 aircraft owned by the Coast Guard," were used to test the "effectiveness and suitability of an airborne CEC."[11]

The Department of Defense noted that its 1995 accomplishments included completing "analysis of Developmental Testing/Operational Testing (DT/OT) lessons learned to fully support continued developmental efforts in CEC system design and fleet operations and tactics . . . [And they] continued development of airborne CEC for integration with E-2C aircraft."[12] Also accomplished was the "modeling and simulation of ship-based over-the-horizon cruise missile defense with airborne surveillance and tracking to develop operational concepts for deployment jointly with the Army and Air Force. [And] work to design a system to transfer Cooperative Engagement Capability (CEC) data to [an] Army Patriot battery for analysis of future development and in preparation for simulated Army missile-firing events."[13]

Just as the early 1996 CEC tests were getting underway off the island of Kauai, Undersecretary of Defense for acquisition and technology, Paul G. Kaminski, gave a speech at the Redstone Arsenal in Huntsville, Alabama:

> We have seen equally encouraging field demonstrations of the Navy's Cooperative Engagement Capability, which has been deployed in TMD [theater missile defense] exercises with the [aircraft carrier] *Eisenhower* battle group off the Atlantic coast and in the Mediterranean over the course of the past twelve months as a part of the JTF-95 [Joint Task Force] exercise activity.

So CEC testing was not limited to the sterile environment of the missile range off Kauai.

During phase one of development, the focus on the cruise missile defense was "the detection and engagement of beyond-the-radar-horizon cruise missile targets. The goal was to detect, track, and successfully engage cruise missiles at ranges beyond the radar line-of-sight of surface-based air defense units.[14] Sensors were placed on a Hawaiian mountaintop, giving the altitude to simulate an aircraft acting in concert with an AEGIS cruiser and a U.S. Army Patriot battery "to detect, track, and engage target drones at ranges beyond the radar lines of sight of the surface-based air defense units."

This was a joint Navy/Army testing and development program, with the Navy as lead service. The scenario resembled what the military planners saw as the limited war capability in the remote hot spots of the world. Two AEGIS cruisers from the Atlantic fleet participated, the *Anzio* and the *Cape St. George*, as well as the carrier *Eisenhower*, a Customs Service CEC-equipped P-3, an Army Patriot missile battery and a USAF E-3A AWACS aircraft, a Marine Corps Hawk missile battery, and a sensor-equipped aerostat.

Several air defense scenarios were run in January and February of 1996 off the Hawaiian Islands at the Kauai Pacific Missile Range Facility, in order to test the rapidly developing high-tech program. As confidence built, the scenarios began to be tested "in jamming and radar-clutter environments."[15]

Instead of using expensive cruise missiles, the Navy's target of choice while developing CEC has been the BQM-74E drone produced by Northrop-Grumman. Configured to closely resemble a cruise missile, the BQM-74E can be remotely controlled or preprogrammed to fly a specific route. An aircraft resembling a BQM-74E drone would be photographed later in the same area, during the same time frame, where Flight 800 was shot down. Where the BQM-74E drone flies, things are being shot into the air.

Nine of these drones were used during the Army/Navy test of this CEC concept. All were destroyed. Two AEGIS cruisers used CEC to defend themselves, firing Standard missiles to destroy the drones. "The ships also communicated with a nearby Army Patriot anti-missile radar and AWACS"[16] in order to successfully engage and destroy the BQM-74E drones.

The USS *Lake Erie*, one of the AEGIS cruisers involved in the January 20 and 21, 1995, tests off Kauai, used a Standard missile, "*modified for remote engagements*, to kill the BQM-74E drones, which were flying out of radar range at an altitude of fifty feet."[17] [Emphasis added]

The second set of tests, February 1 and 2, 1996, "were far more complex ... These exercises added Army and Air Force assets"[18] as well as a CEC Customs Service P-3. Two additional

AEGIS cruisers, the USS *Anzio* and *Cape St. George*, were joined by the USS *Lake Erie*.

The scenario used for the test included the AEGIS vessels' arrival in a hostile littoral environment. "The battle group was confronted with two drones, launched from the island."[19] Each drone employed its own "self-screening" jammers as they streaked toward the AEGIS battle group, less than 50 feet above the ocean. The BQM-74E drone jammers "blinded all the cruisers. The *Lake Erie* alone regained the track in time."[20] Because the radar data is shared by all CEC-equipped AEGIS ships, even the *Anzio* and *Cape St. George* computer systems could track the oncoming drones. Each was able to launch a Standard missile and destroy a drone.

One month later, the Secretary of the Navy, John H. Dalton, testified before the Senate Armed Services Committee:

> A second successful investment in emerging technologies is our Cooperative Engagement Capability, or CEC. Beginning with highly successful live firing tests in the summer of 1994 and continuing through a series of challenging demonstrations and exercises in the past year, CEC continued to exceed our most optimistic expectations.
>
> Most recently, CEC was a key element in the Advanced Concept Technology Demonstration, better known as Mountain Top, which took place in Hawaii last month. In Mountain Top, the Navy proved that it can conduct surface-to-air engagements of cruise missiles while those threats are still located far beyond the ships' own radar location.
>
> The true significance of Mountain Top is that our surface combatants will have the capability to provide effective air defense of forces ashore, debarkation ports, and airfields against low-flying, Tomahawk-like cruise missiles. Secretary Perry has declared CEC the most significant technological development since Stealth.[21]

Secretary Dalton's emphasis on the Navy's ability to protect Army and Marine forces onshore should not be minimized. Future testing of CEC as it continued its march toward combat certification required an increasing level of testing providing a realistic setting. That included Army and Navy CEC assets working in conjunction, drone missiles launched in land clutter, and an ever-increasing level of jamming, until the system could be proven to successfully function in a realistic combat environment, all the while maintaining the ability to distinguish military from civilian aircraft while simultaneously locating a drone coming out of land clutter in the same area as the civilian and military planes.

And, as a Navy document explained shortly before Flight 800 was shot down: "The Navy also has begun a study to investigate the difficulties inherent in shipboard sensors in littoral environments." Shipboard sensors are synonymous with AEGIS radar. Littoral means land in the vicinity of which a cruise missile attack can be launched.

The same document warns of Anti-Ship Cruise Missiles (ASCMs): "Increasingly available throughout the world, these sophisticated, relatively inexpensive weapons can be launched from the air, sea, or land. The limited time available to react to them, once airborne, could pose difficulties for existing anti-air defenses, particularly in littoral operations where naval forces may be patrolling very close to the shore or in physically constrained bodies of water. A number of countries in regions vital to American interests, including the Gulf, now possess advanced ASCMS."²²

The Department of Defense 1996 plan was to complete "Initial Operational Capability (IOC) certification for the shipboard system ... Continue development of airborne CEC for integration with E-2C aircraft ... [and] Modify Naval Research Laboratory (NRL) and fleet-owned P-3 aircraft to provide dedicated airborne support for CEC test programs."²³ In other words, when CEC was being tested, there would be a modified P-3 in the air monitoring the test.

By 1996, CEC was headed for its initial certification for use by the Navy in combat. The CEC development project was now described as, "coordinating all Battle Force sensors into a single, real-time, composite track picture having fire-control quality."[24]

While tedious, the military definition of CEC in its advanced stage of development is essential to understanding the complex system that may have failed at a critical moment during one of its final tests prior to combat certification: "CEC distributes sensor data from each ship and aircraft, or cooperating unit (CU), to all other CUs in the battle force through a real-time, line-of-sight, high-data-rate sensor and engagement data distribution network. CEC is highly resistant to jamming and provides accurate gridlocking between CUs. Each CU independently employs high-capacity parallel processing and advanced algorithms to combine all distributed sensor data into a fire-control-quality track picture, which is the same for all CUs. CEC data is presented as a superset of the best AAW sensor capabilities from each CU, all of which are integrated into a single input to each CU's combat weapons system. CEC will significantly improve our Battle Force in depth, including both local area and ship defense capabilities against current and future AAW threats. CEC is designed to enhance the AAW war fighting ability of ships and aircraft and to enable coupling of the Force into a single, distributed AAW weapon system and toward more effective use of tactical data and the cooperative use of all the Force sensors and weapons. These capabilities will provide the ship defense flexibility needed to meet the threat brought about by increasing numbers of highly sophisticated weapons held by potentially hostile third-world countries.

"CEC consists of the Data Distribution System (DDS),

the Cooperative Engagement Processor (CEP), and Combat System Modifications. The DDS encodes and distributes on-ship sensors and engagement data, is a high-capacity, jam-resistant, directive system providing a precision gridlocking and high throughput of data. The CEP is a high-capacity distributed processor which is able to process force levels of data in a timely manner that allows its output to be considered real-time fire-control data. This data is passed to the ship's combat system as fire-control-quality data for which the ship can cue its onboard sensors or use data to engage targets without actually tracking them."[25]

A Pentagon document, in typical military techno-jargon, described the test CEC would have to successfully pass before being certified for combat: "The Cruise Missile Defense (CMD) Advanced Technology effort includes an Advanced Concept Technology Demonstration (ACTD), Phase 1, which demonstrates that an AEGIS ship (or other surface-based missile launch platform), using one or more surrogate airborne sensor partners, can provide greatly expanded air defense capabilities leading to a robust capability against overland cruise missiles beyond surface-based radar line-of-sight."[26]

The Naval Surface Warfare Command (NSWC), East Coast Operations (ECO), located at Dam Neck, Virginia, "was selected as the CEC test site due to its existing hardware resources and physical location with respect to the Virginia Capes surface ship operating area. Particular existing NSWC ... hardware assets being used for the CEC test site include ... SPS-48E air search radar, SPS-49V5 search radar, SPS-48C search radar ... air intercept control facility, and test control central ... ECO (East Coast Operations) NSWC (Naval Surface Warfare Command) is located on the shore directly adjacent to a live gunfire range and the Virginia Capes Operating Area. This arrangement facilitates tests of tactical computer programs with live shore-based radar and communication equipment with ships and aircraft operating at sea. The actual operational environment provides extremely valuable test data that is used to upgrade the tactical computer programs to meet fleet needs. Additionally, ECO NSWC employs a direct microwave link to the FACSFAC air search radar to provide live radar displays for training and testing. ECO radar act as backups in the event of problems with the FACSFAC radar."[27]

ECO NSWC was also responsible for:

• CEC land-based test site management.
• Air logistic support of CEC battle group in Virginia Capes operating area.

So the Naval Surface Warfare Command, East Coast Operations, located at Dam Neck, Virginia, had the technical expertise to closely monitor all CEC activity in the restricted zones and warning zones that extend from Virginia to just south of Long Island. These tests are monitored and tape-recorded for training purposes. And aircraft are in the air with monitoring equipment to enhance the collection of data.

This monitoring equipment certainly recorded the events that led to the destruction of Flight 800, a few miles northwest of active warning zone W-105. The Navy had significant assets in the immediate area. The only question is, have the tapes been destroyed?

We know CEC was in the final testing phase prior to being certified for combat. The testbed for the final months was the area between Long Island and Virginia. The monitoring system for the tests is headquartered at Dam Neck, Virginia. Aircraft outfitted with monitoring equipment were under their control. The entire radar monitoring system was even plugged into the military version of the FAA, at Oceana, Virginia, FACS/FAC. These military air controllers monitor military traffic in the area where CEC is tested.

After Flight 800 went down, nothing more was heard of the need to test CEC's ability to operate with an air asset, in land clutter as well as when being jammed. There was no longer a need to have friendlies and commercial aviation on the screen being read by the AEGIS computer. A kinder, gentler CEC testing program surfaced far away from civilian traffic and a mere shadow of itself in the recent glory days, when overconfidence prevailed.

Introduction
1. *Soldiers of Misfortune, The Men We Left Behind, The Downing of TWA Flight 800.*
2. NTSB "Chairman's Report," November 15, 1996. The report then suggested that an explosive event from aviation fuel may have been able to cause the same explosive damage.
3. The government has admitted that this did not constitute obstruction of justice.
4. House Aviation Subcommittee, July 10, 1997.

Chapter 1
1. Supreme Court Justice Brandeis' dissenting opinion, 48 S.Ct. 564.
2. Brown v. Mississippi, 56 S.Ct. 461.

Chapter 2
1. The NTSB's lead investigator, Al Dickinson; FBI agent Jim Kinsley, and five or six other unidentified people.
2. Trial transcript, pp. 239-240.
3. Tom Bowman, *Baltimore Sun,* "Flight 800 Theorists Stick to Their Guns," September 19, 1999.

Chapter 3
1. E-mail to Ian Goddard.
2. May 15, 1998.
3. Jerry Cimisi, *Dan's Papers* [Long Island], May 15, 1998. Statement of Lisa Perry.
4. The FBI and CIA characterize every sound every witness heard as the explosion. Angelides, an engineer, is actually describing the sounds made from a missile launch, flight and explosion—three distinct and separate sets of sounds.
5. Cmdr. William S. Donaldson, USN ret, "Interim Report on the Crash of TWA Flight 800 and the Actions of the NTSB and FBI," July 17, 1998, p. 89.
6. Ibid., p. 89-90.
7. David Hendrix, The *Press-Enterprise* [CA], October 20, 1997.
8. Tom Stalcup interview. Stalcup, President of a FIRO, a small group of university and other professional people, joined together in an attempt to provide a means of objectively gathering and analyzing Flight 800 evidence. Stalcup was on Ed Wagner's boat at the precise location where Wagner had first observed the "white flare" when the interview took place.
9. Ibid.
10. Stalcup interview.
11. Joey MacLellan, *Suffolk Life* [NY], Flight 800: Accident or Terrorist Attack?
12. Stalcup interview, 1-28-98.

13. Ibid.
14. Op. Cit., Donaldson, p. 91.
15. David Hendrix, The *Press-Enterprise* [CA], October 20, 1997.
16. Retired Navy Commander who has investigated Flight 800 for the last two years.
17. New York Air National Guard pilot who was about eight miles from Flight 800 when it was hit by a missile.
18. Op. Cit., Donaldson, p. 94.
19. Patricia Milton, *In the Blink of an Eye*, (Random House, 1999), p. 50-51.
20. Ibid.
21. W-105 was activated for a 48-hour period beginning 0500 EST, July 17, 1996.

Chapter 4
1. When questioned by *Insight* Magazine's Kelly O'Meara on this point, NTSB's Peter Goelz's response was that boaters were not required to be good citizens.
2. This was first revealed by NTSB Chairman Jim Hall's 11-15-96 meeting notes obtained by Sanders.
3. *Press-Enterprise*, David Hendrix, Department of the Navy FOIA response, dated May 20, 1997, Ser N02L1/0173.
4. New York Air National Guard Pilot Fritz Meyer statement.

Chapter 5
1. Sensitive source.
2. Matthew Purdy, "Many Answers in Crash Inquiry, Except the One That Counts," *The New York Times*, December 15, 1996, p. 46. In parentheses, Purdy adds: "Days later, the object was found to be an electronic anomaly." No source was given for this afterthought, nor does he explain the lack of government action—manhunt on land and military/Coast Guard operation offshore—that presents compelling evidence the government acted as if a state of emergency existed.
3. Liam Pleven, *Newsday*, "Searching for Answers," July 19, 1996.
4. Ibid.
5. Sanders interview, April 1997.

Chapter 6
1. Although never revealed by CBS News, this was confirmed by them after weeks of investigative effort.
2. Each bottle holds 110 gallons of water. Pre-flight checks mandate that the bottles must be at least 3/4 full. Since the 747 had just returned from a trans-Atlantic flight, it is reasonable to believe the bottles were below 3/4 and were filled prior to takeoff. The weight of the bottles and 110 gallons of water is about 1,000 pounds.
3. Sanders has a photo of CW-601 taken April 19, 1997. Numerous

holes are visible. The holes disappeared sometime between April 20, 1997, and December 22, 1998.

4. The August 17, 1996, SUPSALV database printout and NTSB November 13, 1996, printout do not list any of the A-TAGS referenced in this exhibit.

5. Referenced in the China Lake report as being from the early red zone. This debris was not logged into the SUPSALV or NTSB database, at least not the unclassified version.

6. NTSB, Metallurgy/Structures Sequencing Group Chairman's Factual Report, Nose Landing Gear Doors Sequence, Materials Laboratory Report No. 97-155, 97-155A.

Chapter 7
1. Title 49, section 1131(a)(2).

Chapter 8
1. Murry Weiss, *New York Post*, September 22, 1996.
2 US Navy document P 102001Z JUL 96, FM FACSFAC VACAPES PCEANA. TO AIG 9934, p4.
3. DOD Briefing, Kenneth A. Bacon, ASDPA, July 23, 1996, 3:30 P.M.

Chapter 9
1. *The New York Times*, Andrew C. Revkin, August 30, 1996, p. 1.
2. Ibid.
3. Ibid., pp. 1 & 6.
4. Ibid., p. 6.
5. This can be inferred. The government hides nothing that does not conflict with its pre-determined crash cause. All 13 pieces were brought from the ocean floor prior to the November dredging operation—pieces recovered during this operation received orange tags. None of the 13 pieces have orange tags. So we know beyond a reasonable doubt that the pieces were recovered during the initial recovery operation. We know each piece not removed from the debris when it first entered the Calverton hangar, was tagged by NTSB personnel. The longitude, latitude and description were then entered into the NTSB computer. Sanders received a copy of this computerized NTSB debris field, dated November 13, 1996, two weeks after all diving salvage ceased and trawler operations commenced. All RSOB pieces not withheld by the FBI were on the NTSB printout received by Sanders in November 1996.
6. Op. Cit., *The New York Times*, p. 6.
7. NTSB Flight 800 Sound Spectrum Study.
8. March 28, 1997, John C. Gannon, CIA Deputy Director for Intelligence, sent a letter to Jim Kallstrom, saying "the initial explosion" occurred at "8:31:07.5 P.M." If this is accurate data, the CIA has just handed Kallstrom proof the CVR was altered—it is not possible for

the initiating event to occur 4.5 seconds before the CVR lost power, without the initiating event being recorded on the CVR. It is highly unlikely such an event could occur without the flight data recorder recording the event.

9. Example: pressure is lower in moving air through a window broken during a hurricane [if the other windows in the house are closed] than the surrounding air inside the structure. This pressure imbalance causes the windows and walls on the far side of the structure to blow out.

10. The L-2 door is the second door from the front, left side.

11. The NTSB designated this area "yellow zone."

Chapter 11
1. Sanders contemporaneous notes, November 24, 1996.

Chapter 12
1. NTSB Chairman's Report, p. 3.
2. Ibid., p. 6.
3. Ibid., p. 9.
4. James Sanders, *The Downing of TWA Flight 800* (Kensington Publishing, April 1996), p. 116.
5. Ibid.
6. Ibid.
7. Ibid., p. 117.
8. Ibid.
9. Ibid., p. 117.
10. Ibid.
11. Ibid.
12. Ibid.
13. Ibid., pp. 117-118.
14. Ibid., p. 118.
15. Ibid.
16. Ibid.
17. Ibid.
18. Ibid.
19. Ibid., pp. 118-119.
20. Ibid.
21. Ibid.
22. Ibid.
23. Ibid.
24. Ibid.

Chapter 13
1. After notes were taken from the tape, Sanders normally taped over the conversations. The December 8, 1996, interview survived only because it was toward the end of the tape and never taped over.

2. Jacqueline Akhavan, *The Chemistry of Explosives* (Royal Society of Chemistry, 1998), p. 93.
3. Pentaerythritol tetranitrate.
4. Cyclotrimethylenetrinitramine.
5. Ibid., p. 11.
6. Ibid., p. 12.
7. January 26, 1997.
8. The first major piece the NTSB/FBI admit left the 747.

Chapter 14
1. From notes taken during the telephone conversation.
2. We know the grand jury process was used no later than Sunday, March 9, 1997, to obtain a subpoena that Jim Kinsley carried to Florida when he flew down to retrieve the radar tapes retired pilot Richard Russell had in his possession. We also know the government needed time to make a final decision on what disinformation line to use to counter the residue story. By Monday morning, March 10, 1997, they had their nameless, faceless leakers of disinformation dialing the phones to reporters they could trust to put out government disinformation as fact.

Chapter 15
1. Riverside *Press-Enterprise*, March 10, 1997, p. 1.

Chapter 16
1. Hearings, Subcommittee of the Committee on Appropriations, House of Representatives, March 11, 1997.
2. David Hendrix, Riverside *Press-Enterprise*, interviewed Kallstrom on that date, at that time; telling him that residue from the hangar had been tested. Hendrix read Kallstrom the elements and percentages.
3. Terry Stacey had been inside the hangar and interviewed by Sanders and Hendrix within the 24-hour period prior to Kallstrom learning the residue was outside his control.
4. James Sanders inspected and photographed rows 17, 18 and 19 on December 22, 1998, under Rule 16, allowing such an inspection post indictment.
5. NTSB Fire and Explosion Group Factual Report, p. 9.
6. Ibid.
7. Tom Stalcup, a graduate student at Florida State University, was the first person to call Bassett about the testing.
8. This portion of the original statement Bassett was going to sign was eliminated at the insistence of NASA attorneys.
9. Charles Bassett signed a notarized affidavit from which this quote was taken. The affidavit was filed with the federal court, E.D.N.Y., as part of the pre-trial motions of James and Elizabeth Sanders. It was a matter of public record at that time, freely available to any reporter.

Chapter 17
1. " ... there is no meaningful distinction between physical and psychological harm inflicted. ..." *U.S. v. Cuervelo*, 949, F.2d 559 (2d Cir. 1991).
2. *Screws v. United States*, 65 S.Ct. 1047. "Separately, and often together in application, Sections (U.S.C. 241, 242) have been woven into our fundamental and statutory law. They have place among our permanent legal achievements. They have safeguarded many rights and privileges apart from political ones. Among those buttressed, either by direct application or through the general conspiracy statute ... are the rights to a fair trial, including freedom from sham trials, to be free from arrest and detention by methods constitutionally forbidden ... (and) from interference with the exercise of religion, freedom of the press, freedom of speech and assembly. ..."
3. Burke, p. 77.
4. *Von Bulow by Auersperg v. von Bulow*, 811 F.2d 136 (2d Cir. 1987).
5. *Von Bulow*, p. 144.
6. *New York Times* Company v. United States, 91 S.Ct. 2143 (1971).

Chapter 18
1. Contemporaneous notes of Andrew Vita, Assistant Director for Field Operations, ATF, turned over to Senator Charles Grassley in 1998 as part of a Senate investigation of FBI activity connected to the Flight 800 investigation.
2. Because the March 10, 1997, *Press-Enterprise* story identified the commercial lab where the residue was tested, the FBI was able to determine that the residue had been received by the lab in late January 1997.
3. Earlier in the message, Kallstrom alleged that: "... at the outset of the TWA investigation, BATF agreed that, since the FBI is the lead criminal investigative agency for TWA Flight 800, they would not produce any independent reports regarding the investigation." This allegation was not substantiated before Senator Grassley's hearing May 10, 1999, and therefore must be viewed with great suspicion.
4. CIA cover letter to James K. Kallstrom, March 28, 1997.
5. Four-page CIA "Analytic Assessment," FBI-00003572, from CIA Deputy Director for Intelligence, John C. Gannon.
6. NTSB Meteorological Factual Report, p. 3.
7. NTSB Witness Group Factual Report, p. 2.
8. The CIA and FBI would have us believe that any witness who saw something rise into the air, abruptly disappear in the evening sky, followed a short time later by an explosion, constitutes an unfathomable anomaly if the witness did not actually see the 747 as it was hit by the missile.

Chapter 19
1. FBI WCAS 302 form, March 12, 1997.

Chapter 21
1. Sensitive source.
2. Trial transcript, p. 716.
3. Trial transcript, pp. 703-705.
4. Trial transcript, pp. 708-710.

Chapter 23
1. FBI agent Jim Kinsley's 6-13-97 field notes.
2. Kinsley's notes.

Chapter 24
1. Author's emphasis.
2. Author's emphasis.
3. R. Jeffrey Smith, *Washington Post* Foreign Service, "Two Planes Crashed, and Judge Points to Smoke Screen," September 26, 1999, p. A31.
4. The government was locked into 3M 1357 HP Adhesive because that is what TWA used to refurbish seats in-house. The seat manufacturer was quoted in a *Press-Enterprise* story stating glue was used only in minute quantities in their refurbishing plant.
5. "The samples were dissolved in a mixture of nitric, hydrochloric and hydrofluoric acid, dried down and taken up in 1% nitric acid. During this process a small (less than 1% residue formed. Samples were analyzed with a magnetic sector inductive coupled plasma mass spectrometer (ICP-MS). The instrument was calibrated with commercially obtained ICP-MS standard solutions. Signed, Vincent J. M. Salters, Science Scholar, and National High Magnetic Field Laboratory."
6. Another of the attacks by nameless, faceless government personnel spread across America by major media.
7. NASA-KSC Report 97-1C0089, May 19, 1997, prepared for NTSB's Dr. Merritt Birky, head of the TWA Flight 800 Fire and Explosion Group, p. 2.
8. Webster's New 20th Century Dictionary, Second Edition.
9. NASA-KSC Report 97-1C0089, May 19, 1997. See p. 2 and Fig. 1 photo.
10. NASA-KSC Report 97-1C0063, May 19, 1997.
11. Sanders interview of Charles Bassett.

Chapter 25
1. A typical FBI scheme to misinform, stating that the vessel was at least 25-30 feet in length because of its speed. No mention was made of the radar signature mandating a certain size. Destroyers and cruisers

can also attain 25-30 knots with ease. The statement should be considered for what it is, a typical disinformation ploy to eliminate from consideration any vessel large enough to cause the government to have to face renewed questions about Navy involvement.

Chapter 26
1. FBI Assistant Director James K. Kallstrom letter with 11-page attachment, dated September 5, 1997, to Congressman James A. Trafficant.
2. NTSB Witness Group Factual Report, pp. 2-3.

Chapter 27
1. CNN transcript, November 18, 1997.

Chapter 28
1. *Pro-Choice Network of Western New York v. Schenk,* 67 F.3d, 395 (2nd Cir. 1995).
2. Ibid.
3. From the back cover of *Necessary Illusions, Thought Control in Democratic Societies* (South End Press, 1988). It is interesting to note that those on the right who frequently and vigorously opposed his views when the Reagan administration was his foil, now support the basic premise of Chomsky's research and writing. It appears to be the only logical explanation for otherwise illogical actions of the major media.

Chapter 29
1. Arrest warrant, p. 6, point 12.
2. WCAS 3500 report, obtained from the FBI under discovery.
3. Title 18, Sections 241 and 242.
4. Terry Stacey grand jury testimony, p. 40.

Chapter 31
1. Some will argue that the door still remains open for someone suffering extreme physical abuse at the hand of federal agents. But it is a hypothesis without factual support.
2. Jeremy Gutman, an attorney specializing in appellate law, wrote this brief. It is substantially quoted because of the clarity of writing and because major media has ignored or misinformed the public. This is the first time the true story has been made available to the American public.
3. "Ask" is synonymous with "sought," the action word used by the Second Circuit.
4. That testimony included Mr. Loeb's claim that "One thing I can say categorically is there is no such thing as a red residue trail in that airplane." This "categorical" denial conflicts with the sworn statement of FBI Special Agent James Kinsley in his November 5, 1997, affidavit

in support of an arrest warrant that "[F]rom Row 17 to Row 28 of the seating area, there is a reddish residue on the metallic frame and backs of the passenger seats" that is "manifested most strongly on seats from Rows 17 through 19.

5.   In a letter to Mr. Sanders attorney, Assistant United States Attorney [Valerie] Caproni asserted that the government had disregarded those regulations because nothing in the March 10 articles indicated that Mr. Sanders was acting as a journalist. This assertion is preposterous in view of the article's extensive discussion (on page 1, above the fold) of Mr. Sanders' journalistic credentials. Indeed, Agent Kinsley's December 5, 1997, affidavit notes that "[t]he articles indicated that the defendant JAMES SANDERS was conducting an independent investigation into the cause of the crash…"

6.   Agent Kinsley's affidavit had gratuitously—and misleadingly— asserted that the lab had informed Mr. Sanders that its tests "were not conclusive that solid rocket fuel was present," and later sent him a written report "summarizing the conclusions of the tests. …" In fact, the lab had sent Sanders only a report identifying the elements contained in the reddish-orange sample, without any analysis or opinion regarding whether those elements were consistent with solid rocket fuel.

7.   As the Second Circuit observed … "[t]he notion of fair play animating[the due process clause of the Fifth Amendment] precludes an agency from promulgating a regulation affecting individual liberty or interest, which the rulemaker may then with impunity ignore or disregard as it sees fit. …" "An agency is bound to follow procedures required by its own regulations, even if these regulations were not statutorily or constitutionally mandated."

8.   Section 1155 also provides for civil penalties.

9.   Defense pre-trial discovery motion.

Chapter 32

1.   Justice Department "MEMORANDUM OF LAW IN OPPOSITION TO DEFENDANTS' JOINT MOTION FOR PRETRIAL DISCOVERY," p. 2.

2.   Ibid. p. 2-3.

3.   Quoting from page one of a letter signed by Valerie Caproni and Ben Campbell, dated April 1, 1997.

4.   Case law defines a "news gatherer" as anyone who is gathering information with the intent to see that it is disseminated to the public. Case law emphatically states that a news gatherer need not have an article or book published.

5.   A factually false statement. Sanders is listed as an author of non-fiction books and can be found in the index of D.C.-based newspapers and periodicals.

6.   Author's emphasis.

7.   Government opposition to discovery, pp. 10-11.
8.   Ibid., p. 12.
9.   Ibid., p. 12.
10. Ibid., footnote, p. 14.
11. Ibid., p. 18.
12. Ibid., 19.
13. Ibid., p. 19.
14. Ibid., p. 20.
15. Ibid., p. 23.
16. Ibid., p. 27.
17. Ibid., p. 27.
18. Ibid., p. 28.
19. Ibid.
20. Ibid., 30.

Chapter 34
1.   Defense reply to prosecution opposition to discovery, p. 3 footnote.
2.   Ibid., p. 5.
3.   NTSB Fire and Explosion Group Factual Report, No. 20A, p. 9.
4.   NASA Director of Logistics Operations, Report 97-1C0154.
5.   See *von Bulow by Auersperg v. von Bulow,* 811 F.2d 136, 142 (2d Cir, 1987).
6.   At pp. 20-21, *United States v. White,* 972 F.2d 16, 19 92d Cir. 1992)
7.   Government memo, p. 14, n. 1.
8.   Plea allocution, December 10, 1997.
9.   *Grosjean v. American Press Co.,* 56 S. Ct. 444, 449 (1936).

Chapter 35
1.   United States District Court, Eastern District of New York, Memorandum and Order 98-CR-013 (JS).
2.   Ibid., p. 3.
3.   Ibid., p. 4.
4.   Ibid., p. 10.
5.   Ibid., p. 10.
6.   Ibid., p. 15
7.   Ibid., p. 16.
8.   Ibid., p. 17.

Chapter 36
1.   Memorandum of Law in Support of Defendants' Pre-Trial Motions, 98 Cr.13 (JS), p. 1.
2.   Ibid., p. 5.
3.   Baker v. F & F Investment, 470 F.2d 778,782 (2d Cir. 1972).
4.   *Time, Inc. v. Hill,* 385 U.S. 374, 389, (1967).
5.   Garrison v. Louisiana, 379 U.S. 64, 77 (1964).
6.   *New York Times Co. v. Sullivan,* 376 U.S. 254, 270, 273 (1964).

7. *Richmond Newspapers, Inc. v. Virginia,* 448 U.S. 555, 575 (1980).
8. *Martin v. City of Struthers,* 319 U.S. 141 (1943).
9. *First National Bank v. Belloti,* 435 U.S. 765. 783, (1978).
10. *New York Times Co. v. United States,* 403 U.S. 713, 728, (1971).
11. *New York Times* Co., 403 U.S. at 717.

Chapter 40
1. Trial transcript, p. 776.

Chapter 42
1. Patricia Milton, *In the Blink of an Eye* (Random House, 1999), p. 63.
2. Ibid., p. 67.
3. Ibid., p. 51.
4. Ibid., p. 80.
5. Ibid., p. 120.
6. Ibid., p. 135.
7. Ibid., p. 135.
8. Ibid., p. 140.
9. Ibid., p. 162.
10. Ibid., p. 162.
11. Ibid., p. 167.
12. Ibid., p. 168.
13. Ibid., p. 169.
14. Ibid., p. 190.
15. Ibid., p. 229.
16. Ibid., p. 236.
17. Ibid., p. 241.
18. Ibid., p. 301.
19. Ibid., p. 305.
20. Ibid., p. 334.
21. Ibid., p. 335.
22. Colonel Phil Corso described this type of operation to Sanders, giving specific examples. At the end of this mini-lecture, Corso told Sanders that he [Sanders] was the first journalist to have "pierced the veil." Sanders, Corso predicted, would be destroyed by the government as an example to the few who dare challenge the imperial bureaucracy. This prediction was made almost four months before Sanders and his wife were indicted.
23. "Jury at Conspiracy Trial Shown Flight 800 Seats," April 8, 1999, p. B6.
24. Robert Kessler, "Couple Convicted in TWA Theft," April 14, 1999, p. A-33.

Chapter 43
1. Sanders to Goelz, August 31, 1999, electronic time stamp: 0817 hours.

2   Goelz to Sanders, August 31, 1999, electronic time stamp: 1119 hours.

Chapter 44
1. Howard Kurtz, *The Washington Post*, August 23, 1999.
2. *Insight* Magazine, August 27, 1999, issue.

Exhibit A[1]
1. This is a slightly modified version of Appendix IV, *The Downing of TWA Flight 800*.
2. David Foxwell, *Jane's International Defense Review*, Technical Feature, Tasks and Threats Multiply for Amphibious Forces, no date, p. 2.
3. Ibid.
4. Ibid.
5. Navy Public Affairs Library, Department of the Navy 1994 Posture Statement.
6. Ibid.
7. Ibid.
8. DoD, FY 95 Annual Report, Cooperative Engagement Capability.
9. Ibid.
10. Ibid.
11. Ibid.
12. Dod FY 97 Descriptive Summary.
13. Ibid.
14. CINCPAC, ACTD Master Plan Cruise Missile Defense Phase 1.
15. CINCPAC, Cruise Missile Defense Phase I.
16. John Donnelly, *Defense Week*, "Joint Exercises Establish Firsts for Cooperative Engagement," February 20, 1996, p. 6.
17. Ibid.
18. John Donnelly, *Defense Week*, February 20, 1996, p. 6.
19. Ibid.
20. Ibid.
21. Secretary of the Navy, John H. Dalton, statement before the Senate Armed Services Committee, March 12, 1996.
22. Maritime Forces, Chapter 19.
23. DoD FY 97 Descriptive Summary.
24. DoD FY 97 Descriptive Summary.
25. Ibid.
26. DoD FY 1997 Descriptive Summary.
27. ECO SSA Technical Narrative.